A GARLAND SERIES

THE ENGLISH WORKING CLASS

A Collection of
Thirty Important Titles
That Document and Analyze
Working-Class Life before
the First World War

Edited by

STANDISH MEACHAM
University of Texas

The Law and the Poor

Edward Abbott Parry

Garland Publishing, Inc.
New York & London
1980

For a complete list of the titles in this series,
see the final pages of this volume.

The volumes in this series are printed on acid-free,
250-year-life paper.

This facsimile has been made from a copy in
the Yale University Library.

Library of Congress Cataloging in Publication Data

Parry, Edward Abbott, Sir, 1863– 1943.
The law and the poor.

(The English working class)
Reprint of the 1914 ed. published by Smith Elder, London.
Bibliography: p.
Includes index.
1. Poor — Great Britain.   2. Great Britain —
Social conditions — 20th century.   3. Poor laws — Great
Britain.   I. Title.   II. Series.
HV245.P28   1980   362.5'0941   79-56966
ISBN 0 8240-0117-6

Printed in the United States of America

THE LAW AND THE POOR

THE LAW AND THE POOR

BY

HIS HONOUR JUDGE

EDWARD ABBOTT PARRY

AUTHOR OF "DOROTHY OSBORNE'S LETTERS," "JUDGMENTS IN VACATION,
"WHAT THE JUDGE SAW," "THE SCARLET HERRING,"
"KATAWAMPUS," ETC.

" Laws grind the poor and rich men rule the law."
OLIVER GOLDSMITH : "The Traveller."

LONDON
SMITH, ELDER & CO., 15, WATERLOO PLACE
1914

To

THE MAN

IN THE STREET

THIS VOLUME IS

DEDICATED,

IN THE PIOUS HOPE THAT

HE WILL TAKE UP HIS JOB AND

DO IT.

CONTENTS

CHAP.		PAGE
	INTRODUCTION	ix
	REFERENCES	xv
I.	PAST AND PRESENT	1
II.	THE ANCIENTS AND THE DEBTOR . . .	20
III.	OF IMPRISONMENT FOR DEBT IN ENGLAND .	36
IV.	HOW THE MACHINE WORKS	58
V.	WORKMEN'S COMPENSATION	76
VI.	BANKRUPTCY	106
VII.	DIVORCE	125
VIII.	FLAT-TRAPS AND THEIR VICTIMS . . .	152
IX.	POVERTY AND PROCEDURE	172
X.	CRIME AND PUNISHMENT	189
XI.	THE POLICE COURT	213
XII.	LANDLORD AND TENANT	233
XIII.	THE TWO PUBLIC HOUSES : I. THE ALEHOUSE .	252
XIV.	THE TWO PUBLIC HOUSES : II. THE WORKHOUSE	271
XV.	REMEDIES OF TO-DAY	285
XVI.	REMEDIES OF TO-MORROW	299
	INDEX	311

INTRODUCTION

" But, say what you like, our Queen reigns over the greatest nation that ever existed."

" Which nation ? " asked the younger stranger, " for she reigns over two."

The stranger paused ; Egremont was silent, but looked inquiringly.

" Yes," resumed the stranger after a moment's interval. " Two nations ; between whom there is no intercourse and no sympathy ; who are as ignorant of each other's habits, thoughts, and feelings, as if they were dwellers in different zones, or inhabitants of different planets ; who are formed by a different breeding, are fed by a different food, are ordered by different manners, and are not governed by the same laws."

" You speak of——," said Egremont, hesitatingly.

" THE RICH AND THE POOR."

BENJAMIN DISRAELI : " Sybil, or The Two Nations."

THE rich have many law books written to protect their privileges, but the poor, who are the greater nation, have but few. Not that I should like to call this a law book, for two reasons : firstly, it would not be true ; secondly, if it were true, I should not mention it, as I want people to read it.

You cannot read law books, you only consult them. A law book seeks to set out the law, the whole law, and nothing but the law on the subject of which it treats. There are many books on Poor Law, there are hundreds of volumes about the Poor, and many more about the Law, but the Law and the Poor is a virgin subject.

ix

INTRODUCTION

It is a wonder that it should be so because it is far more practical and interesting than either of its component parts.

It is as if poetry had dealt with beans or with bacon and no poet had hymned the more beautiful associations of beans and bacon. In the same way the Law and the Poor is a subject worthy of treatment in drama or poetry, but that that may be successfully done someone must do the rough spade work of digging the material out of the dirt heaps in which it lies, and presenting it in a more or less palatable form. When this has been done the poet or the politician can come along and throw the crude metal into the metres of sonnets or statutes or any form of glorious letters they please.

From the very earliest I have taken a keen interest in this subject. I remember well when I was a schoolboy the profound impression made upon me by Samuel Plimsoll's agitation to rescue merchant seamen from the horrible abuses practised by a certain class of shipowner. My father, Serjeant Parry, was engaged in litigation for Plimsoll, and I heard many things at first hand of that great reformer's hopes and disappointments.

There were a class of traders known as " ship knackers," who bought up old unseaworthy vessels and sent them to sea overloaded and over-insured. Plimsoll, for years, devoted himself to prevent this wickedness. There was the usual parliamentary indifference, the customary palavering and pow-wowing in committees until, after six or seven years of constant fighting, the public conscience was awakened, and, in 1875, Disraeli produced a Merchant Shipping Bill. But then, as now, there was no parliamentary time for legislation dealing with the poor, and the Bill was one of the innocents to be sacrificed at the annual summer massacre.

This would have been the end of all hope of reform had not Samuel Plimsoll, in a fine frenzy of rage and disgust, openly charged the Government with being parties to the system which sent brave men to death in the winter seas and left widows and orphans helpless at home, "in order that a few speculative scoundrels, in whose heart there is neither the love of God nor the fear of God, may make unhallowed gains."

This was unparliamentary enough, but it was allowed to pass. It was when he began to give the names of foundered ships and their parliamentary owners and, in his own words, "to unmask the villains" who sent poor men to death and destruction, that he was promptly called to order, and, refusing to withdraw, left the House.

The result of his outburst was entirely satisfactory. The Government were obliged to bring in another Bill and to pass it without delay.

Many years later the unauthorised Radical programme of Mr. Joseph Chamberlain aroused my youthful enthusiasm, and I spent much of my then ample leisure as a missionary in that cause.

We soon lost our great leader, who went away to champion what he considered greater causes, but he was one of the first English statesmen in high places to make his main programme a reform of the law in the interests of the poor, and he left behind him mournful but earnest disciples who have not yet found such another leader. The Workmen's Compensation Act will always, I think, be regarded as one of his greatest achievements, and mauled and mangled as it has been in the Law Courts it remains the most substantial benefit that the poor have received from the Legislature in my lifetime.

Twenty years' service in urban County Courts has naturally given me some insight into the way in which the law treats the poor and the real wants of the latter. I agree that such a book as this would be better written by one who had actual experience of the life of the poor, rather than the official hearsay experience which is all that I can claim to have had.

I think the great want of labour to-day is an Attorney-General, a man who having graduated in the workshop comes to the study and practice of the law with a working man's knowledge and ideals, and gaining a lawyer's power of expressing his wants in legal accents, raises his voice to demand those new laws that the poor are so patiently awaiting.

If there be such a one on his way and this volume is of any small service to him, it will have more than fulfilled its purpose.

Originating in a series of essays published in the *Sunday Chronicle*, it has grown into a more ambitious project, and is now, I trust, a fairly complete text-book of the law as it ought not to be in relation to the poor.

INTRODUCTION

In my endeavour to please the taste of the friend to whom I have dedicated this book I have dispensed with all footnotes, but I have added an appendix of references in case there may be any who might wish to test the accuracy of statements in its pages.

" Thus," as my Lord Coke says, " requesting you to weigh these my labours in the even balance of your indifferent judgment I submit them to your censure and take my leave."

EDWARD A. PARRY.

SEVENOAKS,
1914.

REFERENCES

The number of the page and the number of the line counting from the top are given in the left-hand column.

INTRODUCTION

PAGE	LINE	
xi	11	Hansard. 1875. Vol. 225, col. 1823.
xiii	7	Coke's " Institutes." I. " To the Reader."

CHAPTER I

1	3	Job xiii. 5.
4	20	" The Compleat Constable. Directing all Constables, Headboroughs, Tithing men, Churchwardens, Overseers of the Poor, Surveyors of the Highways and Scavengers in the Duty of their several Offices, according to the Power allowed them by the Laws and the Statutes." 3rd edition. London. Printed for Tho. Bever at the Hand and Star, near Temple Bar. 1708.
8	16	" Shakespeare's Europe. Unpublished chapters of Fynes Moryson's Itinerary, being a survey of the condition of Europe at the end of the sixteenth century. 1903." At p. 67.
9	24	Smollett. " Roderick Random." Chap. XXIII.
12	6	The Trial of Richard Weston at the Guildhall of London for the Murder of Sir Thomas Overbury, 19th October, 13 James Ist, A.D. 1615. Howell's " State Trials," II., 914.
13	21	Boswell's " Life of Johnson." Edited by Birkbeck Hill. II. 130.
14	29	Boswell's " Life of Johnson." IV. 188.
17	8	*Manchester Guardian*, Saturday, January 24th, 1824.

REFERENCES

CHAPTER II

PAGE	LINE	
22	6	2 Kings iv. 1—7.
28	6	Grote's " History of Greece." Part II., c. 11.
32	20	Hunter's " Roman Law." 3rd edition. P. 18.
34	7	Fynes Moryson. " Shakespeare's Europe."

CHAPTER III

IMPRISONMENT FOR DEBT.—The main authorities for the history of imprisonment for debt are the reports of the three commissions.

1840. Report of Commission on the Present State of the Laws respecting Bankrupts and Insolvent Debtors.

1893. Report from the Select Committee on the Debtors Act with Minutes of Evidence.

1909. Report on Select Committee on Debtors (Imprisonment) with Minutes of Evidence.

The Hansard Reports of the debates over the Bills of 1837, 1844, and 1869, contain many clear statements of the argument for, and against, abolition.

37   17   " The Law of Executions, to which are added the History and Practice of the Court of King's Bench." By the late Lord Chief Baron Gilbert.

42   7   Smollett. " Roderick Random." Chap. LXI.

43   1   For the story of the Clerkenwell Spinster and the Debtor, see Sir Walter Besant's " London in the Eighteenth Century," Chap. V., " Debtors' Prisons," at p. 562. This volume contains excellent accounts of the law and the poor in the eighteenth century.

45   8   December 5th, 1837. Lord Cottenham introduced Bill to abolish arrest on mesne process. 1 & 2 Vict. c. 110.

45   30   Thackeray. " The Virginians." Vol. I. Chap. XLV.

REFERENCES

PAGE	LINE	
46	18	Duke de Cadaval's case. Hansard. 1837. Vol. 39, p. 593.
48	2	J. B. Atlay. "The Victorian Chancellors." I., 406.
48	18	Lord Brougham's speech. Hansard. 1837. Vol. 39, p. 574.
49	15	Lord Brougham's speech. Hansard. 1844. Vol. 75, p. 1174.
51	6	See Judgment of Sir George Jessel, M.R., in *Marris* v. *Ingram*, (1879) Law Reports, 13 Chancery Division, p. 341.
55	6	Sir Robert Collier's speech. Hansard. 1869. Vol. 197, p. 421.

CHAPTER IV

PAGE	LINE	
65	5	"Debtors' Imprisonment Report, 1909." Appendix 19, at p. 371.
70	26	Basil Montagu. "Opinions of Paley Burke and Dr. Johnson on Imprisonment for Debt."
75	5	Jeremy Taylor. "A Prayer to be said by all Debtors, and all Persons obliged whether by Crime or Contract." "Holy Living and Dying."

CHAPTER V

There are many books on the Workmen's Compensation Act. That by Mr. Adshead Elliott is as clear and comprehensive as any. The Hansard Debates on the Bills of 1897 and 1906 are full of interest.

PAGE	LINE	
81	12	John Chipman Gray. "Nature and Services of Law." Sections 222—224.
83	13	*The Attorney-General* v. *The Edison Telephone Co. of London, Ltd.*, (1880) Law Reports, 6 Queen's Bench Division, p. 244.
86	5	Gilbert E. Roe. "Our Judicial Oligarchy."
87	17	Mr. Asquith's speech on Employers' Liability Bill. Hansard. 1893. Vol. 8, p. 1948.

REFERENCES

PAGE LINE

92   24   See the judgments of Lord Halsbury and Lord
            Davey, in *Lysons* v. *Andrew Knowles*, (1901)
            Law Reports, Appeal Cases, p. 79.

CHAPTER VI

108   28   Jeremiah xxii. 13.
109   16   See " The Living Wage," by Philip Snowden,
            M.P., for a sensible, practical statement of
            the Socialist ideal.
109   18   Psalms xxxv. 10.
110   11   Carlyle. " Chartism." Chap. I.
119   30   Hansard. 1883. Vol. 277, p. 834.

CHAPTER VII

            The chief authority for this chapter is " The
            Report of the Royal Commission on Divorce
            and Matrimonial Causes," published in 1912,
            cited below as D. C.
125   13   Notes on the Reformatio Legum Ecclesiasti-
            carum. D. C., III., pp. 44—58. Appendix
            II., p. 23.
129   24   J. B. Atlay. " The Victorian Chancellors."
            II., 71.
133   24   Jane and Fred's Case. D. C., II., 390.
134   14   George and Mary's Case. D. C., II., 390.
136   4   Note by Mrs. Tennant. D. C. Report, 169.
137   28   Mr. Justice Bargrave Deane's evidence. D. C.,
            I., 49.
138   16   Alfred and Anna's Case. D. C., II., 390.
139   9   John and Catherine's Case. D. C., II., 391.
140   25   Norah's Case. D. C., II., 391.
143   17   Divorce in France. M. Mesnil's evidence.
            D. C., III., 485.
146   18   Mr. Dendy's evidence. D. C., I., 133.
147   29   German Divorce. Dr. Carl Neuhaus's evidence.
            D. C., III., 472.
147   31   Scot's Divorce. Mr. Lamier's evidence. D. C.,
            I., 277.

REFERENCES

PAGE LINE

150 9   Selden's " Table Talk." LXXXIV.

150 30   D. C. Report, Part IX., par. 50.

CHAPTER VIII

153 18   Carlyle. "Latter Day Pamphlets." "Parliament."

164 28   Dickens. "Oliver Twist." Chap. LI.

169 8   Arthur Hugh Clough. "The Latest Decalogue."

CHAPTER IX

174 6   George Eliot. "The Mill on the Floss." Book II., Chap. II.

175 11   *Lysons* v. *Andrew Knowles*, (1901) Law Reports, Appeal Cases, p. 79.

178 15   Tomkin's "Law Dictionary," *sub tit.* " Barraster."

180 19   See Lord Sumner's judgment in *Dallimore* v. *Williams and Jesson*, *Times* Newspaper, Saturday, March 28th, 1914.

182 1   Swift. "Gulliver's Travels." "A Voyage to the Houyhnhnms."

183 3   Crabbe. "The Borough." Letter VI.

187 24   As to French Conciliation Courts, see Poincaré, "How France is Governed," Chap. X., "Justice."

188 18   Piers Plowman. "The Vision of the Field full of Folk."

CHAPTER X

190 4   Sydney Smith. "Counsel for Prisoners." *Edinburgh Review*, 1826.

192 23   Bentham. "A Treatise on Judicial Evidence." 1825. Book I., Chap. II., p. 7.

193 19   Thackeray. "The Case of Peytel." "Paris Sketch Book."

194 2   Dickens. "Why?" "Miscellaneous Papers." II., 101.

REFERENCES

PAGE	LINE	
195	22	Hansard. 1898. Vol. 54, p. 1176.
196	4	Hansard. 1898. Vol. 56, p. 990.
196	11	See division list on second reading. Hansard. 1898. Vol. 56, p. 1087.
198	7	Hansard. 1907. Vol. 174, p. 282.
198	10	Hansard. 1907. Vol. 174, p. 292.
199	5	Boswell's " Life of Johnson." Birkbeck Hill's edition. III., 25.
200	6	Fuller's " Church History."
201	30	Howell's " State Trials." II., 927.

CHAPTER XI

215	4	" Speech of Viscount Haldane to the American Bar Association at Montreal on September 1st, 1913." Published in " The Conduct of Life and Other Addresses, 1914," p. 97.
227	22	Sydney Smith. " Cruel Treatment of Untried Prisoners." *Edinburgh Review*, 1824.

CHAPTER XII

		As to Housing, see " Report of Her Majesty's Commissioners for Inquiring into the Housing of the Working Classes, 1885," and " Report of the Joint Select Committee of the House of Lords and the House of Commons, 1902."
235	9	*R.* v. *Foxby*, 6 Modern Reports, pp. 11, 178, 213, 239 and 311.
238	4	Dickens " Bleak House." Chap. XVI.
238	32	Charles Kingsley. " Alton Locke." Chap. II.
240	1	Benjamin Disraeli. " Sybil." Book II., Chap. III.
244	10	" History of Housing Reform." Published by the National Unionist Association. 1913.
246	1	" The Land. The Report of the Land Enquiry Committee." Vol. II., p. 28.
250	2	Carlyle. " Chartism." Chap. VIII. " New Eras."
254	21	" The Republic of Plato." Book IV. Translated by Davies and Vaughan.

REFERENCES

CHAPTER XIII

PAGE LINE

255 26   Mr. Balfour's speech on licensing. Hansard. 1908. Vol. 185, p. 98.

256 4   Licensing Act, 1904, § 4, now Licensing Act, 1910, § 14.

256 16   Hansard. 1904. Vol. 133, p. 742.

258 21   Dickens. "Our Mutual Friend." Book I., Chap. VI.

265 19   "Letters and Memories of Charles Kingsley." I., 270.

CHAPTER XIV

272 15   "Report of the Royal Commission on the Poor Laws and Relief of Distress, 1909."

274 24   Coke's "Institutes." III., Chap. 40, p. 103 (note).

275 16   Horn's "Mirror of Justices." Selden Society. Vol. 7, Book IV., Chap. XVI., "Of the Judgment of Homicide."

276 2   Horn's "Mirror of Justices." Book I., "Of Sins Against the Holy Peace."

279 11   "Report of Royal Commission on the Poor Laws, 1834," p. 307.

280 17   "Poor Law Report, 1909," p. 728.

CHAPTER XV

285 1   2 Samuel xv. 4.

290 12   Walt Whitman. "Song of Myself."

292 14   "Report of Select Committee of the House of Lords on the Debtors Act." William Johnson's evidence, p. 164.

294 12   Manitoba Laws.

CHAPTER XVI

299 2   Marcus Aurelius. "Meditations." Book IV., par. 31.

303 3   Rudyard Kipling. "The Five Nations." "Stellenbosh," p. 194.

THE LAW AND THE POOR

CHAPTER I

PAST AND PRESENT

In a word we may gather out of history a policy no less wise
than eternal ; by the comparison and application of other men's
fore-passed miseries with our own like errors and ill-deservings.
SIR WALTER RALEIGH : " History of the World."
Oxford edition. Vol. II., Preface v. and vi.

I OFTEN feel that if that excellent patriarch Job
had been alive he would have sent me a postcard
indited, " O that ye would altogether hold your
peace ! and it should be your wisdom." I have an
anonymous friend who sends me frank criticisms of
that kind on postcards. The sentiments are the
same as Job's text, but the language is fruitier.
Nevertheless, I like to hear from him, for he is an
attentive reader of all I write. But, honestly,
although I was always sorry for Job and glad when
he came into his camels and donkeys in the last
chapter, yet I never sympathised with his attitude
of taking his troubles lying down. After all, if one
has gained a little practical experience of the law and

the poor by living and working with them for twenty years it seems a pity to take it with you across the ferry into the silence merely because you have a bashful and retiring disposition. It is right, of course, to give your views and services to Select Commissions and the like,—but that is no better than hiding a lump of gold in a hole in the ground. The wiser plan is to try and tell the law-makers of the future—the men in the street—what is wrong with the machine, so that when they take it over, as they must do some day, they will not scrap it in mere despair, but tune it up to a faster and nobler rhythm. Job, great, good, patient soul that he was, had his sour moments—a medical friend of mine believes that he had a liver,—I am sorry not to take the patriarch's advice, but I do not see my way to hold my peace about the law and the poor, and that is why I propose to try and point out how and why the law as a system is hard on the poor, and wherein the governors and great ones of the earth may further temper the wind to the shorn lamb. I myself do not expect to enter into the promised land of legal reform, but I am as sure that the younger generation will see it, as I am sure that they will see the rising sun if they ever get up early enough. The man at the door of the booth who beats the drum and calls out to the young folk in the fair to walk up and see the show plays a helpful part, though the old gentleman knows that he is doomed to stand outside and never make one of the audience. Moses was like that, but he did useful work in booming the promised land.

An eminent socialist complained to me with tears

in his eyes that nothing was being done for the poor. I do not agree. Not enough, certainly, but something, and every day more and more. The world is a slow world, and Nature, like all such artisans, does her building and painting and decorating with exasperating deliberation. Geology is slower than the South Eastern Railway. But no doubt Providence intended each of them to go at the pace they do for our good. And it is impious to grumble. Nevertheless, if I were a sculptor called upon to design a symbolic statue of Nature, I should model a plumber. Slow, hesitating, occasionally mixing the taps and flooding the world's bathroom or exploding the gas mains in the cellars of the earth, but in the end doing the job somehow—such is the way of Nature. You cannot cinematograph the growth of the world or its rocks and trees and human beings—to study Nature you want long life and a microscope. And the only way to make out whether the tide is coming in or out is to place a mark upon the shore and wait and see. It is the same if you are travelling an unknown road—you measure your progress by the milestones. In this matter of the law and the poor, if we want to know where wo are to-day and where we are likely to be three hundred years hence, the only sane way to make the experiment is to go back to what we know of things in the past, and, by measuring the progress made in bygone centuries, take heart for the morrow. That is what Sir Walter Raleigh meant when he told us how to gather a sane policy for to-day out of the blunders and troubles of yesterday.

THE LAW AND THE POOR

As I grope my way back along the main road of the history of the law into the dark ages I seem to find the milestones of reform set at longer and longer intervals. This puts me in good heart for the happy youths whose lot it will be to set their faces towards the morning breezes of the future. Their milestones will come at shorter intervals every day, until the burden of the law drops from the shoulders of the poor at the wicket gate.

There is no greater folly than to sing the praises of the good old days. Anyhow, the law had no good old days for the poor. Stroll down to the dockyards with Samuel Pepys; take a walk down Fleet Street with Dr. Johnson; or, even as late as the days of Charles Dickens, go round the parish with Mr. Bumble. You will learn in this way better than in any other how the law has treated the poor in the good old days. I have a quaint little volume written for the Dogberries of the early eighteenth century called "The Compleat Constable." It is amazing to read of the tyranny of the law towards the poor and the homeless of those days.

The statutes made for punishing rogues, vagabonds, night walkers and such other idle persons are, says the anonymous legal author, " a large Branch of the Constable's Office, and herein two things are to be known :—

" (1) What is a Rogue and who is to be accounted a Vagabond ?

" (2) What is to be done unto them ? "

The charming impersonal technical spirit of this little work is beyond all praise. Not a word is ever used to remind you that, after all, a rogue and a vagabond is a man and a brother. You are taught first to diagnose him as Izaak Walton would teach the young angler how to discover the singling that did not usually stir in the daytime, and having captured your rogue and vagabond, you are then enlightened as to the various methods of killing or curing him.

And first you are to note that all persons above the age of seven, man or woman, married or single, that wander abroad without a lawful passport and give no good account of their travel are accounted rogues. Then follows a very lengthy list of such as are " of a higher degree and are to be accounted as Rogues, Vagabonds and sturdy Beggars." Such are all Scholars and Sea-faring men that beg, wandering persons using unlawful games, subtle crafts, or pretending to have skill in telling of fortunes by the marks or figures on the hands or face, Egyptians or Gypsies. All Jugglers or Slight-of-hand Artists pretending to do wonders by virtue of Hocus Pocus, the Powder of Pimper le Pimp, or the like ; all Tinkers, Pedlars, Chapmen, Glassmen, especially if they be not well known or have a sufficient testimonial. All collectors for Gaols or Hospitals, Fencers, Bearwards, common players of interludes, and Fiddlers or Minstrels wandering abroad. Also Persons delivered out of Gaols who beg their fees, such as go to and from the Baths and do not pursue their License, Soldiers and Mariners that beg and counterfeit certificates from their commanders. And, lastly : " All Labourers which wander abroad out of their respective Parishes, and refuse to work for wages reasonably taxed, having no Livelyhood otherwise to maintain themselves, and such as go with general Passports not directed from Parish to Parish."

In a word, all the unfortunate poor who would not do as they were told by their pastors and masters and wanted to work and amuse themselves in their own way were rogues and vagabonds. And it is not without interest to run your eye over this list, for the statutory rogue and vagabond is still with us and our Poor Law of to-day suffers from its direct hereditary connection with the Poor Law of the eighteenth century.

The duty of "The Compleat Constable" was, in the words of Dogberry, to "comprehend all vagrom men" and he was liable to a fine of ten shillings for every neglect. Moreover, if you were a stalwart fellow, you could apprehend your own rogue and vagabond and hand him over to the constable, who was bound to receive him.

Having dealt in accurate detail with the classification and identification of rogues, we come next to the chapter on treatment, which is best given in the simple words of the original. "The Punishment is after this manner. The Constable, Headburrough or Tythingman assisted by the Minister and one other of the Parish, is to see (or do it himself), That such Rogues and Vagabonds, etc., be stript Naked from the middle upwards and openly Whipped till their Body be bloody and then forthwith to be sent away from Constable to Constable, the next straight

6

way to the place of their Birth ; and if that cannot be known then to the place where they last Dwelt, by the space of one whole Year before the time of such their Punishment ; and if that cannot be known then to the Town through which they last passed unpunished." If, however, none of these habitats was discoverable, the vagrom man was sent to the house of correction or common gaol, where he was put to hard labour for twelve months.

It is only fair to remember, " that after such Vagabond is whipt as aforesaid he is to have a Testimonial "—is this the origin of people asking for testimonials ?—" under the Hand and Seal of the Constable or Tything-man and the Minister testifying the day and place of his Punishment ; as also the place to which he is to be conveyed, and the time limited for his own Passage thither : And if by his own default he exceed that time then he is again to be whipt—and so from time to time till he arrive at the place limited."

In the good old days of Merrie England the chief entertainment of the villagers must have been to crowd round the stocks and the whipping post on the village green—some of which are existing to this day —just as their city cousins swarmed along the road to Tyburn. And if you had suggested that the players or the fiddlers were a more wholesome amusement for the people than these cruel sights, you would not only have shocked the minister but would have rendered yourself liable to be treated as a vagrom man and to receive a testimonial from the constable. It is easy to-day to see the wrongdoing

7

of much of this, but it was not to be expected that the citizens of the time should see any evil in the everyday cruelties they were used to. The law seems to have been hard on the poor then, but very few worried about it.

History is constantly showing us that in matters touching the imperfections of our own system of law we are colour blind to the cruelties we commit ourselves and easily moved to indignation by the horrors and wickednesses committed by foreigners, especially if they are foreigners who have never known the blessings of the particular religion we profess. When Fynes Moryson was travelling in Turkey at the end of the sixteenth century, he set down with reasonable detestation some of the gruesome things he observed. " Touching their Corporal and Capital Judgments," he writes : " For small offences they are beaten with cudgels on the soles of the feet, the bellies and backs, the strokes being many and painful according to the offence or the anger of him that inflicts them. Myself did see some hanging and rotting in chains upon the gallows."

Yet in England he might have seen many of his fellow countrymen hanging and rotting in chains, for there was at that date and for many years afterwards no country with a more evil record than England for the practice of capital punishment for minor offences. As to mere corporal punishment, there was not a village in England without its whipping post, and a common sight in the streets of the city was to see a poor wretch being whipped at the cart's tail. In ordinary cases the journey was from Newgate to Ludgate, or from Charing Cross to Westminster, but for really bad cases it was extended from Newgate to Charing Cross. And not only did these punishments exist in England, but the populace enjoyed them. One of the sights of London was to see the women whipped in the Bridewell. The Court of Governors held their board meeting, presided over by a magistrate, and the sentence was executed in their presence and continued until the President struck the table in front of him with a hammer. The cry, " O good Sir Robert, knock ! Pray, good Sir Robert, knock ! " which the victims screamed out whilst under the lash, became a common slang cry among the lower orders in the streets of London in the seventeenth century.

There can be no doubt about the horrors of the old prisons, but it was only men and women of especial insight who recognised that there was real evil in them. Literature and art did much to arouse the public conscience. There is a strong description of the Bridewell in " Roderick Random," where Smollett makes Miss Williams tell her life story. In this prison, she says, " I actually believed myself in hell tormented by fiends ; indeed, there needs not a very extravagant imagination to form that idea ; for of all the scenes on earth that of Bridewell approaches nearest the notion I had always entertained of the infernal regions. Here I saw nothing but rage, anguish and impiety ; and heard nothing but groans, curses and blasphemy. In the midst of this hellish crew I was subjected to

THE LAW AND THE POOR

the tyranny of a barbarian who imposed upon me tasks that I could not possibly perform and then punished my incapacity with the utmost rigour and inhumanity. I was often whipped into a swoon and lashed out of it, during which miserable intervals I was robbed by my fellow-prisoners of everything about me even to my cap, shoes and stockings · I was not only destitute of necessaries but even of food, so that my wretchedness was extreme."

No one need suppose that Smollett is guilty of exaggeration, for the well-known plate of Hogarth shows us the actual scene and the records of the place are numerous. There were, of course, just as many good and charitable men and women then as there are now, but the possibility that a Bridewell was a thing that the world had then no use for was entirely beyond the thought of the eighteenth century citizen. In the same way how few of us recognise that there is much room for reform in the penal system of to-day.

It is natural that it should be so. We arrive in the world knowing nothing much about it, we are brought up to believe that everything that has been going on for the last few centuries has been for the best, and the tired old ones who are leaving us are never tired enough to leave off telling us that they have made every possible reform that it was safe and advisable to make. In the few years of hustling life and in the scanty hours that he can spare from earning his daily bread the average citizen has little time and opportunity to investigate the social system of which he is a unit, or to understand how or why the wheels of the world machine are grinding unevenly. When we read of the horrors of two or three hundred years ago, it should not be to cast a reproach against our fathers, but rather to learn who were the men and women who moved the world of that day to see things as they were. These glorious spirits have enabled us to enter upon our inheritance free from the worst degradations of the past and we may best render them thanks and praise by learning to follow their example.

I make no doubt that most of us are much like old Fynes Moryson, who, being an ordinary average Englishman, saw the everyday horrors of his own country, but was in no way impressed by them, yet was moved to grave indignation at the wickedness and cruelties of foreigners. Truly the seventeenth century Turk was a cruel beast. Moryson tells us with honest reprobation, but in gruesome detail, of the Turkish methods of impaling, where a " man may languish two or three days in pain and hunger ; if torment will permit him in that time to feel hunger for no man dares give him meat," and of casting down malefactors to pitch upon hooks and other nameless horrors. Yet if he had been in London on October 19th, 1615, and dropped into the Guildhall, he might have heard the Lord Chief Justice of England, the great Coke, using much persuasion to Richard Weston, who, being accused of the murder of Sir Thomas Overbury, stood mute, refusing to plead.

Coke and his brother judges, having failed to persuade the wretched Weston to utter a plea of

not guilty, the Lord Chief Justice repeated for his
benefit the law of England at that time and reminded
him that the prisoner who wilfully stood mute must
undergo the *peine forte et dure*, the extremity and
rigour whereof was expressed in these words, " *Onere,
frigore et fame.*" " For the first," continued his
Lordship, " he was to receive his punishment by
the law, to be extended and then to have weights
laid upon him no more than he was able to bear
which were by little and little to be increased. For
the second, that he was to be exposed in an open
place near the prison in the open air, being naked.
And, lastly, that he was to be preserved with the
coarsest bread that could be got, and water out of
the next sink or puddle to the place of execution,
and that day he had water he should have no bread,
and that day he had bread he should have no water ;
and in this torment he was to linger as long as
nature could linger out so that often times men
lived in that extremity eight or nine days ; adding
further that as life left him so judgment should
find him. And therefore he required him upon
consideration of these reasons to advise himself to
plead to his country."

Notwithstanding this advice the wretched man
continued mute, but after a consideration, during
an adjournment of three or four days, of the law
of procedure as laid down by Lord Chief Justice
Coke, Weston thought better of it and pleaded not
guilty, and was duly convicted and executed.

How illogical it seems that a citizen whose State
executed this form of torture on its prisoners should

hold up the holy hands of horror at the variations
of cruelty that satisfied the lust of the unspeakable
Turk ! The *peine forte et dure* remained one of the
pillars of our law until the reign of George III. and
was carried into execution in the reign of Queen
Anne and George II.—so obstinately do we cling
to our ancient precedents and so fearful are we of
facing the narrow paths that lead to better things.

When Oliver Goldsmith wrote, " Laws grind the
poor and rich men rule the law," I do not know that
he wished to make any specially unkind attack
upon the rich. I imagine he merely intended to
state a fact which seems in all ages to have been
universally true. I do not suppose that in the
middle of the eighteenth century anyone in the
least recognised the actual horrors that were going
on around him unless it was some poet and dreamer
like Oliver himself. The strong, sensible men of
that generation were as assured of their own
righteousness as they are to-day.

Dr. Johnson told Dr. Maxwell that " the poor in
England were better provided for than in any other
country of the same extent ; he did not mean little
cantons or petty republics. Where a great proportion of the people (said he) are suffered to languish
in helpless misery that country must be ill-policed
and wretchedly governed ; a decent provision for
the poor is the test of civilisation. Gentlemen of
education, he observed, were pretty much the same
in all countries ; the condition of the lower orders,
the poor specially, was the true mark of national
discrimination."

THE LAW AND THE POOR

The good Doctor rolled all that excellent stuff out one evening in 1770 to the Rev. Dr. Maxwell, the assistant preacher of the Temple, who, like Boswell, faithfully recorded what he remembered of it in the morning—I doubt not that if Dr. Johnson had lived in 1670, or 1870, or 1970, or had flourished under Caligula or Nero, he would have rolled out the same sonorous complacent nonsense to some sort of faithful human gramophone who would have recorded the utterances of his master's voice with a canine credulity in its omniscience.

There is nothing extraordinary in the divergence of the views of Oliver Goldsmith and Dr. Johnson about the law and the poor. The good Doctor held the strong, sensible, Tory view that the system of treating the poor handed down to us by our forefathers was the right and proper system, that it was at least as good as any other system, that nothing anyhow could be learned from the hated foreigner, and that to pander to dreamers and busybodies, who found fault and wanted to alter things, was to start down the broad road of destruction. Oliver Goldsmith might have thought the same thing if he had been an Englishman, but he had the saving grace of Irish blood in his veins, and the true Irish have the power of looking beyond the present, and are often prophets and dreamers of dreams, seeing signs and wonders that we wot not of.

" Sir ! " said Dr. Johnson on another occasion, and when he began like that you knew that wisdom was about ; " the age is running mad after innovations ; all the business of the world is to be done in a new way ; Tyburn itself is not safe from the fury of innovation."

It having been argued that this was an improvement—" No, sir (said he eagerly), it is not an improvement ; they object that the old method drew together a number of spectators. Sir, executions are intended to draw spectators. If they do not draw spectators, they don't answer their purpose. The old method was most satisfactory to all parties ; the public was gratified by a procession ; the criminal was supported by it. Why is all this to be swept away ? "

And Boswell and Sir William Scott nodded approval, just as you and I would have done or do now when some important old gentleman lays down the law about something of which he knows perhaps even a little less than we do and we are too courteous or cowardly to tell him that at the back of our minds we believe he is talking nonsense.

If you would be gratified by a Tyburn procession, you may see one any day for yourself in Hogarth's print of the awful end of the Idle Apprentice. The ragged men, women and children bawling dying speeches about the streets, the criminal in the cart sitting beside his coffin, the chaplain exhorting the poor outcast, who, if he still courted popularity, scoffed openly, shouting to his friends on St. Sepulchre's steps where they stood with their nosegays to give their pal a last greeting. What a solemn impressive scene ! All the way up Holborn there is a crowd so great that every twenty or thirty yards the cart is pulled up, and now someone brings out wine and

THE LAW AND THE POOR

the malefactor drinks a last toast. And when he reaches the fatal tree the ribald mob swears and laughs and shouts out obscene jests. Amid these noises a psalm is sung and the sound of it drowned in filthy tumult. So was the life of a fellow sinner brought to an end in the eighteenth century.

And there were men and women who wanted to abolish it all. It was too much for Dr. Johnson. "Tyburn itself not safe from the fury of innovation!" Fancy that! What a terrible outlook! The law deserting the poor and giving them no more cheap excursions to Tyburn—well might the good Doctor shake his dear old head and prophesy woe.

And when Dr. Johnson upheld the English treatment of the poor in 1770, we may suppose he knew as much about it as a literary professor of to-day knows about what is going on in the workhouse, or the police court, or the County Court of our own time. The belief that the world is the best possible of worlds has its value in making for the stability of things, but mere ignorance of the facts of life, coupled with that strange form of piety which accepts whatever system was good enough for a past age as the only possible system for this, renders the pace of social reform as imperceptible to the human mind as the movements of glaciers.

If a history of the law and the poor were to be written, it would be a story of the lower classes emerging out of slavery into serfdom, out of serfdom into freedom of a limited character, and every age finding new abuses to remedy and trying in some small way to rid the law of some of those traits of

16

barbarism which linger in its old-world features. To each new generation the terrors of the past iniquity of the law are mere nightmares. We can scarcely believe that what we read is true any more than our grandchildren will be able to understand how we were able to tolerate some of the everyday legal incidents of our daily courts.

Less than a hundred years ago at Salford Quarter Sessions there were over two hundred prisoners, all poor and mostly very young, and the law thought nothing of transporting them for life or fourteen years as a punishment for small thefts. And horrible as all this cruelty was, yet I make little doubt that the judges of the time, with very few exceptions, administered the law as humanely as they do to-day. Sir Thomas Starkie, the learned Chairman of the Salford Epiphany Quarter Sessions in 1824, no doubt felt very grieved when he sentenced Martha Myers, aged sixteen, and Mary Mason, twenty-four, to seven years' transportation. I expect he thought he was "giving them another chance." Perhaps he was. We do not know. They may have become the mothers of big-limbed colonial aristocrats instead of peopling the Hundred of Salford with another generation of feeble-minded criminals.

Nowadays there is a tendency among the less discerning of mankind to set down all the rough edges and inequalities of the law to the fault of the judges, though in truth they have but a small part in the making of new laws, and I do not think they can be rightly blamed for harsh administration. They get the blame because they are the figure-heads of the show, so to speak, and the public know nothing of the difficulties under which the judges labour. It is their duty to administer the complicated modern laws turned out by Parliament in a somewhat haphazard fashion, and they are bound to keep alive old-world laws that ought long ago to have been shot on to the rubbish heap. Nearly all the law relating to the poor will be found to be defective to our modern sympathies, just because it is a patching up of the ancient cruel pagan law of past ages and does not break bravely away from the old superstitious uses and close for ever the volumes of laws that were made in the days when liberty and equality and fraternity were words of anarchy and rebellion.

The poor are suffering to-day at the hands of the law because in the evolution of things we have a lot of old derelict law made by slaveowners for slaves, by masters for serfs, by the landlords for the landless. It is law that has no more relation to the wants of to-day, and would be of no more purpose to a Ministry of Justice—if we had one—than crossbows and arquebuses would be to the War Office, or coracles to the Admiralty. And, instead of cursing the judges, who, poor fellows, are doing their best, I wish our parliamentary masters would look into the history of the matter. They would find, I think, that in the last few years enormous reforms have been made in modifying the cruelty of the law to the poor, and might discover, by marking back on the track of ¹·ast reform, the lines upon which further evolution may be hastened. One thing, I think, they will be convinced about : it is not the judges who are hard on the poor, it is the law. It is the sins of the law-givers of the past that the poor are expiating to-day.

CHAPTER II

My thoughts are with the Dead, with them
  I live in long-past years,
Their virtues love, their faults condemn,
  Partake their hopes and fears,
And from their lessons seek and find
  Instruction with a humble mind.
ROBERT SOUTHEY:
" My Days among the Dead are past."

I FIND this question of the debtor, and our modern method of imprisoning the poorer variety of the genus, in the forefront of any consideration of the problem of the law and the poor, because to my mind it is a clear and classic instance of the way in which it comes about that the law with us is a respecter of persons.

The physiological tutor will take his pupils into the laboratory and cut up a rabbit to show them where their livers ought to be, the microscopist will choose a newt to exhibit to you the circulation of the blood, and in like manner, for my purposes, the debtor seems to me to possess all the necessary legal incidents in him through which one can give an excellent object lesson on the law and the poor. There is no legal mystery about a debtor; he is a common object of our legal seashore, as ancient of lineage as the periwinkle and sometimes almost as difficult to get at. Everyone has in his life at some time or other been a debtor, though not all of us have attained to the dignity of a co-respondent, a mortgagor, a garnishee, a bankrupt or a *cestui que trust.*

It seems to me that to demonstrate to the man in the street the unfairness of our law of imprisonment for debt is such a feasible proposition, that I have come to regard the subject as very fitting for the citizen's kindergarten education on legal reform. Once understand the history, and the causes of the continued existence, of imprisonment for debt, and its evil effect on right action, conduct and social life, and you will find it easier to diagnose the more obscure legal diseases which are partially the outcome and partially the cause of much real distress among the poor. Carlyle tells us to " examine history for it is philosophy teaching by experience," and, if we take his advice in this matter of imprisonment for debt, we shall, I think, be bound to admit that what is going on among us day by day in the County Courts of this country is in historical fact a relic of a very ancient barbarism.

It is the more extraordinary to me that this relic should still be venerated, since history also makes it clear that teachers, prophets and law-givers of all ages have testified to their sense of the cruelty and injustice of the law which thrusts a man into prison because he does not pay his neighbour what he owes him. I propose, therefore, before I set down exactly what we are doing to-day, to trace the pedigree of our present system of dealing with debtors and show you historically and cinematographically, as it were, how the world has treated its debtors in the past and what the saner men of different ages thought about it at the time. In this way the man in the street of to-day will have the material for forming a sound judgment on the question of what we should do with the poor debtor.

And to begin with the Old Testament. Let us remember with gratitude the remarkable action of Elisha in the matter. Elisha went the length of performing a miracle to pay the bailiffs out. There are many poor widows in the mean streets of our own cities looking down the road for the Elisha of to-day who cometh not. Miracles do not happen nowadays ; people don't do such things. Still it is interesting to know that there was imprisonment for debt in Elisha's day, just as there is now—for the poor and only for the poor—and it is encouraging to know what Elisha thought about it.

What happened was this :—

The County Court bailiffs of the County Court of Israel, holden at Samaria, went with a body-warrant to seize the two sons of a poor widow on behalf of a creditor of her late husband, just as they might do to-day.

Fortunately, the deceased had been a servant that did fear the Lord, and Elisha, hearing of the trouble, went down to the house, and in that simple, kindly way that the dear old prophets had of putting little troubles straight for members of their congregations and also no doubt to show the contempt he had for the proceedings of the County Court of Samaria, sent the widow out to borrow empty vessels of her neighbours. These he miraculously filled with oil of the best, and the only pity of it was that there were no more vessels to fill, for Elisha was in form that morning, and was sorry to stop. When it was over he said to the widow : " Go sell the oil and pay thy debt and live thou and thy children of the rest."

I am very fond of that story. I like to believe it really happened. I wish it could happen to-day, for there are many poor women in much the same straits as that poor widow. I have never heard the text referred to in churches and chapels, and I am not surprised. A minister who preached about it would have to explain that he could not do miracles of that kind himself, and if he were to do the next best thing and preach about the iniquity of imprisonment for debt straight from the shoulder—as I am sure Elisha would have done— the respectable credit draper, the pious grocer, and all the noble army of tally-men would get up in their pews and walk out of his church or chapel in disgust.

The days of miracles are past, but if it was worth while for a holy man like Elisha to show what he thought about imprisonment for debt, by means of a miracle, surely, after all these ages, we might have improved that particular piece of barbarism off the face of the earth.

But no. The poor are worse off now than they were then. The bailiffs come for their bodies on behalf of their creditors still. And they look down the road in vain. There is no Elisha.

And when you come to the New Testament the matter is laid down even more clearly. Matthew vi. 12 has the actual words of Our Lord's Prayer to be, " And forgive us our debts as we also have forgiven our debtors." If the forgiveness of our debtors is a condition precedent to our own forgiveness, most of us are in a parlous state. But is it too much in this Christian country of ours to suggest that, even if the highest ideals of the Master are beyond our attainment, we need not insult our belief by continuing a barbaric pagan system of cruelty which has been singled out for special disapprobation by the Word that we cannot shut our ears to ?

You remember the parable of the king that took account of his servants which Matthew sets out in his eighteenth chapter. How a servant owed the king ten thousand talents and, as he had not wherewith to pay, his lord commanded him to be sold, and his wife and children, and all that he had, and payment to be made. Note that in those days the wife and children were actually sold into slavery. We do not do that : we remove the bread-winner, only, to gaol and care for his wife and children in the workhouse. It is encouraging to find this much reform after nineteen Christian centuries.

The servant, you will recollect, pleaded with the king, saying, " Have patience with me, and I will pay thee all." Debtors have not altered much since that date, and the text has a familiar ring in the ears of a County Court judge. The lord of that servant, being moved by compassion, released him and forgave him the debt. This is important to remember, for the servant being forgiven his debt was without excuse for his subsequent contemptible conduct. And, indeed, I have often found that men who have been most leniently treated in their own failures by those in a better position, are themselves most greedy in extorting the uttermost farthing from their smaller victims. Speaking generally, it is not the most desirable class of trader that makes use of the debt-collecting system of the County Court.

The servant of the parable was the meanest of curs. He " went out, and found one of his fellow-servants, which owed him a hundred pence : and he laid hold on him, and took him by the throat, saying, Pay what thou owest." Here, again, we may flatter ourselves on our superior procedure. If this had happened in Lambeth, the servant would not have been allowed to go for his fellow servant with such jubilant audacity. Nowadays everything would be done in legal decency and order. The debt being for a hundred pence, and, therefore, being within the jurisdiction of the County Court, a summons would have to be issued, fees would have to be paid to the Treasury and the Court officials, and a lot of money spent and added to the debt before imprisonment followed. Still the rough-and-ready methods of the earlier centuries were certainly cheaper, and the result was much the same. For we read that, though the fellow-servant pleaded in the same formula, " Have patience with me, and I will pay thee," the creditor of the hundred pence stood firm for his rights and cast his fellow servant into prison till he should pay his due.

And if this had been a repertory drama and not a parable, the curtain had fallen on that scene and one would have come away depressed with the abjectness of human nature and with a cold feeling that the world was a drab uncomfortable place. But the ancient dramatic stories always have a happy ending. There is more of the spirit of the old Adelphi than of the Gaiety Theatre, Manchester, about the parables. The lord hears of his servant's scurvy behaviour and, to the delight of all sane men of child-like and simple faith, the wicked servant is delivered to the tormentors till he shall pay all that was due.

I confess that my legal mind has been haunted with the thought that, the lord having forgiven the servant his debt, it was rather a strong order for him to go back on that forgiveness. Doubtless there was no consideration for the forgiveness, it was *nudum pactum*, or there may have been an implied contract that the servant should do unto others as he had been done by, but I rather expect the lord and his advisers only considered the justice of their act rather than its technical legal accuracy. But one thing we can rejoice in. There is the dramatic story, and no one can construe it into approval of any form of imprisonment for debt.

I know that many who do not regard the Bible as an authority will not be troubled about this testimony ; probably many more who do read the Scriptures for guidance will be pained that anyone should make use of holy words to upset a system that they find so useful in the commercial weekdays of life. Moreover, some will shake their heads and remind me that " the devil can cite Scripture for his purpose." That is true enough. But it will be a very clever devil who can cite any Scripture in support of section 5 of the Debtors Act, 1869.

And I will pass away from scriptural precedents to others which, though to me they possess a less compelling sanction, will perhaps have more weight with men of the world. In the history of ancient Greece the debtor played an important part. Let me remind you what the Archon did.

The particular Archon I refer to is Solon.

Solon knew all about imprisonment for debt, and his evidence on the subject is most convincing. It is well to remember, too, that Solon was a business man—I have this from Grote, who got it, I fancy, from Plutarch. Exekestides, Solon's father, a gentleman of the purest heroic blood, " diminished his substance by prodigality," and young Solon had to go into business ; in modern phrase, he " went on the road," and saw a lot of the world in Greece and Asia. I mention this because I am always told that if I knew anything of business I should under- stand the necessity of imprisonment for debt. Solon was emphatically a business man. Solon was also a poet, which perhaps was his best asset as a social reformer, but he was no sentimentalist if, as some say, when he was a general attacking a rebellious city he ordered the wells to be poisoned to put an end to the strife.

THE LAW AND THE POOR

When Solon in a time of grand social upheaval was made Archon, he found the poorer population, including particularly the cultivating tenants, weighed down by debts and driven in large numbers out of freedom and into slavery. Let me set down the condition of things in the careful words of Grote lest I appear to exaggerate.

" All the calamitous effects were here seen of the old harsh law of debtor and creditor—once prevalent in Greece, Italy, Asia, and a large portion of the world—combined with the recognition of slavery as a legitimate status, and of the right of one man to sell himself as well as that of another man to buy him. Every debtor unable to fulfil his contract was liable to be adjudged as the slave of his creditor, until he could find means either of paying it or working it out ; and not only he himself, but his minor sons and unmarried daughters and sisters also, whom the law gave him the power of selling. *The poor man thus borrowed upon the security of his body* (to translate literally the Greek phrase) and upon that of the persons in his family."

The words I have italicised are interesting as exactly defining the principle of all imprisonment for debt. A wage earner to-day who runs up bills with tally-men and grocers obtains credit upon the security of his body.

I have heard from the wife of a poor debtor an apt but unconscious translation of the Latin maxim, *Si non habet in aere luat in corpore.* Her allegation was that a tally-man had said to her husband, " If I canna 'ave yer brass I'll tek yer body." In the north

28

country, among the more old-fashioned bailiffs and their victims, warrants of arrest are commonly known as " body warrants." No doubt the imprisonment of to-day is different in degree from the slavery of debtors in Greece five hundred years before Christ, but it is absolutely the same in principle, founded on the same idea, and worthy to be maintained or abolished by the citizens of this State for the same reasons that were found good by the citizens of Athens.

Thus it is that it is worth while finding out what Solon thought about it. I wish Solon's tract, " What the Archon Saw," had come down to us, and we could have quoted actual instances of the wickedness of imprisonment for debt in his day, but at least we know what he thought of it, and, what is really important to us, what he did. Solon had a pretty wit in titles. He called his bill *Seisachtheia*, or the shaking off of burdens. The relief which it afforded was complete and immediate. It cancelled at once all those contracts in which the debtor had borrowed on the security of his person or his land ; it forbade all future loans or contracts in which the person of the debtor was pledged as security ; it deprived the creditor in future of all power *to imprison* or enslave or extort work from his debtor, and confined him to an effective judgment at law, authorising the seizure of the property of the latter.

This was indeed a shaking off of burdens. For here we find, not only was imprisonment for debt abolished lock, stock and barrel, but a law enacted protecting the land of the cultivator from being

seized for debt.   This is akin to what in some of our
colonies is called a homestead law, and I have
always contended that in the interests of the State
the few sticks of furniture which a poor man and his
wife and children always call " the home " should be
protected from arrest for debt, just as the bread-
winner's body should be exempt from imprisonment.
I could have got along with Solon.

And when one is told the old tale that continues
to be put forward by those who wish to retain imprisonment for debt—that the workman will starve
for want of necessary credit and that trade will
stagnate owing to timid creditors refusing to trade
—let us remember with pleasure that that was not
what the Archon saw as a result of his beneficial
measures.   On the contrary, the testimony is overwhelming that there grew up a higher and increasing
respect for the sanctity of contracts.   The system
of credit-giving, and especially of moneylending,
assumed a more beneficial character, and " the old
noxious contracts, mere snares for the liberty of a
poor free man and his children "—the flat-traps of
to-day—disappeared.   What happened was what
will happen here when we abolish this degrading
system of giving credit on the sanction of body
warrants.   What happened in Athens was that,
although there were some fraudulent debtors, the
public sentiment became strongly in favour of
honesty, and it is agreed that the prophecies of
Solon's failure were not made good, and " that a loan
of money at Athens was quite as secure as it ever was
at any time or place of the ancient world."   Further-

more, it is acknowledged by the better authorities that what I expect and believe will happen in the mean streets of England when imprisonment for debt is abolished, actually did happen in Athens, and, to use Grote's words, " the prohibition of all contracts on the security of the body was itself sufficient to produce a vast improvement in the character and conditions of the poorer population."

Of course, I am not putting forward " What the Archon Did " as an example to the Archons who Didn't of to-day. The theory of evolution teaches us that in two thousand years the Solon type must have improved, and that the Solon that we see in the latter-day armchair of State must be a far, far better thing than anything that obtained in Ancient Greece. Possibly, the world having no use at all for Solons, the type is extinct. Be that as it may, I am more than ever puzzled since I have studied the records of What the Archon Did. If the world had got so far in the question of imprisonment for debt five hundred years before Christ, why are we where we are now nineteen hundred years since the Master set before us the true doctrine of forgiveness of debts?

The Roman laws against the debtor upon which we have ultimately modelled our own were equally harsh and would nearly satisfy the moneylender or tally-man of any age. Upon notice, a debtor had thirty days in which to discharge his debt. If he did not do so his creditor carried him off in chains. Note, however, that he was not a slave, but his creditor had to keep him in chains for another sixty days, during which time he had to bring the debtor out on three successive market days to give his friends an opportunity of paying up and releasing him. The creditor had also to provide the debtor with a pound of bread a day. In these socialist days we take that burden off the creditor's shoulder and a generous State feeds the imprisoned debtor at the cost of the community. On the third market day, if the debtor's friends were still backward in coming forward, the debtor was killed and thrown into the Tiber, or his body was divided among his creditors, which was the only dividend they received. If there was any market for him he was sold into slavery. It seems that in the very early days of Ancient Rome each creditor had a right to carve his pound of flesh from off the debtor. Portia's point against Shylock :

> . . . nor cut thou less, nor more,
> But just a pound of flesh : . . .

was foreseen and provided for in the drafting of the Twelve Tables. It is enacted in the Third Table : " After the third market day the creditors may cut their several portions of his body : and any one that cuts more or less than his just share shall be guiltless." Unless, therefore, the laws of Venice amended or repealed the Twelve Tables, Shylock's case seems to have been wrongly decided. What is at least curious is that the ancient idea of debtor and creditor law embodied in those ancient statutes should be the foundation of one of the most popular plays in the English language.

Some good people have found a difficulty in understanding Shylock's outlook on life and cannot comprehend why a creditor should enjoy killing a debtor. But, after all, it is equally strange why a creditor should take pleasure in imprisoning a debtor. Yet to-day thousands of debtors go to prison because they have not means to pay their creditors. The difference between killing and imprisoning a debtor is a difference in degree only. The principle is the same. The object of the creditor is, perhaps, in the first place, to get repaid his debt ; when he finds this is impossible the death or imprisonment of the debtor merely satisfies his desire for revenge. The ancient Romans were, in one way, a more practical people than ourselves, for they threw the costs of this revenge direct upon the creditor, whereas we throw it upon the taxpayer. If this particular impost were made upon me in any direct manner it would almost persuade me to be a passive resister.

I am glad, however, to remind you that in historical times at all events the Romans did not carry out the law of the Twelve Tables to its uttermost cruelty. The popular way of dealing with a debtor seems to have been to sell him into slavery and then to credit him in your ledger with the price he fetched— less the out of pockets— much as we do to-day when we issue execution against chattels. In later years the slavery of debtors was abolished and imprisonment much like our own was substituted, but the Romans never had a lawgiver as wise and powerful as Solon to get rid of imprisonment for debt altogether. And the Roman imprisonment for debt in some shape or other runs through the social systems of the Middle Ages, being harsh in one place and less cruel in another, and mitigated at one date and aggravated at another. Always we find a feeling among the more thoughtful of mankind that it is in itself a harsh and cruel system and a desire among at least a few to help the victims of it in their distress.

Fynes Moryson, who was in Rome in 1594, tells us of a practice which then prevailed in the Pope's State which might be introduced into Protestant England to-day in a lively belief that it would be in accordance with the tenets of the Christian faith and a certain hope that it would relieve many a poor wretch in misery and despair. " If," he writes, " a man be cast into prison for debt, the judges after the manner visiting frequently those prisons, finding him to be poor, will impose upon the creditor a mitigation of the debt, or time of forbearance, as they judge the equity of the case to require, or if by good witnesses they find the party so poor as really he hath not wherewith to pay his debt they will accept a release or assignment of his goods to the creditor and whether he consent or no will free the debtor's body out of prison."

At all periods of time we find the same uneasiness in the minds of rulers and governors about keeping a poor man in prison for debt when he cannot pay. The governors of English gaols will tell you that 90 per cent. of the debtors lying in prison to-day for civil debt, rates, maintenance or bastardy orders and small fines are too poor to pay. Yet here in England our legislators cannot even get as far as the Papal State of the sixteenth century in an exercise of charity to the poor and distressed. Pending the abolition of imprisonment for debt, a Home Office visitation with power to release the really unfortunate on the lines of the practical experiment which Fynes Moryson wrote home about three hundred years ago would be something to be going on with.

This, however, is a matter which is concerned with methods of reform. But, before we deal with amendments of the law, it is necessary to trace clearly and accurately the evolution of imprisonment for debt in England, in order that we may understand how and why it exists to-day as a law that can only be put in force against the poor.

CHAPTER III

OF IMPRISONMENT FOR DEBT IN ENGLAND

> Oh let me pierce the secret shade
> Where dwells the venerable maid !
> There humbly mark, with reverend awe,
> The guardian of Britannia's law ;
> Unfold with joy her sacred page,
> The united boast of many an age ;
> Where mixed, yet uniform, appears
> The wisdom of a thousand years.
>
> SIR WILLIAM BLACKSTONE :
> " The Lawyer's Farewell to his Muse."

I AM honestly sorry to have to inflict a chapter of
legal history upon anyone, but for the life of me I do
not see how the imprisonment for debt of to-day can
be intelligently appreciated until one knows something of its lineage.   To begin with, it may be news
to some folk to learn that in the merry days of
Henry III there was no imprisonment for debt at
all.   If Godfrey the garlic seller or Hogg the needler
owed Rose of the small shop a tally for weekly pur-
chases and would not pay, Rose, poor woman, could
not get an order to send them to gaol.   Yet there is
no evidence that trade was thereby injured, or that
there was any difficulty in Rose regulating her
credit-giving, or in Godfrey and Hogg and the rest
obtaining as much credit as they deserved.   The

36

first thing to remember is that England at one period had no use for imprisonment for debt.

It occurs to me that, if I can persuade the man in the street to understand how imprisonment for debt began and continued until it became a great public scandal, and show how in the last hundred years little by little its evil influence and extent have been abated with good results, we shall be making great strides towards the restoration of that liberty in England which in the matter of debt was the citizen's privilege in the days of Henry III.

But the reason for the absence of imprisonment for debt in these early feudal days is not so satisfactory to modern ears as one could wish. Lord Chief Baron Gilbert, that crisp and accurate lawyer of the eighteenth century, puts it very clearly when he says : " But there was no Capias for the Debt or Damages of a Common Person, because the party having trusted him only with personal Things his remedy was only on the personal Estate, and the King had the Interest in the Body of his subject ; and the Lord in his *Feudatory* or *Vassal* to be called out to War or to labour for him ; and therefore none but the King could imprison him."

And this seems clear, that the reason a creditor could not imprison a debtor was because in those days a debtor had only a limited interest in his own body. The fighting part of his body belonged to the king, the labouring part of his body belonged to his lord, and the king and the lord were not going to have their rights and property in his body interfered with because the subject and vassal had been foolish

THE LAW AND THE POOR

enough to run into debt with another subject and vassal who wanted his money.

You will, indeed, find that the whole history of the law and the poor seems to be a long struggling of the poor out of slavery and serfdom where they had a certain guaranteed amount of food and protection from their masters, similar in nature to that given to the ox or the ass or anything that was his, into a state of freedom, so-called, in which they had given up their rights to food and protection without getting any certain rights of wages or the equivalent of wages in return. We are in the middle of adjusting these things to-day, and the story of imprisonment for debt, and why it is retained at the present only for poor people, is a page in the curious English history of social progress.

As long as the debtor was a vassal having certain duties to perform for the lord of the manor his lordship thought him as much worth preserving as the game or venison within the curtilage of his park. It was for this reason you could not take his body in execution. As you may know, when you obtain a judgment in a court of law the next thing to do is to proceed to execution; that is to say, the judge having given you judgment a writ is granted to you whereby you get the sheriff to take your part and seize for you either the goods or body of your opponent. The history of these ancient writs is full of amusing folk-lore for those who love such things, and we still call them by their old dog-Latin names, not for any scientific purpose, but for much the same reason that the doctors write their prescriptions in hieroglyphics and priests mumble Latin or English—but always mumble—in a cathedral. It is the essence of a profession that it should be mysterious and incomprehensible, otherwise the common herd would not respect it and pay its fees.

And, prior to Henry III., if you got a judgment against your neighbour for money owing by him to you, your remedies of execution were these. By a writ of *fieri facias* the sheriff could be commanded to seize the goods and chattels of the debtor in satisfaction of the debt. This dear old writ, the *fieri facias*, affectionately alluded to as the *fi. fa.* by attorneys, bailiffs and others who have the handling of the fellow, is still with us. I agree that without him the delivery of judgments in courts of law would be mainly of academic and rhetorical interest. For as Gilbert—not William Schwenck, but Sir Geoffrey the Chief Baron—puts it, if a party trusts a man with personal things, then his remedy should be against the personal things of the debtor, and this seems a principle of common law and common sense as just as it is homeopathic. As our latter-day Gilbert would have put it, " the punishment fits the crime."

But when you come to our other writ, the *capias satisfaciendum*, or " *ca. sa.*" as it is written in the absurd legal shorthand of the day, or " body warrant " as it is still termed with brutal accuracy in Lancashire, then you will find that in old days different considerations prevailed. You were not allowed to seize a man's body for debt, but only his goods. And I am glad to find myself setting forth

39

high Tory doctrine and asking my fellow citizens to return to the earliest common law of the land, for this seems clear that originally, unless the action was for trespass *vi et armis*, which was in the nature of a criminal matter, there was no remedy against the body of the defendant. The *ca. sa.* whereby the sheriff was ordered to seize the body of the defendant in execution could not issue at the instance of a successful plaintiff at common law. In other words there was no imprisonment for debt.

Our forefathers recognised what we seem to have partially lost sight of, that as credit could only be given commercially to a man with goods, it was fair and just that his goods should be seized if he did not carry out his contract. But for reasons of their own—no longer sound as reasons to-day, it is true— they refused to allow a man to mortgage his body for goods. Body warrants only issued against criminals or in actions of a semi-criminal character. It will be reassuring to those conservative minds who fear the abolition of imprisonment for debt to remember that there was a time in England when it did not exist, and that if we abolish it to-day we are working on old fashioned and constitutional lines. Imprisonment for debt has not the sanction of antiquity, and a desire to sweep it away must not be put down to the wild and wicked desires of a political futurist architect, but rather to the pious hopes of one who is in deep sympathy with the best features of the Norman and Early English social institutions of his native land.

To tell the long story of the statutory evolution

of imprisonment for debt from the Statute of Marlbridge, 52 Henry III. c. 23, to the Act for the Abolition of Imprisonment for Debt—so-called—of 1869, would be out of place here. It is enough to know that little by little the principle of the right of one man to seize the body of another in an execution for debt became recognised by statutes and by custom until the wrongs it caused reached such a scandalous pitch in the eighteenth century that some reform of it became inevitable.

The more modern contests over its partial mitigation from time to time throw a direct light on the differences of opinion upon the matter of to-day. It will be seen that there have always been two schools of thought among politicians. One school was clear, that to tamper with imprisonment meant ruin to trade ; the other held—what I take to be the true gospel—that a man ought not to be allowed to obtain credit on the security of his body.

Until the end of the eighteenth century the harshness and cruelty of imprisonment for debt received little attention. The history of the debtors' prisons, the Fleet, the King's Bench, the Marshalsea and the City Compters, are pages of the story of our law that no one can read to-day without shame. Yet the Howards and Frys who called attention to the facts met with just as little encouragement and attention from the rulers of the country as anyone does to-day who desires to put the coping stones on the completed work, the foundations of which were laid by these great reformers.

The extraordinary results that took place through

imprisonment for debt as it existed in the eighteenth
century are surely beyond parallel in any legal
system. The plays and fictions of the time are full
of instances. You remember when Roderick
Random finds himself in the Marshalsea he meets
with his old friend Jackson and asks him about his
amour with the lady of fortune : " You must know,"
replies Jackson, " that a few days after our adventure
I found means to be married to that same fine lady
you speak of and passed the night with her at her
lodgings, so much to her satisfaction, that early in
the morning, after a good deal of snivelling and
sobbing, she owned that far from being an heiress
of great fortune she was no other than a common
woman of the town who had decoyed me into
matrimony in order to enjoy the privilege of a
femme couverte, and that unless I made my escape
immediately I should be arrested for a debt of her
contracting by bailiffs employed and instructed for
that purpose." Upon hearing this poor Jackson
escapes and serves for a few months as surgeon of
a sloop, but, on his return, is arrested for a debt of
his wife's and comes to live at the Marshalsea on
half pay.

Nor is there anything wildly improbable in the
story. Smollett had been in a debtor's prison
himself, and very likely had heard the story at
first hand, for many equally extraordinary stories
in real life are well authenticated.

There was the strange case of the lady who
married a man under sentence of death to get rid
of her debts, and was greatly upset when her husband

was respited and sent to the colonies. But perhaps one of the most curious stories is that of the dear old blind spinster of Clerkenwell, with a fortune of a thousand pounds, who took a deep interest in the career of an industrious shoemaker's apprentice and made him presents of clothes and a watch and lent him ten pounds. When he was out of his articles and was about to go home to Leicestershire and settle down there, he was arrested for the loan and the attorney's bill of costs and the " garnish " at the lock-up to which he was taken. After a few days the kind-hearted lady visited him and offered him three alternatives. He might pay the money ; go to the debtor's prison for the rest of his life ; or marry her. He chose the last alternative and was kept in the sponging house until his wedding day.

These stories are but a sample of the iniquities that were going on in that day, and yet then, as now, the feeling of legislators and business men seems to have been that it was dangerous to trade and business to sweep this horrible system away, so blind are people to the wrongs they see every day, so dull are ears to cries of pain and distress that are continuous and never cease. It would seem as though the conscience of mankind can only be startled into action by some catastrophe, some tragedy obviously brought about by bad government and bad laws, and not until then will it translate its knowledge of evil into demand for reform.

The tragedies of imprisonment for debt occurred, but they took place behind closed doors and the world only heard of them by slow degrees. At

length, however, the constant repetition of the
miseries of the poor debtors who languished in
prison, wasting their lives and eating out their
hearts in despair, began slowly to convince the man
in the street that there really was something wrong
with the world and that the cup of human misery
of some of their fellow creatures was slopping over
into the saucer of despair. Timid reformers began
to think something might be done. The arguments
then, as now, were all one way, but then, as now,
there was no one to listen to them. Good men had
raised their voices to point out the wrong-doing that
was going on, and the unnecessary wretchedness that
was being caused, but nothing much came of it.
There were a few desultory and ineffective movements towards discharging poor debtors, but the
matter did not greatly interest mankind, and there
seemed to the eighteenth century mind no very clear
reason why a debtor once in prison for debt should
ever be released. To-day, in the same way, it is
difficult to persuade the average citizen that there
is any injustice in a debtor being sent to prison for
debt. The attitude of mind about the thing is not
greatly altered, though happily the amount of
injustice and wrong-doing has been lessened.

It was not, indeed, until the beginning of the reign
of Queen Victoria, a time of great hope for the poor
and distressed, a period which has not inaptly been
called " the springtime of social reform," that any
practical movement was made. I myself keep
March 31st as the birthday of the movement for the
abolition of imprisonment for debt, but anyway it is

a red-letter day in the history of English literature and worthy of great honour. For on that day, in the year 1836, the first number of " Pickwick," appeared and there is no doubt that the account of the Fleet prison in that volume has made it the popular text-book of legal reform in these matters. If " Pickwick " in 1836 was not the *causa causans* of Lord Cottenham's Bill to amend the law of insolvency which was introduced in December, 1837, there is no doubt that Dickens' stories of the cruelty of imprisonment for debt supplied the motive power necessary to pass it by rousing the public conscience to insist upon something being done.

The point of particular reform aimed at by the Bill was to abolish what was called arrest on mesne process. It is an absurd term, and it was a still more absurd thing. The wonder is that it had survived as long as it did. Mesne process, translated into English, means middle process, and the idea was to lock a defendant up in the middle of the trial and keep him there in case it turned out at the end of the proceedings that he owed the money. It was as popular with the sharks of the eighteenth century as the present imprisonment is with the moneylenders and tally-men of to-day. Any person who would make an affidavit that another owed him twenty pounds or more could lock him up pending the trial and, unless the victim could find the money and pay it into Court, he remained in the sponging house until the trial came on. Harry Warrington was served so, if you remember. Two gentlemen came from over the way, " one of them takes a strip of paper out of

45

his pocket and, putting his hand upon Mr. Warrington's shoulder, declares him his prisoner. A hackney coach is called and poor Harry goes to sleep in Chancery Lane." Certainly Harry owed the money and had been reckless and extravagant enough, but even then the method of arrest strikes us to-day as a little high-handed. Nor was it always made use of with honesty. To bold rascals it was a very perfect machine for the wickedest blackmail. An affidavit of debt—and eighteenth century affidavits were no nearer the truth than those of the present century—was all that was required, and if in the end the affidavit was found to be false, the only remedy was to prosecute the swearer of it—if you could find him.

A case that Lord Denman mentioned in the debates in 1837 created a good deal of uneasiness in the public mind. A certain Portuguese nobleman, the Duke de Cadaval, on landing at Falmouth, or when he was residing at Plymouth, was arrested on a pretended debt, thrown into prison, and obliged to pay a large sum of money to procure his release. He afterwards recovered in an action for malicious arrest heavy damages, but he never received a penny of them, nor is there any record that the false witnesses were punished for perjury. There are many stories of this kind, and it was an obvious result of the system of arrest on mesne process. One would have thought that there would have been no difficulty about abolishing a legal machinery that brought about such injustice, but, in truth and fact, it was quite otherwise. Indeed, the people who wanted to abolish the excellent and business-like system were

46

regarded as very pestilent and turbulent busy-bodies by the average citizen.

Another incident of imprisonment for debt at this date was that if a creditor preferred to issue a *ca. sa.* to a *fi. fa.* and took the body of the debtor in preference to the property of the debtor, he thereby discharged the debtor. If, therefore, the debtor preferred imprisonment to paying his debts, the law afforded the creditor no other remedy. There were instances of debtors remaining in prison for over twenty years well able to pay their debts, but preferring to live in luxury within the rules of the prison. *Re Pickwick* is perhaps the popular leading case on this point. But whilst we remember with pleasure how the law enabled our dear friend to outwit for a time those wily attorneys Dodson and Fogg, do not let us forget the terrible sights he saw in the Fleet.

The Chancery prisoner, the fortunate legatee whose lawyers had had the thousand pounds legacy, and who was in the Fleet, mending shoes for twenty years because the loom of the law had woven a shroud of costs round him and buried him in prison — he was no fiction — His heart was broken when his child died and he could not kiss him in his coffin. There he remained living a solitary lingering death, lonely amid the noise and riot of the Fleet, until God gave him his discharge. This and many another case was before My Lords and known to the intelligent Commons when the question of the abolition of arrest on mesne process came up for discussion in 1837.

It is to Lord Cottenham, as I have said, that we

47

owe the statute which, to use Mr. Atlay's phrase,
" abolished the bane of Mr. Micawber's existence,
imprisonment for debt on mesne process." Nor
must it be thought that it was done without a
struggle.   Lord Lyndhurst said, and no doubt truly,
that, judging from the petitions, he should be within
the truth in saying that the Bill was very unpopular.
The petitions were at least ten to one against the
Bill. There was no more enthusiasm about mitigating imprisonment for debt then than there is to-day.
The history of these things is always the same ; the
traders objected to the abolition of imprisonment for
debt, the newspaper propiietors strenuously opposed
the reduction of the Stamp Acts, the doctors fought
against national insurance.   Yet, when the horrible
thing is done, we find them smugly prospering on the
reform.

Lord Brougham, who from the very first had always
held instinctively the true faith in these matters,
pointed out to a reluctant House how credit was
imprudently given to the real injury of the customer
who is induced to buy what he cannot pay for, and
to the injury of those who do pay what they do owe,
but who pay the dearer in proportion to the bad
debts which the tradesman is led to let others contract with him.   Further, he emphasised the wrong
done by clothing an insolvent person with an
appearance of credit by lending him more goods
which serve as a bait or decoy to others that have not
yet trusted him.   He laid down the principle that
debt should never be treated as a crime and still less
as a crime to be punished at the sole will and pleasure

of the creditor, and eloquently called upon the peers to wipe out this foul stain from our civil code.

Arrest on mesne process was abolished, not ungrudgingly it is true, but it came to an end, and a commission was set up in 1839 to inquire and report upon the whole system of imprisonment for debt. This commission ultimately reported in favour of abolition. In 1844 another Bill was introduced to distinguish between cases where it could be shown that the debtor was an innocent fool and not a culpable contumacious defrauder. It was not of much avail as a social reform, but may be fairly described, perhaps, as a worthy effort. The brightest reading in its history for us to-day is the debate in which Lord Brougham, with savage eloquence, rubs it in—the modern slang expresses Brougham's method so accurately—and jeers at the opponents of imprisonment for debt now that all their Cassandra prophecies over the abolition of imprisonment by mesne process have proved themselves to be worthless. Abolition of this system had not diminished credit, and had not raised any difficulty in citizens obtaining credit. Then, as now, these were the trade arguments against reform solemnly used by business men, officials and lawyers, and though, on each occasion when the reform has taken place, they have been found to be the hollowest nonsense, yet they are repeated to the reformers of to-day with the same pompous effrontery with which they were offered to Lord Brougham.

We now come to 1869, in which year the present state of the law was created, and it is this law which

seems to me so unjust to wage earners and poor
people who are in debt, placing them as it does in
conjunction with the Bankruptcy Laws in such a
wholly inferior position to that of the well-to-do
citizens. In order to understand the exact legal
position it is, I fear, necessary to deal with the
matter in some little detail.

The intention of the Legislature at the time
seems to have been right enough. It was desired,
no doubt, that a fraudulent debtor should be
punished and that an honest debtor should not.
If a means could be invented to carry out this
principle no one would utter a word against it. A
fraudulent debtor is, I take it, a man who, having
ample means over and above the reasonable necessi-
ties of himself and his family, conceals them or
places them in fictitious names and then defrauds
his debtor and refuses to pay him.

I should be in favour of more stringent measures
being taken against the fraudulent debtor, for one
meets him every day, well-to-do and smiling, with
a bill of sale on his furniture and everything in his
wife's name. But he is the curled darling of the law.
He makes use of the law to protect himself and his
frauds, and the Debtors Act, which was intended to
abolish imprisonment for debt, has no terrors for
him, whilst under its provisions hundreds of weekly
wage earners are imprisoned.

As Sir George Jessel said, the real intention of the
Debtors Act, 1869, was to abolish imprisonment for
debt for honest debtors and to retain the right of
judges to punish fraudulent debtors. Many of the

sections of the Act are framed, and to some extent assist, in the excellent aim of making it hot for the naughty and wicked debtor who has cheated or defrauded his creditors. Why is such a person punished ? asks the Master of the Rolls. I give the answer in his own words. " Simply because he is a dishonest man. He need not perhaps be called a thief in so many words, but he is a man who takes or keeps money belonging to other people, and he is punished accordingly." Instances of such are defaulting trustees and similar misdemeanants, and, so far as the Act provides for their punishment, we have no quarrel with it.

Now no one would contend that the system of imprisonment for debt as carried out in the County Courts is a system directed in the main against dishonest men. Improvident, careless, foolish and childlike these poor defendants in the County Court may fairly be described ; but if a day of judgment audit could be carried out, and a balance struck on the item of " honesty " as between the working-men debtors and the class of traders who give them credit, I make little doubt which class, as a class, would show the better figures. No, we do not imprison in the County Court for dishonesty *per se ;* dishonesty may or may not be a feature of any particular case, but it is not an essential.

The order for imprisonment is made under section 5 of the Debtors Act, 1869. That is the tally-man's charter. I am sorry to bore anyone with all these sections and statutes, but there is such a lot of inaccuracy written and talked about the matter

THE LAW AND THE POOR

that it is best to set down the actual enactment.
We must remember then that the Act, being an
Act for the abolition of imprisonment for debt, had
begun by enacting in the fourth section that "with
the exceptions hereinafter mentioned no person
shall be arrested or imprisoned for making default
in payment of a sum of money." These last words
state quite clearly the true principle of what the law
ought to be. Unfortunately for the poor the
special exception made for them has only too truly
proved the rule.

The opponents of abolition were but too successful
in their endeavours to make inroads upon the
thoroughness of the proposed reform, and one of the
exceptions was called "a saving power of committal
for small debts." It might have been better
described perhaps "as a saving power to imprison
poor debtors." This is the famous section 5 of the
Debtors Act, 1869, over which so much controversy
has since arisen, on the working of which two
important commissions have sat and reported, and
under which we may proudly claim to be one of the
last civilised countries that clings to a system of
imprisonment for debt.

It is necessary to set out the section at some
length, for it has a googlie element about it and is not
so innocent as it appears on the surface. It first
sets out "that any Court may commit to prison for
six weeks any person who makes default in the
payment of a debt or instalment due in pursuance of
a judgment." That, of course, is plain sailing
imprisonment for debt. Then, however, follows the

sub-section—I again apologise for troubling you with all this, but it is really a good citizen's duty to understand it—which causes all the worry. It is enacted in sub-section (2) " that such jurisdiction shall only be exercised where it is proved to the satisfaction of the Court that the person making default either has *or has had* since the date of the order or judgment the means to pay the sum in respect of which he has made default and has refused or neglected or refuses or neglects to pay the same."

It is the words that I have printed in italics that hit the poor man and the weekly wage earner, for of course it is generally provable that, although he has no present means to pay a debt, he *has had* since the judgment means to pay which he has spent on the maintenance of his family, or, if you will, on beer or tobacco, or picture palaces, or, in a word, as good solvent middle class people would say— improvidently.

The further matters enacted are all sensible enough, granted you approve of the main principle of im- prisonment for small debtors. They deal with proof of means of the person making default, allowing such proof to be given in such manner as the Court thinks just, and for these purposes the debtor and any witnesses may be summoned and examined on oath according to the prescribed rules.

The other material points of the section are that a County Court judge must exercise his jurisdiction in open Court, he may order the debt to be paid by instalments, he may also make continuous committals on each unpaid instalment, he may vary and rescind the order, and the imprisonment when suffered does not distinguish or discharge the debt or other remedies of the creditor. The debtor can take his release in payment of debt and costs.

Anyone who studies this Act of 1869 and comes to the conclusion that this system is anything less than imprisonment for debt, and not imprisonment for fraud, must, I think, be driven to argue that the men who drafted the Act called the Act an Act for the abolition of imprisonment for debt, called section 5 a saving clause for continuing imprisonment for small debtors in certain cases, and did not understand their business. As a matter of fact they knew their business very well indeed, and they carried it out faithfully and well.

What happened undoubtedly was this : Parliament as a whole was out to abolish imprisonment for debt. There were a lot of old-fashioned folk then as now, who wanted to retain it. Compromises were made. It was agreed that there should be abolition, it was also agreed that there should be exceptions. The exceptions readily granted were cases of fraudulent trusteeship and the like. This was not enough for the old gang, so the promoters of the reform threw in poor persons owing small debts. The poor had as few friends in Parliament as the fraudulent and they were huddled together into the same bundle of exceptions as a sop to the opponents of the Bill. When folk describe our present system in the County Court as anything other than imprisonment for debt, a legitimate offspring of its noble Norman ancestor *capias ad satisfaciendum,* they do it in ignorance of the legal and political history of the Debtors Act, 1869.

I should like to have set out much of the debate in the House of Commons on the second reading of this Bill. Sir Robert Collier, the Attorney-General, openly expressed his regret that imprisonment for debt was going to be retained in the County Courts, and several members spoke wisely about the hardships then inflicted on the poor and the undesirability of continuing them. But the following extract from a speech of Mr. McMahon shows that no one at that time was under any delusion about what was going to be done. " When," he said, " arrest on mesne process was abolished shortly after the passing of the Reform Bill it was then said that credit would be disturbed, and that traders would not be able to carry on their business. But these forebodings were purely imaginary, and in the same way he believed no evil would attend the good that must undoubtedly result from the final abolition of imprisonment. If, however, they allowed the rich man to escape under the bankruptcy system they ought not to admit the poor man to be liable to imprisonment, for by so doing they would certainly be open to the charge of having one law for the man in broadcloth and another for the man in corduroys."

Here the warning is clearly given by a man on the spot, that what they were about to do was to set up a system unfair to the poor, and there was really no doubt in the minds of any of the legislators of the day that they were deliberately retaining imprisonment for debt for the poor. I want to insist on this point because one of the stumbling blocks in the way of reform to-day is the strange belief, fostered by the tally-man and his friends, that in some mysterious way imprisonment for debt has really been already abolished and that the working classes really go to prison for contempt of court or some other reason. There is no truth in this whatever.

The Attorney-General who introduced the Debtors Act, 1869, may surely be credited with understanding what it was intended to do. He knew well enough that his Bill was going to abolish imprisonment for debt for the rich and retain it for the poor. He pointed out that he was making bankruptcy cheaper and more stringent. It would be obviously absurd, he said, to make a day labourer a bankrupt, and that brought him to the very difficult question of County Court jurisdiction. At that time the County Court had a jurisdiction to punish for fraud as an incident of debt and also to imprison for debt. He proposed to take away the jurisdiction to imprison for fraud and to leave fraudulent debtors, both rich and poor, to the Criminal Courts. " But then," he continued, " came the other question of County Court imprisonment where a man was able to pay his debt, but would not do so. He did not regard that imprisonment as a mere punishment for a past offence *but it was a process of imprisonment for the purpose of compelling the payment of a debt*, and it was a process very analogous to the principle of the Bankruptcy Law." He came to the conclusion, after further argument, " that this power of imprisonment in the one case he had mentioned must be retained."

When an Attorney-General in 1869 brings in a Bill to abolish imprisonment for debt and deliberately tells us that he retains one class of imprisonment for debt, it is inconceivable why people to-day should strive to make out that the system we are working is not imprisonment for debt, but something else. Unless it be that the advocates of imprisonment for debt know in their heads that it is an evil, out-of-date system, and they have an instinct that it smells more sweetly under some other name.

From 1869 to the present there has been no further reform. Many hope that there never will be any, but for my part I have no doubt it will come along, not in my time, perhaps, but whenever the right moment may be. From 1869 until to-day over three hundred thousand English citizens have been actually imprisoned who have not been guilty of any crime whatsoever. They have been imprisoned mainly for poverty or, if you will, for improvidence—that blessed word that so insidiously describes in the poor that failure in economic asceticism, that lack of cold self-denial of luxury and extravagance, that absence of patient thrift and simplicity of life—characteristic features which are never wanting in the beautiful lives of those social classes above them that the poor must learn to look up to and to imitate.

CHAPTER IV

HOW THE MACHINE WORKS

Roll on, thou ball, roll on !
Through seas of inky air
    Roll on !
It's true I've got no shirts to wear,
It's true my butcher's bill is due ;
It's true my prospects all look blue—
But don't let that unsettle you !
        Never *you* mind !
        Roll on !
    W. S. GILBERT : " To the Terrestrial Globe."

I FEAR the earth will do a lot of rolling on before
we abolish imprisonment for debt, but very likely
I am exhibiting a somewhat senile haste in the
matter which is unbecoming. To me it appears
strange that, whilst in every other science the
professors of it are making earnest efforts to place
the result of their studies to the credit of mankind,
the law seems more incapable than theology of
assimilating new ideas and getting into step with
the march of time. I have no hesitation in saying
that the County Court, as a debt-collecting machine,
is a one-horse wooden antiquity only fit for the scrap
heap. If you went down to Euston and found them
coupling up Puffing Billy to the Scotch Express
and the engine driver dissolved in tears, you would
understand the kind of hopeless feeling that oppresses

me every morning when I sit down to try a hundred judgment summonses.

For how can they be said to be tried in the sense in which an Englishman is supposed to be tried before he is deprived of his liberty. There is very little evidence, often the defendant makes no appearance and does not even send his wife to tell the tale for him. He cannot afford to leave his work and she ought not to be asked to leave her babies. The word, therefore, of the plaintiff, or, more probably, the debt collector—and many of these men, making it their business and dealing daily with the Court, are far more accurate and careful than the plaintiffs themselves—this is all you have to go by. The law, as I told you, left it entirely to the taste and fancy of the judges what evidence they should receive, and though nowadays all judges honestly endeavour, I think, not to carry out the law to the full extent of its cruelty, yet naturally different men hold different views of the rights and liabilities of the poor, and so there is no sort of equality in the treatment they receive in different districts.

Thus we have in the working of imprisonment for debt everything that is undesirable. The liberty of the subject is at stake, but there is no right of trial by jury, such as the fraudulent bankrupt or any other misdemeanant is entitled to ; the evidence on which the debtor is convicted and sent to gaol is any evidence that the judge thinks good enough, and within the limit of six weeks the imprisonment is anything that each particular judge determines. There is, of course, no appeal, and when the prisoner

comes out of gaol he still owes the debt, though he
cannot be imprisoned again for the same debt or
instalment. The multiplicity of these proceedings
is appalling. There are over a million small debt
summonses issued every year and nearly four
hundred thousand judgment summonses, of which
about a quarter of a million are heard. What a
waste of time and energy it all means. Judges,
registrars, solicitors, bailiffs, debt collectors, the
piling up of costs and fees on to the original debt,
the dragging off to gaol of an occasional debtor
pour encourager les autres, the breaking up of some
poor home, the blackmailing of friends and relations
very little better off than the poor debtor himself,
the squeezing of the pittance out of the bellies of the
little children to keep the father out of prison—
what a picture to leave on the canvas of our own
generation for our grandchildren to scoff at.

And the business result of it! Even when the
debt is paid—if it is paid—after years of waiting and
hours spent coming down to the Courts seeing if the
money is yet paid in—or 20 per cent. paid to
a debt collector to do it for you—when all is finished,
would it not have been far better if you had recognised that you had made a bad debt and stood
yourself a few shillings worth of righteousness in
forgiving your debtor his indebtedness? Certain it
is that the system is useless to, and very little used
by, the respectable individual creditor. Indeed, if
he tries to use it, he stumbles into so many pitfalls
and finds the procedure of it so troublesome and
uncanny that he very often fails to stay the course,

and, after a few wasted days, goes his way and leaves the debtor to go his. The best customers of the County Court, indeed the only people to whom the system of imprisonment for debt is of any real service, are those traders who carry on a business which can only be carried on and made to pay by reason of the sanction of the shadow of the gaol which is of the essence of the contract.

The tally-men, the moneylenders, the flash jewellery touts, the sellers of costly Bibles in series, of gramophones and other luxuries of the mean streets, these are the knaves the State caters for. For these businesses are based, and soundly and commercially based, on imprisonment for debt. The game is to go forth with a lot of flash watches, persuade a workman in a public-house or elsewhere to sign a paper that he has bought one—he always says, silly fellow, that he thought he had it on approval—and when he fails to pay his instalments put him in the County Court. I have known a pigeon-flying working man earning thirty-five shillings a week buy a watch priced eight pounds which had a second hand and a stop movement for timing that momentarily overcame his better sense of economy. Without imprisonment for debt it would not have paid the servant of the Evil One to have led him into the temptation.

To these traders the County Court is of real value. They issue their plaints in bundles, they take out judgment summonses in batches of thirty, fifty, or a hundred at a time, they can afford to have a skilled clerk well versed in the procedure of the Court to fill up the papers, and can run the machine which a complacent State puts at their disposal with very good results to themselves. I remember a firm starting in Manchester with the sale of some sort of horse medicine—good or bad is really no matter. The method of business was delightfully simple. The proprietor travelled round in Herefordshire and Devonshire and persuaded the farmers to try some of the horse medicine. A form was signed which was a contract of sale and a promise to pay in Manchester. This gave the Manchester Court jurisdiction to issue the summonses, which were for sums of under two pounds. Letters came complaining that no contract had been intended, that the stuff was worthless, etc., but no one turned up and judgment went by default. The success of the business was its ruin. The plaintiff, tired of filling up the forms of the Court and well knowing that none of his customers would pay without process, actually had affidavits of his own ready printed, and this cynical admission of the fraudulent nature of his trade—for an honest man would not expect nearly all his customers to refuse to accept goods ordered—led to his undoing. Inquiries were made, one or two farmers were induced to appear and give evidence, and his business career came to an end.

I am not, of course, saying that the County Court exists only for those who have the courage and effrontery to make the full use of the machine as an accessory to shady trading. But it can be demonstrated that imprisonment for debt is the mainstay of such trades as moneylending and credit drapery

HOW THE MACHINE WORKS

and all those low trades that make their profits by
foisting shoddy luxuries on to working men and their
wives.

Some time ago I made a careful examination of
some 460 judgment summonses taken consecutively.
The figures were from the Manchester Court. I
found the following were the trades represented :—

<pre>
        Drapers 154
        General dealers   .   .   . 130
        Jewellers   60
        Grocers 35
        Moneylenders 24
        Doctors 10
        Tailors   5
        Miscellaneous traders issuing less
            than four summonses .   . 42
                                          ───
                                          460
</pre>

General dealers, it must be remembered, are
traders in a large or small way of business who will
sell furniture, drapery, clothes, cutlery, or anything
you like, on the instalment system. Their methods
of trading are tally-men's methods.

If this list be looked at, it will be seen that the
general public make very little use of imprisonment
for debt. The substantial shopkeeper and ratepayer
is scarcely represented at all, the grocers and a few of
the big general dealers being the only people who pay
rates. Some of these general dealers it should be
remembered are limited companies having numerous
agents paid by high commissions and spending large

sums in advertising. Their prices are apparently low, but the quality of their goods leaves much to be desired. Now what worries me is, why should the State keep Courts going for men of this class ? The only creditor in that list for whom one can have the least sympathy is the doctor, and the National Insurance Act has now put him on a cash basis, so that in a list taken to-day he would not appear so often. It is clear from these figures that at a cost to the general body of taxpayers you are encouraging a bad class of parasite traders to choke the growth of thrift among the working classes.

For unless you make it ruinous to the creditor for the credit to be given you will never stop it. How can a man at work hinder credit being given through the agency of the wife when the law permits it and caters for it by providing the trader who lives by it with a special debt-collecting machine without which this class of trader were impossible. I have known cases where a working man's wife was dealing with nineteen different Scotch drapers. What wages can satisfy such an orgy of drapery as that ? How often, too, do men and women buy watches to pawn them for drink or a day at the races ? What is this but an evil and ruinous form of moneylending ? And what makes these things possible among our poor people ? The law siding with the knave against the fool ; the saving clause for the imprisonment of poor debtors in the Act of 1869.

And whereas I shall show you that bankruptcy and divorce are the luxuries of the rich, so it is only fair, I think, to allow that imprisonment for debt is a distinctive privilege that the law reserves for the poor. A man among the well-to-do classes is never imprisoned for debt; the wage-earners are practically the only people who are subject to it.

The governor of a gaol reported a case to the last Select Commission that sat and did nothing on the subject. A labourer was sent to his custody for twenty-one days in default of payment of four shillings and costs, five and ninepence in all. How can a State for very shame prate about the extortion of moneylenders when it adds forty per cent. on to a small debt like this for costs? The man was a widower with four children, the eldest of whom was thirteen, and the youngest two or three years old.

When father went to prison the children went to the workhouse. That is all part of the system. The debt was a tally-man's debt for clothes supplied to his late wife. The governor sent it as a typical case for the Commission to consider. "As I believe," he wrote, " that there is an idea of having the law on imprisonment for debt amended."

The good governor was, of course, entirely mistaken about that. There is no such idea, except in the heads of dreamers and visionaries like Elihu and the good governor and myself, and we do not count. So his report ended in nothing, and remains on record as a typical result of the working of imprisonment for debt in a civilised European State in the early part of the year of our Lord 1909.

I should like to leave the matter there as a horrible example, for so it is, but I am a man of truth—and, in fact, the poor labourer was not kept in gaol. It was afterwards discovered that the good governor, when he investigated the man's case at 9.30 a.m. on the morning after his arrest, had paid his debt for him and set him free. You remember that Elisha in a similar case performed a miracle by filling several jars with oil. For myself, I think the good governor's was an even nobler deed.

And when the supporters of this wretched system tell you that very few people actually go to gaol, that is, in a sense, true. There are only about six or seven thousand, say, who go to prison on a hundred and odd thousand warrants issued. The number too, is decreasing. This is not, however, to the credit of the law, but because, as I shall show, the law is not strictly administered, and also because the public conscience, what Lord Haldane so graphically described under the German title *Sittlichkeit*, is against it. The habit of mind, custom, and the right action of good citizens do not sanction enforcing debt by imprisonment. It is only the greedy, low-down citizens who deign to use it. But the matter is lightly regarded. A few thousand poor people doing time for trumpery debts cannot, anyhow, be allowed to trouble the sleep of the middle-class voter, and what am I but an untaught knave to bring their slovenly, unhandsome corpses betwixt the wind and his nobility ?

It is not only the very poor who are dragged to gaol that suffer. The system is really one for blackmailing the poor man's friends and relations. You ask a debtor when he comes before you on a second instalment of a debt : " But you managed

66

to pay the first instalment ? " " Yes," he replies ; " but I had to borrow it from my brother-in-law, and I have not paid him back yet, and he can ill-afford to lose it."

I have heard that story hundreds of times, and I know it is often a true one. Bailiffs will tell you that on the road to gaol a prisoner will ask to be allowed to call at various houses, looking for an Elisha, and if he cannot find anyone to work miracles nowadays he does very often find someone with five and ninepence and a kind heart. The poor are very good to one another in distress, and it is better that a brother man should be saved from gaol and restored to his home and children than that the land-lord should have his next week's rent.

In the bad old days a County Court judge openly said that he found it better to commit to prison for six weeks rather than any shorter period, for he found that the longer the period for which he committed people to prison the shorter the term served, " because when they were committed for the whole six weeks they moved heaven and earth among their friends to get the funds to pay."

Friends of the system of imprisonment for debt call this " putting the screw on." I think " black-mailing " is the straighter English—but any dirty old phrase will do.

And an enormous evil, the extent and results of which can only be guessed, is that the power to send a fellow citizen to gaol for debt, the power to issue or not to issue a warrant for his arrest at any moment after he is in default, places a man and his family so entirely at the mercy of his creditor that, if the creditor be a man of bad character, terrible results may follow. Few of us probably have not heard stories of an evil-minded creditor using his power to seduce the virtue of a wife in her husband's absence. There is certainly truth in such stories. Human nature is the same in narrower lanes than Park lane. The tally-man plays on the wife's love of finery, she gets into debt, her husband knows nothing of it. As long as the wife is complacent nothing is heard of the debt. I do not say such scandals are common, but I have heard enough of such stories to know they are not fairy tales. Human nature being what it is the wonder is that these dramas are not more often enacted. When the poor have their Divorce Courts no doubt the evidence of them will be forthcoming, meanwhile they rest mainly on the complaints of women of insults offered to them, which may be fabrications, but are not always so. What a responsibility rests on a State that maintains a system which leads to such evils.

Another and less terrible affair is the political influence wielded by a grocer or draper over the free and independent voter whom he can put in gaol for twenty-one days if he fails to see eye to eye with him at election times about Disestablishment or Tariff Reform. Yet this is one of the minor evils of the working of the Debtors Act of 1869. In a hard-fought Lancashire election which ended in a tie there was a great flutter and to-do caused by the arrest on the eve of the poll of some earnest debtor of one colour by an equally earnest creditor of another colour. It may, of course, have had nothing to do with the election—but one never knows. Anyhow, it happened, and it was certainly not a desirable incident from the point of view of the losing candidate.

The theoretical arguments against the abolition of imprisonment for debt are few. The chief one is that a working man would be unable to get credit in times of distress. Personally I do not believe it. The argument has been used on every occasion when any legislative step has been taken to mitigate imprisonment, for always the prophecy has been : trade will suffer and individuals, for want of credit, will starve. On every occasion the facts have obstinately refused to honour the prophecy after the event. I am inclined to back history against prophecy in this matter. Credit will be given to a working man of good character to a reasonable amount, but he will not be tempted, as he is to-day, to mortgage his future wages on the security of his body for every passing whim. Beer is a cash business, betting is a cash business, picture palaces, railway trains, tram cars, slot machines, are all run on a cash basis, yet no one will pretend that the working man does not get as much as he wants of the goods and services of all of them.

To-day the temptation, and very largely, I am sorry to say, the practice, is for a workman to make the brewer and the betting man first mortgagees of his weekly wages, whilst the draper and the grocer are too often very ordinary shareholders indeed, obtaining an irregular dividend ranking after the

Treasury fees of the County Court. Can anyone
honestly say that it would not be better for the
draper and the grocer to have their working-class
business put on a cash basis. Abolish imprisonment
for debt and the grocer and draper will demand cash
in advance or, at the worst, weekly bills. The
workman will then be face to face with the immediate
question of whether he prefers to spend his wages in
drink and pleasure for himself or food and clothes
for his wife and children. I have no doubt what his
answer will be. The working man is of the same
nature as ourselves. In the old days of general
imprisonment for debt everyone lived in debt. The
middle classes were tempted to live beyond their
means and did so, and the Micawbers of the world
were always being carried off to prison, leaving their
families in tears. Now such a state of things is
unknown. Through the great private and public
stores the middle classes buy for cash the best
material at the cheapest prices and live within their
incomes. The result in their lives is matter of
social history. Why is it to be supposed that any
different result will be arrived at when the working
classes are no longer tempted by a false system of
credit ?

" The motive of credit," says Dr. Johnson, " is
the hope of advantage. Commerce can never be at
a stop while one man wants what another can supply ;
and credit will never be denied whilst it is likely to
be repaid with profit. He that trusts one whom he
designs to sue is criminal by the act of trust : the
cessation of such invidious traffic is to be desired and

no reason can be given why a change of the law should impair any other. We see nation trade with nation where no payment can be compelled. Mutual convenience produces mutual confidence and the merchants continue to satisfy the demands of each other though they have nothing to dread but the loss of trade."

This argument was against imprisonment for debt as the worthy Doctor saw it in his own time, but it is just as convincing to-day about our own or any other form of imprisonment for debt. It goes to the principle and the root of the matter and, like many another of his best sayings, is the knock-out blow on the subject.

Further, we have proved in our own country the beneficial effects of the abolition of imprisonment for debt, and other countries have set us the good example of doing away with it altogether. In Germany they have a strict system of enforcing judgments against well-to-do debtors who seek to cheat their creditors, a class to whom we are somewhat indulgent, allowing many fraudulent persons to live at the expense of tradesmen by the simple expedient of putting goods in their wife's name. But this procedure is not available against working men, and the result is that they have to pay their way as they go along. Dr. Schuster, an English barrister and a Doctor of Laws of the University of Munich, explained the German system of debt collecting to the Commission of 1908. Not only did he make it clear that the German workman had, in the absence of imprisonment, acquired habits of thrift that our system discourages, but he pointed out that the insurance funds against sickness and accident, the trades unions, the co-operative societies, and charitable relief, enabled a German working man to tide over bad times without hanging a millstone of debt about his neck as he has to do in this country.

In the same way in France there is no imprisonment for debt for the poor, and so far from the French admiring our debt-collecting system in England they think it so expensive and futile that French traders absolutely give up all hope of recovering small debts in England and prefer to write them off as bad. And, indeed, I have more than a suspicion that if one could get an accurate financial history of the collection of a forty shillings' debt in the County Court by means of imprisonment for debt, one would find that, when Treasury fees, solicitor's costs, and creditor's time wasted had been duly paid for, there was very little balance to credit in the plaintiff's ledger. The more one sees of the system the more is one convinced that it is only serviceable to those creditors who use it in a wholesale manner to recover undesirable debts.

And though in theory I can find no serious argument against the abolition of imprisonment for debt, yet there is one practical difficulty in carrying it out which will have to be faced. The County Court registrars in the small courts are unfortunately paid by fees on the number of plaints issued. A moneylender or tally-man who cleans up his books once a year and brings into Court a few hundred plaints automatically raises the salary of the registrar. If this debt-collecting business is swept away, compensation for the disturbance of these salaries that have been calculated on this basis for many years must certainly be made. Probably it is this real practical objection that stands between the debtor and freedom.

I am not alone in thinking that the time is fast coming when the inconvenience of having as the registrar of a Court a solicitor in private practice paid by fees on the number of plaints will be so fully recognised that the country will demand a sweeping alteration in the system. The abolition of imprisonment for debt will give the Courts time to entertain jurisdiction for divorce and other matters where the poor are entitled to the same legal favour as the rich. When these reforms are made it will be found necessary, I believe, that the registrar of each Court or group of Courts should be a whole-time permanent official.

One other point remains to be mentioned. It is commonly said of those who desire to abolish imprisonment for debt that they have a lower sense of honesty than their opponents, that their views tend to encourage the man who runs into debt and will not pay when he can. For my part I care not how strict the law is made against dishonesty and debt resultant from dishonesty, but let the imprisonment be imprisonment for dishonesty and not for debt. If the debtor has acted criminally, let him be tried in a criminal court and punished for dishonesty. In the old days a County Court judge had powers to imprison for dishonesty, now he has only power to imprison for debt.

It is because I believe that the abolition of imprisonment for debt will improve the character of our citizens, as it improved the character of the Athenian citizens more than two thousand years ago, that I have put in so many hours overtime in the advocacy of its abolition. But whilst I would abolish imprisonment and should like to see the English workman paying his way like his German brother, whilst I am eager to see the poorer classes freed from the misery that debt and extravagance brings upon them to-day, yet no one, I hope, recognises more clearly than I do the sacred duty of a debtor to pay an honest debt. Every penny that he can save after his first duties of maintenance of wife and family should be devoted towards the repayment of debts. But this is a personal obligation on a man, like speaking the truth, or treating mankind with courtesy, and, in a word, is only a branch of the golden rule of doing to others as you would be done by. The breach of this obligation ought not, as it seems to me, to be treated nowadays as more than a case of a flagrant breach of good manners, and I would rather imprison a man who forgets to shut a railway carriage door when he gets out on a winter night than a man who omits to pay me the five shillings he borrowed yesterday. Both are ill-mannered fellows and must be dealt with socially, but not, I think, by imprisonment. Debt, except from misfortune, is really " worse form " than drunkenness. When that is generally understood no Debtors Act will be necessary.

HOW THE MACHINE WORKS

And the right feeling of a respectable debtor towards his creditor seems to me stated in very apt and beautiful words by old Jeremy Taylor in one of his " Prayers relating to Justice," in which he sets out the correct petition to be made thus : " And next enable me to pay my duty to all my friends, and my debts to all my creditors, that none be made miserable or lessened in his estate by his kindness to me, or traffic with me. Forgive me all those sins and irregular actions by which I entered into debt further than my necessity required, or by which such necessity was brought upon me ; but let them not suffer by occasion of my sin."

And if all debtors were moved by the aspirations included in this noble prayer, and if all creditors refused credit to poor folk unless they believed them to be men of such a character that the ideas of the petition were really living in their hearts, then, I think, there would be no need of imprisonment for debt or for County Court judges either. Indeed, the millennium would be at hand. But short of that great day, we are surely entitled to act as though the majority of mankind preferred right action to wrong action and not to encourage a class of debtors and creditors whose *nexus* is force and imprisonment rather than friendship and goodwill. The working man should be able to say with Piers Plowman : " Though I should die to-day, my debts are paid," and the law should help him to that end.

CHAPTER V

WORKMEN'S COMPENSATION

Your Plea is good ; but still I say, beware !
Laws are explained by Man—so have a care.
POPE : " First Satire of Second Book of Horace."

AN interesting volume might be written about historical litigants and their deeds of heroism. There was the dour Coggs who let in his friend Bernard over the brandy cask, there was the astute Scott who never paid Manby, the draper, for his wife's dresses, there was Wigglesworth who built himself an everlasting name in the Hibaldstow trespass case, and the hero of our own time, Dickson, who actually bested a railway company in the matter of Dutch Oven, the tail-less hound—these and many others are names enshrined in our dusty tomes of law, but if you would read them for mere delight, has not Sir Frederick Pollock done our leading cases into the most melodious verse.

If I were a bencher I would like to promote a pageant of these grand old litigants in honour of their service to the English law. I think my favourite among them all is little Priestley, the butcher's boy. You will find his simple story in the third volume of " Meeson and Welsby." How many know that it was at the Lincoln Summer

WORKMEN'S COMPENSATION

Assizes of 1836 that the brave butcher's boy began it, and started a train of legal thought reaching out to the workmen's compensation system of to-day ?

It was Priestley's duty to deliver meat, and one day Fowler, his master, sent him out with such an over-load of beef and mutton that the cart broke down and poor Priestley broke his thigh. Priestley brought an action against his master, and the jury gave him a verdict for one hundred pounds, but on appeal the judges would not have it, and so poor Priestley never got it. A servant, they said, is not bound to risk his safety in the service of his master; he may decline any service where he apprehends injury to himself.

Lord Abinger, C.B., who presided in the Appeal Court, admitted that there were no precedents either for or against such an action, but he was hard put to it to explain in legal terms why the little butcher's boy, who was certainly a brave explorer into legal hinterlands, was not to be allowed to peg out the claim the jury had awarded him. His Lordship was driven back to " general principles." The most learned lawyer of our day, the late Mr. Danckwerts, once said to me when I was a very young man at the Bar and talked glibly in consultation about the " broad grounds of truth and justice" : " If we have nothing better to rest our case on than that, God help us in the Court of Appeal." He then proceeded to show me some cases on the subject which my ignorance and inexperience had failed to discover. And it was not that the great man was not a lover of truth and justice, but that he knew that law meant, not what he and I and our client thought to be truth and justice, but what all generations of calm thinking men outside the dispute ought to think to be truth and justice, and that was to be found in the decisions in similar cases which he knew as no other lawyer ever did and about which I showed the common ignorance of my contemporaries.

Lord Abinger, then, having no cases to guide him, played a lone hand, and naturally played it from the point of view of the man who held the cards. If, he said, the master be liable to the servant in an action of this kind the principle of the liability would carry us to an alarming extent. For instance, if a master put a servant into a damp bed or a crazy bedstead or gave him bad meat to eat he might be liable in damages to his servant. " The inconvenience, not to say the absurdity, of these consequences," afforded a sufficient argument against poor Priestley and all other servants in like case. Priestley broke his leg and lost his case, and legal history does not record his future career. But, though Lord Abinger was against him, he might fairly have said in the phrase of a celebrated and eloquent Manchester surgeon that, " This day he had lighted a candle which would bring forth good fruit."

Several minor heroes made legal efforts to get behind this judgment, but the judges were too many for them. It was strongly endeavoured to make masters liable to their servants for injury caused by the negligence of a fellow servant, but the judges declared that, when a servant enters a service he contemplates all the ordinary risks of his work, including the negligence of his fellow servants, and that allowance is made for this by the master in fixing his wages. This " doctrine of common employment," as it was called, was, of course, largely a figment of judicial imagination, and it set back, or rather kept back, the hour of industrial reform for more than one generation.

There never really was a law of that kind. It is what is rightly called judge-made law. The judges said that it was " inconvenient " and " absurd " for masters to be responsible for negligence of their servants. So, of course, it was—to the masters and in 1836 that finished the matter. Thus it came about that in a railway accident, if it was caused, let us say, through the negligence of the company's signalman, every ordinary passenger got compensation out of the company, but the engine driver, the stoker, the guard, and their widows and orphans got nothing. Note, however, that if the signalman had belonged to another company it would have been quite otherwise.

In the old days when Druids sat under oak trees I daresay judge-made law was all very well, though no doubt the personal prejudices of the Druids were manifest in their decisions. But since the days of the Ten Commandments it has been recognised that statute law, carefully considered and simply expressed and written down on tables of stone or otherwise, is a better-class article for ordering the affairs of a modern community.

THE LAW AND THE POOR

No doubt the judges of 1836, being men connected with the upper middle classes of the day, could not conceive how civilisation and social order could exist side by side with a wicked system whereby a master had to compensate a workman injured in his service. The thing was as incomprehensible to the judicial mind of that date as the fifth proposition of Euclid is to many a third-form schoolboy to-day. Some of our judges are still in the third form in their ideas of sociology. That is one of the dangers of judge-made law. It is bound to put the stamp of old-fashioned class prejudice on its judgments. If the judges had been labour leaders they would have discovered an implied contract for the master to pay compensation with equal complacency.

The fact is that *natural justice* is merely justice according to the length of the judge's foot, as the common saying is. And the length of a judicial foot will depend on the evolution of the judge. That is to say, according as he and his ancestors have rested their feet cramped in pinched shoes under the mahogany of the wealthy or tramped barefoot along the highway in the freedom of poverty, so will a judge's principles of natural justice favour the rich or the poor.

We cannot get away from the fact that our judges make a great deal of law. The idea that a law is somewhere in existence and that the judges merely adopt it will not, I think, hold good for a moment. It is, indeed, a legal fiction. As a great American jurist, Professor John Chipman Gray, of Harvard, asks : " What was the law in the time of Richard

Cœur de Lion on the liability of a telegraph company to the persons to whom a message was sent ? " The answer to this question is obvious.

When one reads from time to time of decisions of the Courts that are upheld for a generation and finally overruled it is against the truth to speak of a pre-existing code of laws which the judges merely administer and expound. And the reason this is not openly acknowledged and that this mysterious bogey of pre-existent law is worshipped in our Courts of Justice is, as Professor Gray tells us, that there is an " unwillingness to recognise the fact that the Courts, with the consent of the State, have been constantly in the practice of applying in the decision of controversies, rules which were not in existence and were therefore not knowable by the parties when the causes of controversy occurred. It is the unwillingness to face the certain fact that Courts are constantly making *ex post facto* law." This is why we maintain the fiction of the continuous pre-existence of law.

The fear among those in authority seems to be that it would be unwise to openly recognise the real extent of the judicial power, as it would be unpopular and widely rebelled against, and that under the soothing fiction of the existence of an imaginary body of law and by the constant humble assertion of the judges, that they are not there to make laws, but only to administer them, the man in the street is deceived for his own good. For myself I have grave doubts whether this juggling with facts is to anybody's benefit. If it were recognised that in giving decisions at common law, and also in the interpretation of statutes, judges were not only declarers of existing law but makers of new law, then it would be possible to discuss and perhaps control or direct the law-making power of latter-day judges which from time to time manifests itself in unbalanced social judgments.

When the telephone was invented by Alexander Graham Bell, the Postmaster-General of the day claimed that it was a species of telegraph within the meaning of the Telegraph Act, 1869. Scientifically, of course, it was no such thing. Economically and in the interests of the community it was essential that the telephone should not be handed over to a public department predetermined not to give it a fair chance of development. Lord Kelvin and others pointed out what was the right policy in the matter, and, if the affair had gone to a parliamentary commission, his words would have had weight and a Telephone Development Act might have brought about excellent results. In that case the future of the telephone would have been settled by parliamentary law.

It was, in fact, settled by Mr. Justice Stephen in 1880, who declared that the telephone was a telegraph within the meaning of the Telegraph Acts, 1863, 1869, although the telephone was not invented or contemplated in 1869. In this way its proper development in this country was arrested for more than a generation. This is a remarkable instance of judge-made law. Why should an individual citizen just as unversed in science and business as the man in the street have the right to enact what should or should not be done with an entirely new invention which was not in existence when the statute which he pretends to apply was enacted. If the judges decided that an aeroplane plying for hire was a hackney carriage it would in law remain liable to all the statutory hackneydom of carriages until Parliament otherwise ordained. Is it not becoming time when judges, instead of making new and often reckless law, should be satisfied with declaring that in the case before them there is no law to their knowledge, and it is for the Legislature to consider and enact some. If this had been Mr. Justice Stephen's decision in *The Attorney-General* v. *The Edison Telephone Co. of London, Ltd.*, how much better for all of us to-day!

Again, in the Workmen's Compensation Act, Parliament, it is known, intended and desired to express many things which the judicial interpretations of the Act have altered and amended out of all recognition. It is scarcely true that these interpretations are all of them due to the verbal inaccuracy of the parliamentary draftsman, because one often finds the Court of Appeal taking one view of the meaning of the words and the House of Lords another. The real parliamentary object of the Act is now very difficult to understand and ascertain from the language used in the judgments interpreting it. If law were really a science and the interpretations of statutes by judges merely an ascertaining of parliamentary intention, one would not expect to find such different interpretations put upon the same words and the parliamentary intention so openly

83   G 2

THE LAW AND THE POOR

ignored.   In America grave popular discontent has
arisen over the law-making propensities of judges
and their bold refusal to carry out the intentions of
the Legislature.   We have no such widespread feeling
in this country, nor are we likely to have, but, all the
same, if we were to recognise the law-making power
of our judges and openly discuss it and endeavour to
define and limit it, there would be less fear in the
future of a rupture between the people and the judges
when futurist laws of far-reaching social reform come
to be administered by the Courts.   The lamentable
failure of consistent interpretations of the Compensation Acts is not calculated to raise the judiciary
in the affections and respect of the working classes.

   This matter is really one of grave importance, for
though in a sense and up to a point, whatever a
judge decrees is for the time the law—that time may
only be short.   In the end the law must express the
wills of those who rule society.   Professor Vinogradoff well says, in that excellent little treatise
" Common Sense in Law," we ought to " realise that
law has to be considered not merely from the point
of view of its enforcement by the Courts : it depends
ultimately on *recognition*."   When, then, we openly
confess that our judges are making new law every
day we shall have to impress on them—especially in
social matters—that the new law they make should
be, like new parliamentary law, founded on the best
aspirations of modern hopes and thoughts of the
future life of our people, rather than on the musty
creeds and traditions in which the individual human
beings who are judges have unfortunately for the

84

most part been educated. Judge-made law, like any other law, can only be of value to the community by popular recognition of its wisdom. The more the judges can keep to the real administration and interpretation of laws already existing the better for everyone, but new points of difference and a new social order of things naturally bring before the judges cases which can only be decided by their making new laws. When it is freely acknowledged that this is so, not only the community but the judges themselves will be called upon to consider and decide the ideals and principles by which they ought to be actuated in their capacity of lawgivers.

The law that was laid down to meet the case of the butcher and his boy became the law under which every railway servant, every miner, every mechanic, every navvy—the huge industrial army working under impersonal boards and committees of limited liability companies—risked his life in his daily work at his own expense. From 1836 to 1880 men were killed and injured by the thousands in industrial work and there were no pensions for the widows and orphans, no compensation for the wounded. Moreover, such a system discouraged employers from spending money on safety devices. No doubt many good and wise employers did a great deal to safeguard their men; equally no doubt, servants, being but human, were often injured and killed by their own carelessness and recklessness. The deplorable part of it was that the law had taken up an attitude against the poor in this matter and, as things stood, it was to no company's interest to spend their money and decrease their dividends by safeguarding the lives and limbs of their servants. This is still so in America, where on the railroads one man is killed for every two hundred and five employed and one is injured in every nine. " War is safe compared to railroading in this country," is the comment of Mr. Gilbert Roe, the American jurist.

Of course, at all times much was done by private charity of employers and others to help those who fell in the industrial fight.

In great colliery, shipping, or railway disasters subscriptions were made, no doubt, just as they are to-day, but the little obscure cases that mount up to many thousands in the annual statistics of the industrial killed and wounded were left to chance and charity.

The Employers' Liability Act of 1880 gave certain workmen limited rights of action in special cases. It was a prudent conservative measure brought in by a Liberal Government, and, of course, it was predicted that it would ruin every industry in the country. It must have cost industry a big bill in lawyer's fees. Every case under the Act was fiercely litigated, and might go from the County Court through two Courts of Appeal to the House of Lords.

I do not like to write ill of the poor statute. It is not actually dead, but moribund, and in the years gone by, when we were both young fellows I had many a good outing at the old fellow's expense, and he did me very well indeed. Therefore, of the Employers' Liability Act of 1880 I will say no more

than the man in the gallery did about the bride when
the minister asked, " Who giveth this woman
away ? " " I could, guv'nor, but I ain't going to."

But when we come to the Workmen's Compensation Acts that is another matter altogether. The
County Court judges have never received a penny
for the extra work thrust on them by these Acts, and
therefore there can be no indelicacy or indiscretion
in speaking one's thoughts plainly about the system.

And of the idea, and to a great extent of the
achievement, of Mr. Chamberlain's scheme—for to
him must the praise and honour be given for bringing it about—one cannot speak too highly. The
theory at the bottom of it is exactly the opposite
of the theory at the bottom of the judges' decision
against poor Priestley. It is best put in these
memorable words of Mr. Asquith :

" *When a person, on his own responsibility and for
his own profit, sets in motion agencies which create
risks for others, he ought to be civilly responsible for his
own acts.*"

That is the Magna Charta of workmen's compensation. It cannot be better stated. And the
promises and intentions of the new Act were splendid.
For Sir Matthew White Ridley said that the Act
would prevent uncertainty, and the parties would
know what their rights were, and that it provided a
simple and inexpensive remedy and would prevent
litigation. Mr. Chamberlain pointed out that up
to then, in 1897, only 12 per cent. of accidents
were dealt with, but that he hoped that now the
other 88 per cent. were to be brought in.

THE LAW AND THE POOR

His plan was so simple. An injured man in certain trades had only to ask for compensation, and receive it according to a fixed standard. State-paid doctors and arbitrators were to settle the details of the man's injuries and the amount to be paid to him. In his own words, " We wish to avoid bringing in again under another name the old principle of contributory negligence." A man was to receive compensation when injured in the service, even if he himself had been negligent.

I often think if Mr. Chamberlain had had health and strength to see the workmen's compensation business properly through he would have dealt with the lawyers who mangled his excellent scheme much as Theseus did with Procrustes when he met him on the banks of the Cephisus. Procrustes, you will remember, was a robber of Attica with a quaint sense of humour and a bedstead. If a traveller asked his hospitality he invited him to the bed, to which he tied him. If his legs were too long he cut them off, and if his legs were too short he pulled them out to the right length. Procrustes had the calm judicial mind of the Court of Appeal, and within his narrow limits knew exactly what he wanted to do and how to do it. But it was rough on the traveller.

And it is rough on a humane, simple, wise scheme for the benefit of the poor on leaving the hands of that great reformer and statesman, Mr. Chamberlain, to find that it is being martyred by the Procrustes of the law so that it may fit his narrow bed of justice. I think some of the decisions of the Court of Appeal would have been too many for

WORKMEN'S COMPENSATION

Mr. Chamberlain, and he would have severed their
connection with the workmen's compensation business as Theseus severed Procrustes' connection with
the bedstead business.

It is certainly not putting it too strongly to say
that the judicial body, speaking generally, did not
love the Workmen's Compensation Act.   The idea
at the base of it that a man should compensate
another outside the scope of contract or wrong was
to them out of harmony with the English law.   There
never was a more honest or single-hearted judge than
A. L. Smith, who was Master of the Rolls when the
earliest cases came up for decision in the Court of
Appeal.   The social creed of " A. L." was something
between that of the Church catechism and the
Sporting Times.   He was beloved by rich and poor.
His ideal world was one where a good-natured
aristocracy would confer kindnesses on a well-
mannered democracy, who should receive them in a
jovial and grateful spirit.   There is no doubt that he
endeavoured, as did all the judges of the Court of
Appeal, to rightly interpret its provisions; there is
equally no doubt that the spirit of many of the
interpretations placed upon the draftman's words
did not give effect to the intentions of Mr. Chamberlain and those who had passed the Act.   This one
can only trace to the habits of mind and social creeds
of judges like " A. L." who were wholly out of touch
with the beliefs and hopes of industrial democracy.
The Act of Parliament ought not to have been sent
to the Court of Appeal at all.   It was not founded
on any legal principle, it was an insurance scheme

that wanted business men to work it, and, as **Mr.** Chamberlain had foreseen, lawyers and litigation could in no way assist its working.

It cannot be gainsaid that the legal history of the Workmen's Compensation Act is not a thing for lawyers to boast about. No one has a greater respect for the Court of Appeal—and, indeed, for all my spiritual, legal, and worldly pastors and masters— than I have. Humility towards those who are called to any honour amongst us is my foible. I admit I have but a poor stomach for law and that I often find the learned judgments of Appeal Courts a little indigestible, but I remember the Irishman sampling the twopenny racecourse pies, and piously murmur to myself, " Glory be to God, but they're dam weighty." No one would deny the learning, subtlety and weight of the judgments in the Court of Appeal on the Workmen's Compensation Act, but, speaking as a common arbitrator who has to work the Act at first hand and make it human food for shattered men and widows and orphans, they have not tended to make my task easier, they have not simplified and assisted the scheme as a compensation scheme, and they have not been in harmony with the spoken intentions of the author of the scheme.

This, I think, to be due, in the first place, no doubt to the imperfections of the Act, in the second, to the fact that the appeals come before learned judges who have never administered the Act in cases of first instance and have had no practical experience of its working, and, in the third place, to the fact that to much of the higher judicial intellect the

theory of workmen's compensation is in itself
unscientific, and therefore repugnant.

Nearly all the cases, and there are, I regret to say,
many, where the Court of Appeal has overruled the
County Court, and the County Court judgment has
ultimately been restored by the House of Lords, the
error has been in the Court of Appeal striving to find
a reason to hinder the payment of compensation,
rather than searching for the principle which brought
an admitted injury within the scheme that Parliament has made to compensate the injured. After
all, the Act was one for the compensation of workmen, and every case of injury that is found not to be
provided for is a blot on the scheme.

The expense of all these appeals, is of course, a
terrible burden, and to a workman without a trade
union behind him would be impossible. Great confusion has been caused by having to work certain
matters for considerable periods under decisions of
the Court of Appeal that have afterwards had to be
dealt with differently by decisions in the House of
Lords. Very likely if there were a further appeal to
a House of Archangels the Court of Appeal would be
upheld. But to the injured man in the works and
the arbitrator waiting to award him his few shillings
a week what could be more pitiable and exasperating
than the delay and expense that the present method
of working the Act entails? One solid reason why the
appeals in workmen's compensation cases should be
removed from the Court of Appeal is that they cannot
be heard within a reasonable time. The *Law Journal*
of June 13th, 1914, states that there are seventy-

three workmen compensation appeals waiting to be heard, of which no less than ten were entered in 1913. It would be interesting to know how the appellants manage in the interim.

The Act itself was difficult enough no doubt to make into a good working scheme by those who desired to do it ; the hundredweights of handsomely published and learnedly edited reported decisions as to what it really means have made it hopelessly impossible to comprehend and increasingly difficult to administer.

To sum up the position of the Act to-day, with its myriad encircling decided cases, one can only say, with the immortal Sergeant Arabin, that it " bristles with pitfalls as an egg is full of meat."

When you have an Act of Parliament that in at least a dozen reported cases is solemnly decided to mean x in the Court of Appeal and y in the House of Lords, x representing " against the workman " and y " for the workman," what does the man in the street think about it ? And yet I cannot believe there is so much difficulty about construing the Act if the Courts would all steer by those excellent sailing directions of Lord Halsbury and Lord Davey.

Lord Halsbury said :

" The broad proposition, of course, was that the Legislature intended that there should be compensation given to every workman in certain trades when an injury happened to him in the course of his employment."

Lord Davey said :

" I entirely agree with what has been said by my

noble and learned friend on the Woolsack that you ought to construe this Act so as, as far as possible, to give effect to the primary provisions of it."

Now the primary provision of the Act was to compensate workmen for injuries, not to leave them uncompensated, and to do the business promptly and simply. We want more of the spirit of the Act and less of the letter, and a great deal fewer forms and orders and rules. In a word, more business and less procedure. As a dear old lady said to me when, after several efforts to set her affairs right, the registrar and myself had at last got her to fill up the papers necessary, as things are now, to get her case through : " I tell you candidly, Judge, all this filling up of papers and signing things has been more worry to me than the loss of my old man."

And I'm sure she loved her old man—so what must she have thought of us and our Act of Parliament ?

There may be some who think that it is almost indelicate to discuss such a subject as the possible fallibility of the higher judiciary. I agree that it is a subject that can only be treated by one imbued with that reverence for existing institutions that so happily results from a sane middle-class education. Moreover, we cannot shut our ears to the sound of much discussion about what is called judicial bias by the man in the street. In America the sounds are louder and clearer than they are in England, and the problem is so much the simpler to understand—especially for the onlooker. There are great lessons for us to study if we would avoid the troubles which the American judges have been assiduously looking for and are now successfully finding. Two interesting books written from different standpoints, Gilbert E. Roe's " Our Judicial Oligarchy," 1912, and Frederick N. Judson's " The Judiciary and the People," 1913, show the eagerness with which lawyers who have human interests outside the daily problems of their profession are discussing the great questions of the law and the poor.

The judiciary in America is differently chosen from that in this country and in some ways it has greater powers. Its instinct and bias are similar to those of our own judges, but it has not been so successful in instilling into the minds of the citizens a belief in its infallible honesty of purpose. There is no doubt that in America there is a growing distrust of the integrity of the Courts and a feeling that the judges in their sympathies and views are on the side of wealth and against the working man. Much of this arises, no doubt, from circumstances which do not obtain here. But that the middleclass instinct exists on the American bench even more strongly than it does here can be seen in their history of workmen's compensation which to an English lawyer is strange and confused reading.

The common law of America in this matter is the same as the common law of England. The failure of Priestley, the Lincoln butcher boy, settled the law of America as completely as it did the law of this country. And though different Legislatures have endeavoured in different ways to remedy the grievances of employers, the judges have made this not only difficult, but in some cases impossible. In 1906 Congress, with the approval of the President, passed a carefully and well-considered " Employers' Liability Act " relating to common carriers in the district of Columbia. When it came before the Supreme Court of the United States this law was held to be unconstitutional by five judges as against four. To my mind there can be no comparison between the influence and common-sense of the judgments. The counting of heads was against the statute, but the expression of the contents of the heads showed a resultant force of brain power in its favour. The chief argument of the majority was that some of the clauses of the statute were " novel and even shocking," just as Lord Abinger found poor Priestley's contention inconvenient and absurd. Later on, in 1911, the Court of Appeal found the workmen's compensation legislation of New York to be unconstitutional, because it placed a " burden upon the employer without any compensatory benefit." In America the judges have been able, for reasons that would certainly have appealed to the late Master of the Rolls and many of his colleagues, to cancel popular legislation. This has roused a direct conflict in America on the subject of the law and the poor, and there is a growing feeling that the Courts are not discharging their duty in relation to social and industrial justice. The recall of decisions and the recall of judges are popular cries, and there is much public discussion of such themes.

These things are of interest to us because our laws

and our poor come from the same stock and, though we pride ourselves, and I think rightly, on the superiority of our legal machine, yet it is not so perfect that we may not learn something from the troubles and difficulties of our neighbours. If the working class should, even on false premises, come to a conclusion that they could not find justice in our Courts owing to judicial social myopia, it would be a sad day for everybody. For my part, though I quite recognise that there was a bias in the late Lord Abinger, for instance, against poor Priestley's way of looking at things, I do not think that anyone believed then or believes now that he gave his judgment in any unrighteous class spirit adversely to the rights of Priestley and mankind. On the contrary, I think he did his best. He expressed what he and his fellows believed to be the law.

This idea of " bias " in judges is well worth a little consideration. We have not the same problem that America has about our judiciary and, let us hope, we never may have, but no one who knows the working man can fail to have observed that he has been, as he would say, colourably—I modify the adverb—" colourably fed up " with several recent judicial decisions.

It has certainly become too common a thing in England to grumble about our judges, and to say— especially when the costs are taxed and the bill is delivered—that the judge was biassed. But let us remember that it is our birthright to grumble. To grumble, as Cox pointed out to Mrs. Bouncer, is a verb neuter meaning to complain without a cause. In

England we grumble at all our best beloved—our wife, our children, our weather, our constitution, the three-year-old that fails to carry our money to the winning-post, and the stewards who disqualify him when he does. And when we grumble at our judges and say there is bias on the bench it is only our little way.

For what is " bias " ? I have never been able to make out why the word should have a sinister meaning. Bias—as all good bowlers know—is that mysterious weight within a good "wood" or bowl whereby the skilful is enabled to direct it by an arc-like course towards adjacency of " the mark," which is the historic name of the jack. In Lancashire, where the game of bowls is played, as it should be, upon a crown green—and not, as in the South, on a tame, flat rink—the bias and the use of the bias make the glory of the green. By means of bias scientifically used we may reach " the mark " by the circuitous " round peg," or play straight up against " the watershed," as I once heard a geologist among bowlers describe the slope of the green.

What grave problems have to be judicially decided on the green as to the use of " thumb " or " finger " bias before the "wood" is delivered! What anxiety is pictured on the face of the bowler! What contortions of his body are involuntarily indulged in as the bowl speeds on its way and does— or more often does not—carry out the intentions of the bowler!

And therein, I think, lies the secret of the evil meaning we have given to the word " bias." We

see our " wood " careering across the green and hear
it fall with a dull thud on the path beyond, and
instead of blaming ourselves we blame the bias.
Thus, owing to the alarming prevalence of duffers
on the green and in the greater world surrounding
it, the word " bias " has come to be regarded as a
tendency that leads astray rather than a tendency
that keeps straight and is up to " the mark."

And when I am asked whether there is bias on the
English bench, I cheerfully reply that I hope and
believe there is. I have met with unbiassed bowls,
and very poor " woods " they were. I have met
with men almost devoid of bias, and I never found
that they were continuously up to the mark. Bias
is as essential as character to both " woods " and
men. As far as I remember I have never met a
judge without " bias " and seldom seen one whose
bias was not fairly under control. We want bias
on the bench because we like to feel that the men
who decide our disputes are not mere automatic
legal slot machines, but human beings, with likes
and dislikes similar to ours, trained to hear and
determine our disputes and honestly endeavouring
to decide the cases without fear or favour. When
judicial bias carries the judgment beyond " the
mark " we grieve not that the bias is there but that
it has been injudiciously used.

From the true bowler's point of view there is only
one bias, a bias towards things, but in our vulgar
misuse of language we speak of a bias against things.
And if that is to be allowed no one would grudge a
poor working judge his right to a bias against fraud

and dishonesty, greed and oppression. Such a bias should indeed be instinct in him in the same way as a golfer has a bias against bunkers, a terrier against rats, and a mongoose against snakes. But even a good bias requires strict and cunning control. I remember a very excellent and sage judge—in most matters a cool fountain of deliberate justice—whose bias towards purity and a high ideal of man's conduct towards woman was so little under control that in cases, and especially criminal cases relating to these affairs, it was very difficult for him to conduct the case with justice to the accused. His bias against the sin over-rode his judgment of the crime.

The same bias is more often found in juries. I remember a case in which my father, Serjeant Parry, defended a man named Smethurst, charged with the murder of his wife. He was admittedly guilty of bigamy, and so incensed were the jury with his misconduct that their bias carried them right by the mark of the medical testimony and landed them in the ditch of an unjust verdict of murder. The case was taken up by John Bright, one whose bias against all evil was as strong as any man's. The criminal was ultimately punished only for the crime he had committed. No one will contend that a bias against immorality is not a good bias and a good asset in the character of a judge and a man. But the best bias in the world will not aid you in attaining " the mark " unless it is directed by body and brain working together in harmony.

And if it be asked if there are judges on the bench

who are biassed towards or against capital or labour, railway companies, motor-buses, piano organs, Scotch drapers, moneylenders or other products of modern life, I must answer in all honesty that this is very probably the case. A fact that seems to be lost sight of in this insistence on the immaculate judge is that, after all, he is like other human beings, a forked radish with a fantastically carved head quaintly decorated by a horse-hair wig generously paid for by himself out of his slender salary. He is just as much the product of the age as one of yourselves. He has toddled about in the same nursery, learned in the same school, played at the same university and lived in the same society as the rest of the middle classes. Why should you expect in him a super-instinct towards futurist sociology?

In the old days when everyone believed in witchcraft the judges believed in witchcraft. Chief Justice Hale solemnly laid it down as law that there must be such things as witches since there were laws made against witches, and it was not conceivable that laws should be made against that which did not exist. It was not, indeed, until the time of George II. that it ceased to be an offence to endeavour to raise the Devil by magic words and oblige him to execute your commands. Nowadays even the Devil himself is in danger of disestablishment, though my conservative views would lead me to maintain that he is still entitled to judicial notice, and I am inclined to the opinion that he is not yet surplusage in an indictment for perjury. In every age your judge will be tinged with the prejudices of his time and his class, and I cannot see how you can expect to grow middle-class judges in hot-beds of middle-class prejudices without the natural formation of a certain amount of middle-class bias in the thickness of their middle-class wood.

Nor do I think among Englishmen anyone resents such bias as your judges display in their everyday life. Mr. Justice Grantham, like " A. L.," was undoubtedly a man of strong conservative bias and showed it openly enough upon the bench, but he was adored on a working-class circuit, and no man was better beloved by all who practised or appeared before him, and no judge strove more earnestly to do justice. The fact is, bias is recognised among Englishmen as one of the sporting attributes of man and is as necessary to the instruments with which we play the game of life as to the " woods " in our old-world game upon the green.

If there is any bias on the bench that is popularly and justly disliked it is a bias towards formalism and technicalities. Our law of old got a bad name for that, and in quiet places our reputation still sticks to us. There are still men and women in the English country-side who think there is some sort of disgrace attached to a law court. In the quiet County Courts of Kent and Sussex a defendant often complains in an aggrieved tone at being brought to a " place of this kind." It argues to his mind a want of delicacy in the plaintiff, and he states his case without the least hope that it will be decided on the merits. I remember an amusing expression of this feeling. A defendant, a cheery, round, pippin-faced jobmaster with a treble voice was sued by a farmer for keep of his horses in the farmers' field for several week-ends.

" Well, I'll tell you about it," he piped diffidently in answer to my request for information, " for I might as well now I'm here. It was this way. I met Sandy in Crown Lane. I always call him Sandy —you must excuse me if I'm wrong, I've never been in a place like this before—and Sandy says to me, ' Jim, why don't you bring your 'orses down to my field for Sunday like you used to do last year ? ' Well, I brought my 'orses down on Sunday and I did that for some two or three months and then I took them away, and I meets Sandy and he says, ' Jim, why have you taken your 'orses away ? ' and I says, ' Because there ain't no food on your field for my 'orses.' He says to me, ' There's more food on my field than your 'orses is used to.' I says, ' Sandy, you know there's no feed in your field for my 'orses.' He says to me, ' If there ain't no feed in my field for your 'orses there's plenty of recreation for them.' ' Recreation ? ' I says ; ' my 'orses don't want no recreation, they gets recreation in the bus through the week. With that Sandy went his way and we never exchanged another word for three year, and now he brings me to this 'ere place for sixteen shillings and I've never been in a place like this before."

I explained to the defendant that the County Court was really a place intended for an affair of this nature and thoroughly equipped to see it through, but he was not satisfied.

"What right has he to bring me here?" he complained. "I never promised to pay him anything."

"Was there no agreement between you?" I asked.

"Well, we did agree about one thing."

"And what was that?" I asked hopefully.

"We agreed that if we couldn't settle what I ought to pay," he replied, eyeing me with doubt and disapprobation, "that we should leave it to a respectable man."

Now what he really wanted was a judge full of bucolic bias and well acquainted with vaccine and equine learning. It was only I fancy in a veterinary sense that he considered that I was not respectable.

And nowadays when we open the Courts to new applicants, and turn over great schemes of workmen's compensation to judges to deal with, we want judges to work them who are in touch with the needs and lives of the working class, not necessarily folk who want to exalt the poor on to unreal pedestals and clothe them with impossible virtues, but people who know how near their faults and virtues are to those of the rest of mankind.

And when we find American judges deciding that no system of workmen's compensation is to be allowed to become law, and when we note that the most learned judges of our own Appeal Courts differ constantly as to the meaning of the words of our own scheme, thereby causing delay, confusion and expense, it raises a question in one's mind as to whether some far less exalted Court of Appeal—say, three County Court judges who have to try these cases face to face with the men and women who are interested in their decision—would not better meet the wants of the community in carrying out the scheme and come nearer to the ideal of " the respectable man." A bishop has once been a curate, but a Lord Justice of Appeal has never been a County Court judge. The Workmen's Compensation Act is a practical business machine of a complicated character, and it is scarcely a sensible thing that the men who have to keep it going should work under the theoretical direction of men who have never seen it working.

And there is another reason why the appeals in these cases should be removed from the Court of Appeal, and that is a very practical one—the Court is over-crowded and has no time to try them. Even now as I write there are cases, many of them perhaps merely questions of the payment of a few shillings a week, which have been waiting for many months to be reached. From the point of view of everyone concerned, except the lawyer, there is no health in this litigation. In so far as the administration of the Workmen's Compensation Act has been a success it has been because insurance companies and employers and trade unions and workmen have either kept out of Court altogether or, when they have got there, have assisted the registrars and judges of the County Court to work the thing on business lines and have resisted in a large measure the temptation in the uncertainty of the decisions to speculative litigation. There is still enough English common-sense left among us to muddle through most things, but the Workmen's Compensation Act, as interpreted in the Court of Appeal, has tried it fairly high.

CHAPTER VI

BANKRUPTCY

" In a lofty room, ill lighted and worse ventilated, situate in Portugal Street, Lincoln's Inn Fields, there sit nearly the whole year round, one, two, three or four gentlemen in wigs, as the case may be, with little writing desks before them, constructed after the fashion of those used by the judges of the land, barring the French polish. There is a box of barristers on their right hand ; there is an enclosure of insolvent debtors on their left ; and there is an inclined plane of most especially dirty faces in their front. These gentlemen are the Commissioners of the Insolvent Court, and the place in which they sit is the Insolvent Court itself."
CHARLES DICKENS : " Pickwick." Chap. XLIII.

A BANKRUPT is not a person who breaks the bank, as is popularly supposed. On the contrary, he is, or ought to be, by his derivation a person whose bank is broken by others. A learned professor tells me that the Florentines of old had some sort of ceremony in which they marched to their insolvent neighbour's office and broke up his bank, or bench, or money table to show the world that he was no longer commercially sound. Until recently in English law bankruptcy was merely a trader's remedy designed to protect an unfortunate business man from life-long imprisonment for debt resulting from unfortunate business ventures. Latterly the privilege of bankruptcy has been extended to every citizen that has a debt of fifty pounds and ten pounds to pay the fees necessary to filing his petition.

But, in order to become insolvent, it is a condition precedent that at some time or another one should have been solvent. And one difficulty about applying any form of bankruptcy laws to the poor is that they are too often born insolvent, live insolvent, and die insolvent. There must be many fellow citizens in this country of ours who never knew what it was for twelve months of their life to have a living wage and be out of debt. As long as we have imprisonment for debt credit of some kind and on some terms ruinous or otherwise is always obtainable. At the present, bankruptcy is almost regarded as a sign of grace, a condition of honourable martyrdom into which the careless and good-natured ones of the world find themselves after a short struggle in the slough of solvency. To the rich it is a very present help in time of trouble, but the poor, never having been sufficiently solvent, can never make use of its aid.

When the worker has a living wage guaranteed him by the State it will be necessary to make him a new bankruptcy law so that the living wage cannot be attached and converted to the use of the Shylocks of this world. The law protects the infant and the idiot from the results of their own foolishness, and we shall find it advisable in the future to extend similar protection to the grown-up idiots and infants who are all too prevalent in the world. Antonio was a normal business man, but he was no match for Shylock, and, though no lawyer can approve of the way in which the Courts treated Shylock, the real lesson of the story is that laws are necessary to protect Antonio, the fool, from Shylock, the knave.

In order, then, that the full blessings of bankruptcy may be made available to the poor, we must certainly tackle the problem of the living wage, which to my mind is the most urgent social question of our time. So many things seem to hang upon it. Rent, taxation, education, physical and moral improvement, eugenics, all the social discussions of the time, land you back on the question of the living wage. Sometimes, I think, we are on the eve of a new era when every capable honest citizen will have the same right to a living wage that he now has to free board and lodging and stone breaking in the workhouse. I would rather have a legal right to a living wage than a vote, unless I was clear that I could use the latter to obtain the former and many better things to boot.

As a matter of dull, dry, literary history all the prophets and singers and poets, from King David, Isaiah and Jeremiah down to Carlyle, Kingsley, Ruskin, Dickens and Tom Hood, have said or sung the praises of the living wage. There are many who regard Jeremiah as a kind of gloomy dean, but for my part I find him most encouraging. When he says : " Woe unto him that buildeth his house by unrighteousness and his chambers by wrong ; that useth his neighbour's service without wages and giveth him not for his work," I think that he is absolutely right on the spot. I cannot believe that

it was his view that woe would providentially
descend upon the man who paid sweating wages
and that it would come in the shape of lions and
bears or lightning and earthquakes; on the contrary,
I read it, that, in Jeremiah's view, it was the duty of
citizens to see that their fellows did not behave like
this. The prophet intended to tell us that our first
duty was to persuade our fellow citizens employing
labour to give their workmen a living wage, but if we
could not achieve this by reasoning and exhorting
them, then it was our duty to give such anti-social
churls statutory woe, just as we mete out statutory
woe to the naughty ones who get drunk and beat
their wives, and, indeed, for the same social reasons.

David and all his biblical backers were as eager
as Mr. Philip Snowden and his Socialist friends to
promote the living wage, and, as they put it, to
" deliver the poor from him that is too strong for
him." That, in a phrase, is the modern problem of
the living wage. The trust, the combine, the
limited company, the corporation or Government
office are bound in the nature of things to become
the spoilers of the poor and needy unless there is
some power delegated by the State to some judicial
authority to " deliver the poor from him that is too
strong for him."

But it is not sufficient to cite poetry and Psalms
and the " Song of the Shirt "—for then your Thomas
Gradgrind comes along—a man of realities, sir, a
man of facts and calculations, a man who proceeds
upon the principle that two and two are four and
nothing over, and who is not going to be talked into

allowing for anything over—Thomas Gradgrind
shakes his square finger at you and says : " How
are you going to do it ? " And I agree that Gradgrind is deserving an answer. I do not say we must
wait until we convince him, for Gradgrinds are
obstinate, stubborn fellows, but we must satisfy
the majority that we have a fair answer to his objec-
tions and a practical programme to propose. The
problem cannot be shirked for ever. Even in the
prophet Carlyle's day it was a matter in regard to
which " if something be not done something will
do itself one day and in a fashion that will please
nobody."

And shortly the way in which it will come about
is by voluntary conciliation, the erection of joint
boards of employers and workmen with a right of
appeal to a business legal tribunal—something akin
to the Railway Commission—which shall have
power to make and enforce a decree to the worker of
at least so much of his fair share of an industry as
shall amount to a living wage. I can see nothing
revolutionary in this proposal. It really only
follows out the trend of modern legislation. If a
man has a smoking chimney, or pollutes a river, or
goes about in public with an infectious disease, we
fine or imprison him for his anti-social misconduct.
Surely a man who pursues an industry that does not
make a living wage for the workers in it is equally
an enemy of the people, to be dealt with as such by
the law ! As Mr. Justice Gordon laid it down in
the Australian Labour Courts : " If any particular
industry cannot keep going and pay its workpeople

BANKRUPTCY

a living wage it must be shut up." Some day that
will be the law of England. No one can deny the
common sense of it.

A very encouraging sign of the times is that both
sides are discovering the uselessness of strikes. In
Mr. Snowden's frank words, " a strike never did
much substantial gain to the strikers." It is not
only that the strike or lock-out is a crime against
helpless women and children, that it wastes the
substance and savings of employers and employed
and embitters their relations for a generation—all
that we knew before; the new and comforting
message is that the strike does not " get there," it
does not suceed, and therefore, as Mr. Snowden
says, "just as war between nations cannot be
defended either ethically or economically, so labour
disputes are indefensible."

And there are other indications that conciliation
and agreement in labour matters are to have a fair
trial. Already in the railway world an interesting
experiment has been made. I have seen enough of
it in the working to know that it is not such a
spavined animal as some of our political jockeys
would have us believe. When the railway conciliation boards were set up the employers and workmen,
where it was possible, agreed upon an independent
chairman to sit with them in case there was a dead-
lock. Several boards of different companies invited
me to undertake this honourable position. I need
hardly say that I fancied myself not a little at
receiving such flattering invitations, and meeting
a friend, who was an eminent railway solicitor, I

told him the news—not, I suspect, without a note of pardonable triumph in the phrasing.

"What!" he cried; "do you mean to say that the companies and the men have agreed upon you as chairman?"

"That is so," I replied, with dignity, being a little hurt at his surprise and astonishment.

"Well, I'm——. However you'll never have anything to do," he added with a grunt of satisfaction.

"And why not?" I asked.

"Because," he replied, with great deliberation, "if they could agree about you they could agree about anything."

I thanked him for the compliment, but, analysing the saying since, I am not so sure that the commendation I accepted was really proffered to me. Be that as it may, it has turned out to be true. On the few occasions on which my services were required, I have found that things were capable of adjustment and settlement owing to the excellent good feeling on each side and the real endeavour made by everyone to try and understand the other's point of view. This is where the independent chairman is of real service. In explaining to his virgin mind the difficulties of the case, every point in it has to be discussed and explained anew, and in this way the weaker positions of the argument are made clearer to those who are defending them. Thus it becomes easier to give way about some matter of detail, and concession breeds concession.

Without making too much of my own small

experience, it bears out my theoretical expectation, and I am satisfied that a conciliatory court for trade disputes is a live business proposition, calculated to save employers much unnecessary woe, and that if Jeremiah had thought of it, he would have proposed to set one up as a practical step towards the living wage.

Until, then, we have established a living wage for the worker, the question of his bankruptcy is in a large measure academic. At present bankruptcy, like divorce, is rightly regarded as a luxury for the well-to-do. I know that to some minds the word " bankruptcy " connotes poverty, but if you look into the facts and history of the matter, you will find that, though bankruptcy may on occasion lead to poverty, a poor man never does, or can, become a bankrupt.

People fail to the tune of five or six million pounds a year, but when you analyse the list of the insolvent you will not find many poor folk among them. There are lords and gentlemen, solicitors and stockbrokers, merchants and manufacturers, builders and farmers, and butchers, bakers, and candlestick makers.

But the nearest you will find to poor people are lodging-house keepers and coffee-house and fried fish shop proprietors. These are precarious trades, and the working man, being a good sportsman, likes to have a gamble in them with his savings. In this way he joins the aristocracy, and becomes an eligible bankrupt. But the labourer and artisan, the real working men, have no more chance of bankruptcy than they have of election to the Athenæum or the Carlton.

Bankruptcy is a legal status jealously guarded by the caste to which it belongs. The poor man reads in the paper of builders and merchants failing for their thousands, of well-paid accountants carefully investigating the history of their financial fall; he puts his head into the Registrar's Court and hears an amiable official receiver sympathetically tracing the career of the well-groomed bankrupt in front of him; he sees the judge present the unhappy fellow with a clean slate, from which all his debts are wiped away, and hears him announce to the unfortunate insolvent the date upon which the law will allow him to start becoming insolvent again.

And the working man thinks to himself of the twenty or thirty pounds that he owes, and how pleasant it would be if an accountant would add it up and a judge tell him that he need not worry any more about it; but when he begins to inquire further into the subject he finds that bankruptcy is one of the good things of this world that he cannot afford.

Bankruptcy, successful bankruptcy, is not so easy of achievement as you might think. It is not everyone who knows how to become a bankrupt. There are a lot of big, expensive law books written on this subject by clever fellows who spend their lives soothing the bankrupt's last hours and winding him up according to law and order, with costs out of the estate, but you need not study these to learn how to become a bankrupt. Most bankrupts are pig-headed fellows, and achieve bankruptcy in their own foolish amateur way. They read the books about it afterwards.

To begin with, you certainly want money, or at least an overdraft and plenty of credit. Intending bankrupts generally wear very good clothes; especially are they particular about the shine of their silk hat. Bankers and intelligent business men have, in all ages, given credit to top hats, white waistcoats, and gold watch chains. The poor man has none of these, and therefore cannot obtain that overdraft which is one of the first essentials of bankruptcy.

The bankrupt has a curious affection for jewellery. He buys large quantities of this commodity, and sells it again at a loss to stave off the evil day and add to his deficiency. I read in the Board of Trade reports of a failure due to gambling and extravagance, in which the debtor purchased jewellery for £40,000 and sold it the same day for £10,000. If he had been a poor man I think maybe the police would have tried to find a law to give him a rest cure for a few months in one of His Majesty's gaols, but he failed for over £70,000, and the probable value of his assets was £175.

Perhaps he was a bit of an aristocrat. Anyhow the police left him alone. I cannot even tell you his name, for the kind Inspector-General in Bankruptcy, fearful of causing pain to the sorrowing, never tells you the names and addresses of the people whose history he writes. He speaks of him as " No. 1512 of 1911." The poor fellow had no occupation, his cruel father only allowed him a miserable thousand a year, so what could No. 1512 do but run into debt? The wonder is that he failed for so little as £70,000.

No. 614 of 1907 was not much of a record, but he will do as another example. He, too, had no occupation except qualifying for a bankrupt and ultimately failed for £21,292 with assets *nil*. He started his wild career at the age of nineteen with expectations of a fortune when he got to the age of twenty-five. With that charming simplicity and cunning, characteristic of the whelps of the vulgar rich, he proceeded to moneylenders, and at the date of the receiving order had created charges exceeding £430,000 on his reversion of such complexity that every mortgagee disputed the right of every prior incumbrancer. This would not matter so much, as all these victims were doubtless moneylenders and a lot of the money would go to estimable lawyers to smooth out the wrinkled parchment muddle, but then at the back of all those were the unsecured creditors, poor tradesmen and others. They were to get nothing.

No. 1103 of 1908 was an even smaller fellow. This debtor was educated at Oxford and, on leaving the university in 1901, he was in debt to the extent of £4,500. I have a passion for statistics, and I should like to see a balance sheet showing on one side the expenses of the four thousand Oxford undergraduates during three years of residence, and on the other side the earnings of the same four thousand undergraduates for a similar period in, say, fifteen or twenty years afterwards. I fear it would not be much of an advertisement for Oxford. No. 1103's father paid up his creditors to the extent at least of fifteen shillings in the pound, and gave him a fresh start. He was in trouble again in 1906, through betting and extravagance, and failed for £20,392— assets £1,103.

The French have an excellent system of declaring these youngsters to be prodigals and putting them under a committee as we do lunatics with property, and no doubt in money matters they are akin to the insane, and are really to be pitied and cared for. But to the poor it must be strange to see debt and the disaster of debt causing such different results in law to different classes of people, and it must be hard for them to understand why they, too, are not fit subjects for the blessings of bankruptcy rather than gaol.

And what am I to say to my friend Joseph the signalman, at twenty-nine shillings a week, when he shows me some of these spicy stories of the Inspector-General's report cut out of the local paper.

" What has it all got to do with you, Joseph ? "

" Well," he says, " I've been thinking why should not I do a bit of a failure like No. 1512 of 1911 ? I can buy a gramophone and a watch, and a few lucky wedding rings and a family Bible, and a plush drawing-room suite on the instalment system, and I can borrow a pound or two on a promissory note. Of course betting and beer cannot be done on the nod in my class of life, but one can owe a bit of rent, and altogether I see my way to do a failure up to,

say, thirty pounds. Why shouldn't I go bankrupt ? "

" Well, the answer is very simple," I have to tell
him. " The rules of the game are made by the rich
for the rich, and not for you, Joseph, at all. Oh,
dear, no ! In the first place you must have a debt
of fifty pounds."

" Well," replies Joseph, " I think I could bring it
as high as that if I tried."

" And next you must have a creditor to make you
bankrupt, and unless he thinks there is some stuffing
in you or wool on your back a creditor is not going
to waste his time and money making the likes of you
bankrupt."

" But," says my hopeful friend Joseph, " what is
the meaning of a chap filing his own petition ? I've
often read of that. Why shouldn't I file my
petition ? "

" My dear, simple fellow, you surely do not think
the clever ones of the earth who look after your
interests have not thought all that out ? You take
your petition to the Bankruptcy Court and see what
happens. You will find the usual janitor at the
door with his open palm. Of course you are expected
to pay a fee—you have learned enough about English
Courts to know that you do not get ' owt for nowt '
in any of them. But in the Bankruptcy Court, my
young friend, they foresaw you coming along and
they have put the figure too high for you. Ten
pounds, money down ! That's the price. If you
want to set all the pretty little figures working, the
official receiver smiling, the registrar writing it all

down, and the judge nodding on the bench, and the Board of Trade publishing statistics about you—ten pounds into the slot, my young friend, and the figures will work.

" But you have not got ten pounds, Joseph, and you could not raise the sum if you tried, so you will have to go back to work and pay twenty shillings in the pound somehow. And don't go and sell your gramophone and drawing-room suite, for they are on the hire system, and that would put you in the dock, where I hope you may never be. No. 1512 bought his £40,000 worth of jewels out and out, or said he did, and it was a Paris jeweller, anyhow, and I believe he was one of the ' nuts ' and not your class at all, Joseph, but you may take it from me that you must not expect to be treated as he was. Have I said enough, my dear friend ? Are you quite satisfied ? Bankruptcy, I can assure you, is not for Joseph. Oh, dear, no ! "

It is only fair to the law and to the memory of Mr. Chamberlain, who made the law, to remember that when he introduced the Bankruptcy Act of 1883 he invented a system of small bankruptcies called administration orders, whereby poor folk whose debts do not amount to fifty pounds may make a composition with their creditors. Let me set down in his own words exactly what he intended and tried to do. I quote from his speech on the second reading of the Bill :—

" What he now desired to call attention to was the clause which followed and which dealt with the case of debtors who owed less than fifty pounds. That

was the class of debtors who filled our County Courts
with plaints and added very considerably to the
number of the occupants of our gaols. It had always
been felt to be a great hardship that while a large
debtor could with ease relieve himself of all his
liabilities he or his trustees might be prosecuting a
poor man for thirty or forty shillings, and the latter
might be sent to prison without having any means
provided for him to make a composition with his
creditors, and when, after satisfying the debt, he
came out of gaol he was still liable in full to all his
other creditors."

.   .   .   .   .

" But the more important provision which he had
made for dealing with this subject was that under
which a County Court judge might in future make
an order for the payment by a debtor who owed less
than fifty pounds by instalments or otherwise of all
or any part of his debts. A debtor who was brought
up on a judgment summons or a County Court plaint
might state that he was indebted to other persons,
might give in a schedule of his debts and propose an
arrangement for discharging them, and, if the Court
thought it reasonable, it might at once confirm it,
so that a small debtor would thus be in exactly the
same position as a large debtor who had succeeded
in making a composition with his creditors or in
arranging for a scheme of liquidation. Although he
had not abolished in all cases imprisonment for
debt, yet, if these provisions became law, it could no
longer be said that any inequality existed as between
rich and poor. The resort to imprisonment to

secure payment would be much easier, and a large discretion would be vested on the judges to arrange for the relief to the small debtor by a reasonable composition."

I have set this out at length because it is enormously encouraging to know that thirty years ago Mr. Chamberlain's ideal was to destroy the County Court imprisonment for debt and to give the working man who fell into debt a bankruptcy system similar to that of the rich.

Why did it fail?

Well, it has not been wholly a failure, but it certainly has not fulfilled all its author's generous hopes. In the first place the fifty-pound limit is too small, another reason of its non-success is that it is a voluntary system of some complication in competition with the simple, brutal method of the judgment summons and imprisonment for debt, but probably its unpopularity is chiefly due to the fact that the Treasury has always deliberately crabbed it by imposing harsh and unreasonable fees.

No system of this kind will be successful without compulsion and some clerk of the Court in the position of an official receiver to advise the poor how to go about the matter and to see that the order made is carried out. Such a system is in vogue in some Courts and has proved a success in mitigating imprisonment for debt and holding out a helping hand to those who were drifting into insolvency. But the system as it stands depends too much on the initiative of the County Court judge or the registrar. Thus we find on a working-class circuit like Oldham, Rochdale, etc., there will be over six hundred orders made, whereas in Whitechapel only two orders are made in the same year. Systems favourable to the working classes flourish more vigorously in the North than in the South.

You must not suppose the working man is allowed to cast off his debts in the wholesale way in which the thorough-bred, blue-blooded bankrupt does. Not a bit of it. The order made against him is that he shall pay his debts to the extent of so many shillings in the pound at so many shillings a month. If he does not carry out the order there is prison for him for every instalment he fails to pay if the judge so orders, or at the best his order is rescinded and all his creditors are down on him again as before.

But the main drawback to the business is the extortionate fees charged by the Treasury. Here is a poor devil with twenty-five shillings and a wife and family and, let us say, thirty pounds of debt, and the judge gives him an administration order to pay ten shillings in the pound at five shillings a month. The Treasury are at once down on him. Their fees are always calculated, not on the dividend paid, but on the total amount of the debts, and they insist in every case on two shillings in the pound. Thus, in the case of the man with thirty pounds of debt, the Treasury want three pounds money down before the creditors get anything. In 1911 the Treasury took no less than £13,000 in these fees.

In this matter we cannot acquit the law of the

BANKRUPTCY

offence of grinding the poor. Imagine a wealthy
country like this squeezing the insolvent poor out
of their weekly pittances instead of helping them to
pay their debts. I call it a wicked policy for the
State to throw impediments in the way of a working-
class man who is struggling out of the back-waters of
debt into the fairway of solvency.

Do not let us shut our eyes to what it means, for
the Treasury is only our servant and ought to be
doing our will, and the responsibility is yours and
mine. For we know that every penny of that £13,000
comes out of the mouths of hungry women and
children or, at the best, robs them of so many boots
and so much clothing.

What fees do the Treasury receive from No. 1512
of 1911 and his like ? Two shillings in the pound
on the rich man's £70,000 of debt might enable the
Chancellor to treat the poor more leniently. But
the rich man pays his entrance fee of ten pounds and
is a life member of the Bankruptcy Club. The
Treasury never thinks of touching him for a
subscription of two shillings in the pound on the
amount of his debts. Some day there will come
along a Chancellor of the Exchequer who will be a
Good Samaritan, and the Treasury will cease to
strip the poor debtor of his raiment to the tune of
£13,000 a year.

Of course it is very easy to blame a public department and throw ugly words at the lords thereof.
One gets into a bad habit of blaming those in high
places for the inequalities of things. I wonder if I
were Chancellor whether I should get rid of that

123

shameful tax on the poorest of the poor. Perhaps not. After all, the Good Samaritan was speculating with his own oil and investing his own twopence. The oil and the twopence of the Exchequer belong to the public and must be dealt with according to the rules of statecraft.

And there may be some grave national danger beyond my humble ken that makes it necessary for England to dirty her hands with that £13,000.

CHAPTER VII

DIVORCE

" We have thought to tie the nuptial knot of our marriages more fast and firm by having taken away all means of dissolving it ; but the knot of the will and affection is so much the more slackened and made loose, by how much that of constraint is drawn closer ; and on the contrary, that which kept the marriages at Rome so long in honour and inviolate, was the liberty every one who so desired had to break them ; they kept their wives the better because they might part with them if they would ; and in the full liberty of divorce, five hundred years and more passed away before anyone made use on't."

Michel de Montaigne : " Essays."
Translated by Charles Cotton.   Book II., Chap. XV.

NEARLY four hundred years ago Thomas Cranmer, Archbishop of Canterbury, was burned at the stake over against Balliol College, Oxford.   You remember how a few days before, in a moment of weakness, he had signed a recantation, and how when the fire was kindled and the flames licked up the faggots they revived the spirit of the martyr within him, and he thrust his right hand into the flames, crying out : " This was the hand that wrote it ; therefore it shall first suffer punishment."   But if that hand had offended in matters spiritual, in practical matters it had done good work for the State.

Cranmer's " Reformatio Legum Ecclesiasticarum " contains some of the best sense about divorce law

reform that I have ever read. Its proposals are
moderate, sensible and in harmony with the religious
ideas of his day, which seem to have been broader
and more rational than those of to-day. Had
Edward VI. lived a little longer Cranmer's treatise
would have been enacted as the statute law of the
country. It is pitiful to think of the four hundred
years of misery and injustice under which the
citizens of this country have suffered in matters
relating to divorce owing to a change of Government
in 1553. The Scots did better out of the Reformation and have had a more or less satisfactory divorce
law in working order since that date.

Shortly, the propositions that Cranmer proposed
were these, and they will be found, I think, to run
parallel with the views of the common-sense citizen
of to-day. He laid down the command that no
husband or wife may abandon the other of his or
her own free will and, in order that this might be
a practical ideal, he set down the causes for which
the Courts were to grant relief. Divorce was
allowed for adultery, unless both parties were
guilty ; desertion ; the unduly protracted absence
of the husband ; or the deadly hostility of the
parties. Prolonged ill-treatment of the wife gave
her a right to divorce, but even here, as long as there
was any hope of improvement, the duty of the
ecclesiastical judge was to reason with the husband
and make him give bail for good behaviour. Only
in the last resort must " she on her part be helped
by the remedy of divorce."

Great stress is laid throughout the treatise on the

desirability of reconciliation. " Since in matrimony there is the closest possible union and the highest degree of love that can be imagined, we earnestly desire that the innocent party should forgive the guilty and take him back again should there seem to be any reasonable hope of a better way of life." Practical effect was to be given to this principle by the Court before proceeding to divorce.

Cranmer was entirely at one with the more advanced thought of to-day in his detestation of " separation orders." Separation without divorce was, he realised, an overture to immorality.

" It was formerly customary," he writes, " in the case of certain crimes to deprive married people of the right of association at *bed and board* though in all other respects their marriage tie remained intact ; and since this practice is contrary to Holy Scripture, involves the greatest confusion, and has introduced an accumulation of evils into matrimony, it is our will that the whole thing be by our authority abolished." What he would have said about our wholesale police court method of separating married people without giving them any rights to form new ties one does not like to imagine. One cannot turn from the short and pithy " Reformatio Legum Ecclesiasticarum " of the sixteenth century to the colossal unwieldy Blue Books of the twentieth century with any sense of satisfaction. Perhaps the most interesting thing to be got out of the latter is a study in contrasts between the body, flavour, and bouquet of archbishops of different vintages.

Thomas Cranmer's services to the State being no

longer available after the Balliol fire, the choice of his Majesty Edward VII., when he issued his Royal Warrant in 1909 for the Divorce Commission, fell on " The Most Reverend Father in God Our right trusty and entirely beloved Counsellor Cosmo Gordon, Archbishop of York, Primate of England and Metropolitan."

One would have hoped that after four hundred years further consideration of Cranmer's views on divorce—the latter-day representative of Cranmer's Church would have been able to give King Edward VII. at least as good counsel as his predecessor gave to Edward VI. No doubt the Minority Report that he ultimately wrote fairly represents the narrower views of modern ecclesiastics, but it is a sad thing to see the leader of a great Church absolutely out of touch with the practical reforms that those who know the lives of the poor admit to be necessary. I should regret if, in a moment of spiritual insight, it should be made clear to our good archbishop that in signing the Minority Report his right hand had been guilty of offence, or that he should think fit to discipline himself after Cranmer's example ; but if he had thrust his Minority Report into the fire, Church and State might have sung a joyful psalm of conflagration and congratulation. Alas ! Edward VI. passed away without reform, and our brave King Edward VII. changed his world whilst the Commissioners were still commissioning, and maybe it will be Edward VIII.'s turn some four hundred years hence to sign the new divorce law. Let nothing be done in a hurry.

DIVORCE

From Cranmer's day until 1857 no divorce law was passed. In the meantime, if you were a peer with a naughty wife, you got an Act of Parliament passed to divorce her. It was an expensive proceeding and, incidentally, of doubtful legality. But the eugenics of nobility and the purity of breed in the peerage made some such machinery necessary, and so you had " An Act for Lord Roos to marry again," and others similarly entitled. Only the very rich at the rate of two or three a year could avail themselves of this procedure, and, of course, the very poor had not a look in at all.

It was a judge who awakened the world to the iniquity of it all, and he did it by a jest. There are some funny things said in the High Court to-day, but they do not seem to be designed to push the world along as this witty speech did. It was Mr. Justice Maule—a sly dog, the hero of many a good circuit story—that one about the threatening letters, for instance—it was Maule J. in a bigamy case, *Regina* v. *Thomas Hall*, tried at Warwick in 1845, who woke up the country to the fact that there was a divorce problem, and that it wanted solving.

Hall was a labouring man convicted of bigamy and called up for sentence. Maule, in passing sentence, said that it did appear that he had been hardly used.

" I have indeed, my Lord," called out poor Hall, " it is very hard."

" Hold your tongue, Hall," quoth the judge, " you must not interrupt me. What I say is the law of the land which you in common with everyone else are bound to obey. No doubt it is very hard for you to have been so used and not to be able to have another wife to live with you when Maria had gone away to live with another man, having first robbed you ; but such is the law. The law in fact is the same to you as it is to the rich man ; it is the same to the low and poor as it is to the mighty and rich and through it you alone can hope to obtain effectual and sufficient relief, and what the rich man would have done you should have done also, you should have followed the same course."

" But I had no money, my Lord," exclaimed Hall.

" Hold your tongue," rejoined the judge, " you should not interrupt me, especially when I am only speaking to inform you as to what you should have done and for your good. Yes, Hall, you should have brought an action and obtained damages, which probably the other side would not have been able to pay, in which case you would have had to pay your own costs perhaps a hundred or a hundred and fifty pounds."

" Oh, Lord ! " ejaculated the prisoner.

" Don't interrupt me, Hall," said Maule, " but attend. But even then you must not have married again. No, you should have gone to the Ecclesiastical Court and then to the House of Lords, where, having proved that all these preliminary matters had been complied with, you would then have been able to marry again ! It is very true, Hall, you might say, ' Where was all the money to come from to pay for all this ? ' And certainly that was a serious question as the expenses might amount to five or six hundred pounds while you had not as many pence."

" As I hope to be saved, I have not a penny—I am only a poor man."

" Well, don't interrupt me ; that may be so, but that will not exempt you from paying the penalty for the felony you have undoubtedly committed. I should have been disposed to have treated the matter more lightly if you had told Maria the real state of the case and said, ' I'll marry you if you choose to take your chance and risk it,' but this you have not done."

And so the judge gave Hall three months or, as some say, four. But that was because he had not told Maria all about it. It was for not playing cricket, not for breaking the law. And where the parties commit bigamy out of sheer respectability and a desire to placate Mrs. Grundy and have some marriage lines in a teapot on the mantelpiece to show the lady who lives next door, the judges, providing there is no deception, wisely treat the offence as something far less deserving of imprisonment than non-payment of rates. Why the police prosecute in these cases the chief constable only knows.

And the scorn and irony that Maule poured on the law of divorce roused the public conscience, and there was a Royal Commission in 1850 and a Divorce Act in 1857, and the result was the Divorce Court as we know it, an excellent tribunal for the matrimonial troubles of well-to-do people, but of no use to poor Hall and Maria. For Maule's words slightly paraphrased might be as truly spoken to the bigamist of to-day as they were to poor Hall.

And four years ago we had another Royal Commission, and hundreds of witnesses were examined, and papers and reports handed in, and many days spent in collating and considering the same, and much stationery consumed. It was a shabby thing to the poor to institute this long-winded inquiry. There was nothing to inquire into. The mountain has finished groaning, and the expensive and ridiculous mouse has made his appearance—and all it comes to is that what good old Thomas Cranmer said ought to be done in 1550 the majority think might be experimented on in 1914 ; only—the archbishop of to-day is no longer on the side of reform.

That, I suppose, shows us very fairly the pace at which the world moves forward and the Church moves backward. In a great and necessary social reform, such as this, the Church occupies the position of the old-fashioned horse lorry strolling down the middle of the road amiably blocking the modern traffic of the city. It is all very pleasant and reassuring to those nervous folk who fear we are rushing like Gadarene pigs into a sea of legalised vice and immorality, but to visionaries and dreamers like myself who would like, as the children say, " to see the wheels go round " in their lifetime, it has its mournful side.

There are two ways in which those who are satisfied that the world is the best of all possible worlds meet proposals for reform. If they are backed up by popular clamour and agitation they say with some show of reason that it would never do to give way to threats of violence. If, on the other hand, the campaign for reform is conducted by mannerly argument it is commonly said that there is no demand for a change. Comfortable clerical persons are never tired of telling you that there is really no demand from the poorer classes for any reform of the divorce laws.

True, people do not go out in the streets and break the windows of Cabinet Ministers or make themselves politically disagreeable after the fashion of the middle classes who have grievances real or imaginary. But anyone whose advice is sought by the poor in their troubles knows that the demand for divorce exists if it were of any use uttering it aloud to our smug and respectable rulers. Of course the demand or no demand is immaterial to anyone who has grasped the fact that it is a principle of elementary justice that the poor should have the same audience and remedies in all our Courts as the rich.

The real demand for divorce is to be found in the circumstances of the lives of the poor. I propose to set down a few typical cases drawn in every instance from public published records.

Jane married Fred when twenty-two years of age. Soon after the marriage he began to ill-treat her and would not work. Jane's parents helped them in business. Fred continued his ill ways and at length gave Jane a beating. Jane took out a summons, but would not face the Court, and forgave Fred. After five years of unhappy married life Jane went back to her parents taking her two children, Fred agreeing to pay her three shillings a week. At the end of nine months he ceased to send any money and disappeared. For seven years Jane lived with her parents until they died. After their death she found it a great struggle to live and pay the rent. Charles now comes on the scene, he takes lodgings and pays the rent. Ultimately Charles and Jane live happily together and there are two children of the union. Charles provides for Fred's children as well as his own. Charles and Jane would like to marry for their own sake and for their children's. In so far as there is any sin or immorality in this story the promoters of it and the sharers in it are those who stand in the path of divorce reform.

Here is another typical case. George marries Mary, their ages are eighteen and seventeen. Soon after marriage Mary—who comes of an immoral family—starts drinking and going about with other men. Ultimately she deserts George and becomes pregnant by another man and is confined in hospital. The guardians proceed against George for the expenses of the confinement, but he is able to prove to their satisfaction that he is not the father of the child. Mary then disappears to further infidelities and George goes back to live with his mother. Later on Anna appears on the scene and George and Anna have now a comfortable home and healthy infant. " They think a deal of it and wish it could be legitimate."

So, no doubt, do Charles and Jane and many other poor parents in like case. The law says that these people are entitled to have a divorce, only the law erects its Court in a corner of London inaccessible

to these poor provincials, and makes the costs and
fees and services of its judges and officials and
counsellors so expensive that there is no possibility
of Charles and George, and Jane and Anna, and
their little infants having the blessings of legal and
holy matrimony because they have not the cash to
purchase the luxury which is not for the likes of
them anyhow. And when it is suggested that
divorce might be cheapened and made available for
these poor citizens archbishops shake their heads,
and legal bigwigs, with their eye on the fees and the
costs, hold up their hands in amazement. Divorce
is a reasonable proposition for Marmaduke and
Ermyntrude, of "The Towers," Loamshire, but for
George and Anna in Back Tank Street, Shuttle-
borough—not likely. There is no demand for it,
says the Minority Report, and its worthy authors
point out with cynical contempt for the working
classes that they have got a system of separation
orders which is really all they require.

Now if there is one thing which the evidence
before the Commission puts beyond doubt it is that
the law in relation to separation orders induces,
invites, and causes immorality in the poor. Cranmer,
you remember, knew all about that, and looked on
separation without the right to remarry as an
unclean thing. But since the sorrows of the poor
in their marriage shipwrecks were so manifest, and
the Divorce Court was closed to them, systems of
magisterial separation orders, cheap permanent
divorces, without the right to marry again, have
become the order of the day.

There are some six thousand of these decrees made annually. The evidence is overwhelming as to the evils that spring from these orders. As Mrs. Tennant reports, " I believe that separation orders, the general alternative offered to divorce, work badly in working-class houses, and on the whole make for an increase rather than a diminution of immorality. We have to consider housing conditions and economic circumstances which often do not make for clean or wholesome ways of life, and where the relief offered by separation is not only inadequate but positively mischievous."

Put in plainer terms by the witnesses, a labouring man, if he has to find a home for his children, has to find a woman to keep house for him ; a woman of the same class has to pay a rent, which necessitates the taking in of a lodger. Human nature being what it is, it seemed superfluous to appoint a Royal Commission of trusty and well-beloved ones to tell us what would happen. This is a system that the Archbishop of York thinks " probably fulfils its purpose fairly well."

Of course, it all depends what its purpose may be. If it is its purpose to stand in the way of cheap divorce and the rights of the poor to have the same chance of rescue from a shipwrecked marriage that the rich possess, all is indeed well. But if the object of the law is to bring to those who are weary and in misery some hope of a new life and a new home where children can be born without shame and the parties can live in accordance with the wishes of themselves and their neighbours, then with all respect to the Primate of England, the law is probably fulfilling its purpose very damnably.

It is only fair, of course, to remember that the Archbishop of York and his learned colleagues of the Minority Report never meet Fred and Jane and George and Anna in real life, and can know no more about such folk at first hand, and have as little chance of understanding their point of view, as I have of studying and comprehending the sociological limitations of the higher priesthood.

Detestable as I hold these ecclesiastical errors to be in their practical bearing on the lives of the poor, I am hopeful that time and argument will overcome the ecclesiastical veto on reform. I am sure that even a bishop would be converted to healthier views of life if he could have a little home chat with George and Anna. And if their pleading did not convince him, I have a belief that the sight of their babies might touch the heart which even in a bishop, we may suppose beats somewhere beneath the chimere and rochet or whatever the vestments are called in which his lordship disguises his human nature from the lower classes.

Many of our judges and other learned men see very clearly the enormous importance of divorce reform to the poor. Mr. Justice Bargrave Deane put the matter very straightly to the Commission when he said, " The question of divorce is more a question for the poor than the rich. The rich have their homes and their comforts and their friends who are of a different position and who can by their own advice and conduct keep people straight." In so

far as this implies that the standard of morality or
etiquette of decent matrimonial conduct is stricter
among the rich than the poor, I doubt its truth.
The working classes have no leisure for flirtations
and philandering. The behaviour of a fast set
in a wealthy country house—which is generally
more vulgar than really naughty—would probably
scandalise the dwellers in a back street. But what
the learned judge wished to emphasise was that the
consequences of ill-conduct in a husband or wife are
far more serious in the everyday life of the cottage
than in that of the mansion. Here he is undoubtedly right.

What, for instance, can be more terrible than
the effect of persistent drunkenness on the married
life of the poor. Alfred and Anna have two children. The man earns thirty-two shillings and six-
pence a week when in full work and is a thoroughly
decent and respectable man. His wife is an inebriate.
She pawns everything for drink and neglects her
children. Her husband obtains a separation order,
but after three years Anna promised reform, and
Alfred, like the good fellow he was, took her back.
Unfortunately in two months she was as bad as
ever, and furniture, bedding, clothes, all the household gods disappear to the pawnshop. The children are reported upon by the school authorities.
The parents are prosecuted for neglect, and on Anna
agreeing to go to an inebriates' home for twelve
months the bench postpone sentence. When she
comes out she is a wreck, suffering from alcoholic
neuritis which is leading to paralysis. During her

absence Alfred has had to pay seven and six a week
for her maintenance. He now allows her five shillings a week and she lives with her sister. He is
on short time earning twenty-six shillings a week.
The children are without mother, the home is
without a woman's care and influence and his
income is rendered insufficient to provide the
necessaries of life.

Here is another picture—John married Catharine
in 1896. There was one child. When the infant
was nine months old Catharine was forced to leave
her husband on account of his drunken habits.
The child went to its grandmother and Catharine
went to service for seven years. After that time
she met Charles, a widower, with one child. Being
a brave and sensible woman she went to live with
him as his wife. They have two children of their
own now, one is three years old and the other six
months. They have a good home and are very
happy, and would like to be married if the law
allowed it.

Now all that religion has to tell us about these
cases is that marriages are made in heaven and that
heaven having once made these two utter messes
of human affairs, it is impious for human hands
and minds to try and mitigate the evil for which
heaven is responsible. I wish those for whom
these old-world blasphemies have merely a folk-
lore interest would leave this so-called religion
mumbling in its outer darkness and apply their
practical minds to so reforming the law that the
lives of Alfred and Anna and Catharine and Charles

and their innocent babies, and hundreds of other good men and women and innocent children, might no longer have to live in this civilised country under any legal disability or under any social shadow of ignominy or shame. In practice these folk very often do marry again without the blessing of Church or State, as in the last-cited case, and live useful and virtuous lives, bringing up happy children in good homes. The law should assist such citizens in the interest of the State, for the community want good homes and healthy children leading happy lives.

The recommendation of the Majority Commission in this matter is a very conservative one. It is that habitual drunkenness found incurable after three years from a first order of separation should be a ground for divorce. This, coupled with divorce for cruelty or desertion for three years and upwards, would certainly cover some of the sadder cases that were brought to the notice of the Commissioners.

The right of the State to refuse divorce in the case of the insanity of a party to a marriage seems hardly arguable. Here is one of the many sad stories. Norah married a soldier twenty years ago. Fourteen years ago he was taken to an asylum, where he still is, and Norah applied for relief. She was offered scrubbing work at the workhouse from 7 a.m. to 6 p.m. at nine shillings a week and some bread, or two-and-six a week and six pounds of bread, with liberty to take in two lodgers. Norah, to be with her children, chose the latter. John was one of the lodgers. He found his way to

Norah's heart by buying presents of boots and clothing for the children. And so Norah and John became man and wife, save and in so far as the law refused them that status. As Norah told a lady visitor, "I suppose you think it was wrong for me to drift into our present way of living, but it was such a struggle and he was so good to us. I have never been killed with wages, but we are as comfortable as we can be. I often wish we were free to marry because we do not like our children being illegitimate, and people look down on a woman so, if she lives as I am doing."

In this matter it is cheering to know that the archbishop and his learned adherents in their Minority Report are prepared to make some concession. I state this with pleasure, remembering the wise words of that good old Welsh parson, the Rev. John Hopkins, of Rhoscolyn, who said, "Indeed, Judge Parry, remember this, one must be charitable even to dissenters." *A fortiori* one should be just even to archbishops, and it is hopeful that in the matter of insanity where one of the parties is either of unsound mind at the time of the marriage or in a state of incipient mental unsoundness which becomes definite after six months of marriage and the suit is commenced within a year of marriage the Minority Report timidly proposes that such a marriage might be annulled.

What the difference in principle may be between the cases of a mad husband who has been married for six months and a madder husband who has been married for six years the learned ones do not inform us, but we may regard it as a sign of grace that there are some matrimonial miseries that seem to these hard-hearted pundits worthy of sympathy and relief.

No protest seems to be made by the Church against the go-as-you-please divorce methods of to-day among the upper classes, but if divorce by consent does not exist among the rich it shows great rectitude and self-denial on their part. One often reads of a case like the following one. Mrs. A. is neglected by her husband, who leaves her. She asks him to return and he refuses. She files a petition for restitution of conjugal rights. The Court makes a fourteen days' order on the undefended petition. I wonder if such an order has ever been obeyed or was ever intended to be obeyed. On receiving the order Mr. A. writes that he is not coming back, but that he will be found staying at a certain hotel with another lady under the style of Mr. and Mrs. A. Inquiries are made, and this proving true a divorce petition is filed. This again is undefended and the decree *nisi* goes as of course.

It is conceivable that such a procedure might be used by two intelligent persons who did not respect the laws of their country as a method of divorcing each other by consent, but I have no doubt that the well-to-do who constantly go through these forms are far too scrupulous in their observance of the letter and spirit of our divorce law to be guilty of anything that could be construed into collusion.

I do not think that in this country, except among wild and fanatical folk and some of the fast set with whom we need not concern ourselves, there is any demand for divorce by mutual consent. But, even if this were enacted, it does not follow, as Montaigne has told us, that it would be used. The idea that a more reasonable system of divorce will lead to a wholesale system of divorces is an absurd folly, a bogey used by ignorant but honest clericals to frighten good people who rather enjoy being scared to death. The fat boys of sociology love to make their victims' flesh creep, and when they speak of divorce reform constantly suggest that human nature tends to immorality in matrimonial affairs. As a matter of fact human beings naturally prefer marriage and married life where it is at all a successful institution to divorce and divorced life. This is wonderfully illustrated in Belgium where, as M. Henri Mesnil, the French avocat, points out, divorce law " as provided for by the Code Napoléon has remained in force down to the present day : in spite of the long predominance of the Catholic party dissolution of marriage by mutual consent is still possible in that country. I might say that although possible it is a very rare thing. I think only one case of divorce by mutual consent will be found amongst four hundred cases in Belgium."

Here we have the results of a hundred years' experience of a European country not unlike our own. It bears out exactly what one would expect, and it is only by ignoring such evidence and referring to the laxity of State procedure in America, without reminding the reader that there is no evidence of any greater laxity in the state of morality there than elsewhere, that the Archbishop of York and his friends can claim that the " preponderating voice of history and experience "—a charming phrase—is in favour of their Minority Report.

The archbishop treats history as Moses treated the rock. He strikes it with his archiepiscopal staff and there flows forth a gush of watery precedents to rejoice the hearts of the faithful. A poor pagan like myself can only approach the rock with a humble geological hammer and, knocking a few chips off it, report that it does not come of a water-bearing family. Outside miraculous draughts of history there is nothing to be found in the past experience of social life that tells against a reform of our present divorce laws.

But no reform in the law will be of the least use to the poor unless jurisdiction in divorce is given to the County Court. The opposition to this is twofold. It comes from those who object to any reform at all and see that by keeping divorce costly you naturally limit its use, and, again, it comes with even greater force from those who are making their money out of the present system. Very naturally the Divorce Court Bar, having an excellent paying business all to themselves, do not want to share it round with other people. Towards their trade union attitude of mind I have every sympathy. But when it is more than hinted that it would really be beyond the capacity of a County Court judge to try those " very difficult considerations of cruelty, condonation and connivance," I prefer the alliteration of the phrase to the sense of it. There is really no mystery about divorce law. The issue is an absurdly simple one, of grave importance to the lives of the parties certainly, but to a lawyer with a business mind far easier to try than many of the issues that arise every day in bankruptcy, Admiralty and commercial cases, and in arbitrations under the Workmen's Compensation Act.

The daily work of a County Court judge is not less difficult than that of his High Court brother. The complication of a case does not depend upon the amount at stake, and the County Court judge has, if anything, to have a somewhat wider knowledge of law and a far greater knowledge of the lives of the poor than any other judicial person, since the legal subjects he deals in are more varied in character than those met with in other Courts, and he naturally sees more of the daily life of the people. Certainly the High Court judges get better assistance from the Bar, or rather, I should say, more assistance—or should it be assistance of greater length?—but the County Court Bar of to-day contains the pick of the younger men, and is really the nursery of the common law Bar since it is only in the County Courts that a catholic experience in civil advocacy can be obtained. I noted with some interest that in a recent batch of silks seven or eight had been before me, some of them several times within a few months of their taking silk.

When there is a divorce case of any importance—in the same way as if it were a libel case of importance —great advocates with no special knowledge of the mysteries of divorce law are called in to lead the specialists. What is wanted is advocacy, not knowledge of divorce procedure, and the County Courts have excellent advocates to-day. If there is one special branch of law where one would think expert knowledge is essential it is Admiralty, yet important Admiralty cases belong to County Court districts where for aught anybody knows or cares the learned judge and the advocates may not know the difference between a bowsprit and a rudder.

But the real reason why the County Court should be chosen for this work in the interests of the poor is to my mind the real reason why the County Court is popular with business men and the High Court is not. In a properly managed County Court a case is set down for a certain day and, except on rare occasions, it is tried on that day. As Mr. Dendy, the learned registrar, pointed out to the Commission, " There's no doubt it is of very great advantage to a poor man to know the day on which his case is likely to be tried." It is indeed essential. The man himself and his witnesses do not belong to a class who can spend leisured hours flitting about Gothic corridors or waiting to be fetched from public-houses day by day until their case is reached. Certainty of trial and reasonable speed in reaching and disposing of the case are worth much more to business people than abstruse technical knowledge or long experience of the habits and manners of those who commit adultery. No one has more reverence than I have for the views of Lord Alverstone, who thinks divorce

DIVORCE

jurisdiction should not be given to County Courts, yet one must not forget that not only is the opposite view supported by a large number of men and women who know the wants of the poor very intimately, but experts, like Sir John Macdonell and Sir George Lewis, both recognise that if you are going to give a whole-hearted measure of reform with the intention of really putting divorce at the disposal of the poor there is no other Court to which these cases can honestly be sent.

Not only must this be done, but if we are to bring ourselves abreast of what already exists in foreign countries we must do a great deal towards cheapening the procedure even of the County Court for those who are poor.

The French have a very complete system of divorce for poor people, known as " *Assistance Judicaire.*" The effect is that the persons to whom assistance is granted do not have to pay anything whilst they remain poor. The State advances the necessary money. The *avocat* and *avoué*—barrister and solicitor—work for nothing. In case the assisted person comes into better circumstances he may be obliged to repay the State. If the poor litigant succeeds in his proceedings, the unsuccessful party pays the costs. In 1907 there were 20,464 persons who applied for assistance, 11,726 of which were in relation to matrimonial proceedings, and relief was granted to 9,205 poor people, of whom 5,136 were seeking different forms of matrimonial relief.

In Germany and the Netherlands divorce is equally open to poor people, who receive State aid, and in

Scotland there is a well-known system which is known as the Poors Roll, which is said to have existed since 1424. The Scots Parliament Act, which instituted this excellent procedure, commenced as follows : " If there be any poor creature who for lack of skill or expenses cannot nor may not follow his cause the King for the love of God shall ordain the judge before whom the cause shall be determined to purvey and get a leal and wise advocate to follow such poor creatures causes: and if such causes be obtained [won] the wronger shall indemnify both the party injured and the advocate's costs and travail." It is amazing to find in Scotland of the fifteenth century laws for the poor that we are only dimly thinking about in our vague uncertain timid way at the present day.

What actually happens to the poor man of the present day is set out in the following case—a very common one :—

Summoned in the City of London Court for the non-payment of forty-five pounds, his wife's costs in a divorce suit in which he was the successful petitioner, a City messenger said that he received one hundred and seventeen pounds a year, and while the divorce suit was pending he paid his wife as alimony two pounds ten shillings a month. He had paid sixty-five pounds for his wife's costs, and still owed forty-five pounds. He had obtained an order for payment of his own costs against the co-respondent, but as that person was only earning a few shillings a week he did not know if he would get anything.

DIVORCE

Judge Lumley Smith, K.C. : " Does a successful husband always have to pay his wife's costs ? "

Mr. Seyd (for the defendant) : " Yes."

Judge Lumley Smith : " That is rather hard on him."

The defendant added that while the suit was pending he had to borrow fifty pounds from his friends.

Judge Lumley Smith said a judgment debt must come in front of those of his friends, and ordered payment of one pound a month.

This man could not have proceeded *in forma pauperis*, as by our then system this was not open to anyone with more than thirty shillings a week with no means above twenty-five pounds and clothing. If he had done so he would have had neither counsel nor solicitor to plead his cause and the only real benefit he would have obtained would be that he would not have had to pay Court fees.

The self-respect of working men in many cases hinders them from applying for assistance rendered nominally distasteful by the pauper taint. They manage these things better in France, and what the poor want in England, in fact as well as in name, is " assistance." The new rules that have come into force this year go a little way to provide this, but it is too early as yet to say how far they will meet the wants of the case.

There was no need for any Royal Commission on Divorce to explain to any reasonably educated citizen what ought to be done, but I agree that the labours of many good men and women have given chapter and verse for the want and the remedy in a convenient form. Too much time was wasted over the moot points of the theologians, for most citizens are agreed that ecclesiastical opinions on the contract of matrimony as it affects the State are of the same value and no more as ecclesiastical opinions would be on such contracts as a bill of sale or a hire-purchase agreement, which may equally from time to time affect adversely or otherwise the moral conduct of human beings.

" Marriage is nothing but a civil contract. 'Tis true 'tis an ordinance of God : so is every other contract : God commands me to keep it when I have made it." Worthy John Selden did not mean by that that it was to be kept for ever and in all circumstances, but that it was to be kept until such time as the law released the parties from it in the same way as every other civil contract. Nothing is more true and necessary to be repeated in these days than the citizens' view of marriage law. Whatever codes different religious men and women wish to observe they are free to follow. But the marriage law is a question of citizenship for citizens to settle for themselves. It is therefore satisfactory to read in the Majority Report that English laymen seem generally to base their views, not upon ecclesiastical tradition or sentiment, but upon general Christian principles coupled with common-sense and experience of the needs of human life. It is the conclusion of these men and women—not the anathemas of priests—that want parliamentary attention. They have told us " that there is necessity for reform in this country, both in procedure and in law, if the serious grievances which at present exist are to be removed, and if opportunities of obtaining justice are to be within the reach of the poorer classes. So far from such reforms as we recommend tending to lower the standard of morality and regard for the sanctity of the marriage tie, we consider that reform is necessary in the interest of morality, as well as in the interest of justice; and in the general interests of society and the State."

When shall we find time to ease these heavy burdens of the poor and let the oppressed go free?

CHAPTER VIII

FLAT-TRAPS AND THEIR VICTIMS

> Will you walk into my parlour
>   Said the Spider to the Fly
> 'Tis the prettiest little parlour
>   You ever did espy.
> The way into my parlour
>   Is up a winding stair,
> And I have many curious things
>   To show you when you're there.
> Will you ? Won't you ?
> Will you ? Won't you ?
>   Walk in pretty Fly.
>   *Nursery Rhyme.*

IF we could remember half the wise saws and moral jingles that nurse and granny taught us in the nursery and not forget to act upon them in after life, what sensible citizens we should be ! Some day there will be cinematograph lectures to the young people just leaving the elementary schools, exhibiting not only the real spider, but his many human prototypes, who are lying in wait for the working-class man and woman at every corner of their career. A nature lesson on the smaller tally-man would be far more practical in a city school than a botany lecture on the lesser celandine.   Nevertheless, I doubt if it will do much good when it comes about.   Human beings are naturally divided into spiders and flies, and of the two the latter really have the best of it. There is not much fun to be had out of a cramped life in a dingy web counting your gains, even if a white waist-coat and a gold chain conceal your evil conscience. At least the fly buzzes round a bit and thinks he is seeing life before he biffs into the web. And no one need care much about the gay young sportsman bachelor variety—except perhaps his sweetheart, and she has a lucky escape, poor thing ! But the silly old married fly who gets caught in the web and leaves a young wife and family starving at home, or, worse still, the house-mother fly who rushes into the web just to look at the spider's latest fashions which she knows her old bluebottle cannot afford—these are sad cases.

Thomas Carlyle was mightily pleased with him-self, I doubt not, when he hit upon that phrase describing his fellow citizens as " The twenty-seven millions, mostly fools." Those last two words are constantly in the mouth of the odd fool in reference to the 26,999,999 other fellows. Still a long life in the County Court compels me to the conclusion that the fool is not extinct ; he is, indeed, but too prevalent. Furthermore, the old world saying, " that a fool and his money are soon parted," is, like many another old proverb, a true saying.

These being the facts, why does the law side with the inappropriate knave who preys upon the harm-less necessary fool ?

Scientific sociologists will no doubt tell me that if the law were to protect the fool the effect would be to increase and multiply the breed of fools, whereby the human race would become a bigger fool race than already it is. To which my reply would be that the law as it now stands makes the trade of knavery such a lucrative one that the business of it is fast becoming overcrowded, and the best hope of the extinction of the knave seems to lie in the fact that he will soon have to work nearly as hard for his living as the honest man.

It is all very well to smile at the simplicity of the fool, and admire the cunning of the knave, but let us remember that the poor fool has in each generation to discover for himself that this is a world in which skimmed milk is constantly masquerading as cream, and that faith in the honesty of human nature in business affairs is in the poor man the first step on the road to ruin.

I do not want the law to mollycoddle the fool and deprive him of the birthright of an Englishman to make a fool of himself in his own way, but I should like to see the law doing more to stamp out the knave, especially—O, yes, especially— when he is a respectable, pious, well-to-do knave clothed in broad cloth and a well-boiled shirt, tempting the working man to part with his savings in the name of thrift and the preparation for the rainy day.

What misery has been caused by well-advertised and wicked schemes of investment introduced to the working man by lying promises garnished with much prayer and psalm singing !

If a chartered accountant could make out a balance sheet of the losses of the working class from frauds connected with building societies, insurance schemes, house-purchase companies, and the like, from the days of the Liberator onwards, what a terrible indictment it would be of the way in which the law permits the rich knave to rob the poor fool! And yet how few of the promoters of these schemes arrive at their proper destination— the gaol.

We open our prison doors readily enough to the poor debtor, but the rich man who lives on the stolen savings of the poor finds it as difficult to enter the gates of the gaol in this world as he will to reach the wicket gate in the hereafter.

Many societies have been formed under the Limited Liability Companies Acts offering working men facilities for buying their own houses or obtaining old age pensions or future lodgings in some glorious castle of Spain. These have gathered in for years the savings of working men, and when the directors were called upon to redeem their promises it was found that the money had been spent in directors' salaries and commissions, and there was no provision whatever for the policy-holders.

For as the law stands you may make nearly any wild promises you like, for that is not the contract. The contract is the long-worded, obscure policy which is sent to the workman later on. The gaudy booklet with its golden promises and pretty pictures of villas with bow windows which the poor man treasures up has nothing to do with the case.

Sentimental judges may try to find a way out; juries may give verdicts returning the poor man his money ; but all to no purpose. The law stands firm for the solemn contract under the seal of the company, the policy which the poor man has never read and could not understand if he did ; and the sleek directors chuckle at the angry working man, and with the blessing of the Court of Appeal remind him in Shylock's own words :

> Till thou canst rail the seal from off my bond,
> Thou but offend'st thy lungs to speak so loud.

And certainly as the law stands it is necessary to have a Court of Appeal stern and unbending in judgment to uphold the sacred nature of the contract. The doubt in my somewhat sentimental mind is whether transactions of this character between knaves and fools are in any practical business sense really contracts at all ; and if they are to be deemed to be contracts whether power should not be given to Courts of Justice to release the victims from the flat-traps in which they have been snared, and give them at least some of their fur back again.

This has been attempted with the moneylender, but not at present with very great success. For myself I have always thought that the moneylender, if he be a real moneylender and not merely a fee-snatcher, is by no means the worst setter of flat-traps. I have an uneasy feeling that if moneylenders were Nonconformists or Churchmen, instead of being Jews, we should love them better.

For if you get an actual sovereign from a moneylender you have at all events got some concrete thing that you can exchange for food and drink

156

or clothing, and the token has an ascertained value ; moreover, if you know a little arithmetic you know what you are paying for it. But if you buy clothing from a tally-man or a watch from a travelling jeweller, or a walnut suite from an instalment furniture dealer, or a family Bible in parts from an area tout, you can have no idea whatever of the value of the thing purchased or the percentage of profit on the deal.

And, though I should like to see all this class of trading done away with, and know that it causes great ruin and misery, yet to my mind the money-lender and even the lower class of tally-men are angels of light compared with the directors of insolvent collecting societies, who take the savings of the thrifty poor on promises that any sensible person must know to be incapable of performance.

As I have shown elsewhere, the bulk of the smaller flat-trap poachers could be quietly exterminated by the abolition of imprisonment for debt. That alone is the artificial manure which enables these social weeds to flourish. Withhold it from them and they would wither and die, and the world would be well rid of them.

If the man in the street could listen, as I have had to do for the last twenty years, to tales of misery and wretchedness brought about by our absurd credit system he would understand something of my impatience at its continuance. I remember a small household that was ruined by a gramophone. A poor woman, a widow, earned twelve shillings a week, and a son was doing well at fifteen shillings a week. There were two little children. As things go in their world they were well-to-do. The Devil, in the form of a tout, came down the street one Saturday afternoon, with a beautiful gramophone. It was only a shilling a week, and all that was to be done was for mother and son " to sign just there at the bottom of the paper, and, of course, if they did not want to keep it they could send it back."

However, later on, they found that they had signed to buy it ; the boy fell out of work, the case was put in Court, and judgment was entered against both mother and son in default of appearance for two or three pounds. Then the son enlisted and went to India, and I first heard of the case when they brought the widow up on a judgment summons. I asked her why she had signed the guarantee, and her reply was : " Tom was such a good lad and he was in work, and he was that keen to have it I couldn't deny him." Anyone who has ever been any kind of a father or mother will not cast a stone at her for her folly.

That is one of the short and simple tales from the annals of imprisonment for debt.

What match are confiding folk like these for the lying scallywags who tout their inferior wares round the streets ? And instead of our law remembering that we pray daily to be delivered from temptation, and playing the part of a father of the fatherless and a friend of the widows, it keeps alive section 5 of the Debtors Act, 1869, in the interests of about as low a class of knaves as ever disgraced the name of English trade.

FLAT-TRAPS AND THEIR VICTIMS

I know very well that there are many good honest folk who approve of imprisonment for debt and have fears about its abolition. These should remember that in France and Germany and a great part of America there is no such thing, and yet trade does not suffer and the working classes do not starve. I should quite agree that if a man defrauds a trades-man by lying promises or cheating he should be punished, but imprisonment should be for fraud, not, as it is now, for poverty. As I have already pointed out, in America no honest man is likely to get into prison merely for the wickedness of owing money. We cannot say that is true here. In Germany the working man lives on a cash basis. Credit is not largely given, as there is no power of imprisonment for debt.

England is the last civilised country whose law encourages the poor to live on credit, yet nothing is more true than this, that once start living on credit and you cannot get out of it. It is a down-ward path leading to the Slough of Despond. But until the law is amended we must be content to look on and see the poor in the cages of prison whilst those that set the traps and catch them wax fat and shine.

And as soon as a boy or a girl begins to earn wages the Evil One, in the shape of some kind of tally-man, is at his or her elbow with a watch, or a ring, or a family Bible, or a musical instrument, or a shoddy sewing machine, the possession of which can be gloriously enjoyed on payment of the first instalment. I do not say that boys and girls must not buy their experience of the world and pay for it, but the law need not assist the knave in making it more expensive than is necessary. I have known several cases of young servants leaving good places and running off in terror because they have been served with a blue paper, "frightener" with a lot of law jargon about imprisonment upon it, threatening them with dire penalties because an instalment was due on a gold ring. More might certainly be done to prevent back-door trading, and there is no more reason why area touts should be allowed to infest the streets than the lower class of bookmakers. Well-to-do people have very little idea of the number of firms that employ travelling canvassers and touts to hawk their wares from door to door in the mean streets.

I remember once a fairly well-to-do working man —he was the doorkeeper of a public institution in Manchester—had an action brought against him by a street tout because his dog, an Airedale terrier, had bitten the prowling fellow as he was coming in at the back door. The man was badly mauled, and the dog having been proved to have bitten several other people of a like nature, I had, much to my discontent, to give judgment for the plaintiff.

About a year afterwards—having forgotten all about the matter—I was visiting the institution where the defendant was employed, when, as the gentleman I wished to see was engaged, the doorkeeper asked me to step into his lodge and sit down and wait.

"I've often wanted to see you, Mr. Porry," he began, "about that there dorg case."

"What case was that?" I asked.

"That case where you fined me five pounds over an Airedale what tried to gobble up a tally-man."

"I remember," I said doubtfully.

"Well," he continued, "you seemed to sympathise with me like, but you found against me. You see I had bought that dorg for the very purpose of keeping those fellows off the premises whilst I'm away. So I said if the law don't let 'im bite 'em, what's the use of the dorg? and what I wanted to arsk you was, may my dorg bite 'em within reason or did I 'ave to pay five pounds 'cause 'e mauled 'im too much?"

I explained the law in relation to dogs and tally-men as well as I could, and my friend was good enough to say when I had finished :

"Well, I quite see you 'ad to make me pay as the law stands, but it don't seem to mc just. If you can't 'ave a dorg, how can you keep them fellows out of the house?"

That was more than I could answer. We parted friends—and there was, I think, a mutual feeling between us that the law of dogs in relation to tally-men was not all it should be.

And many laws that are made for the best purposes are wrested from their beneficent uses by the wicked ones of the world and turned to the basest advantages. No legislation was hailed with greater delight by social reformers than the Married Women's Property Act, and yet one must admit that the fraudulent use of its provisions is a commonplace. I am not suggesting that it is mainly against the poor that it is misused, though I have known of cases under the Workmen's Compensation Act where goods were alleged to be " in the wife's name " after an award had been made against the husband, and many a poor tradesman and small worker is swindled by this allegation, the victim not having the money to test it in a court of law, and the result being in any case so gloriously uncertain. I am sorry to put matrimony among the flat-traps, but the use of the married status among the dishonest to prevent a successful litigant from obtaining the results of a judgment brings it within this category. Even the poorer classes themselves are beginning to make use of it as a kind of homestead law to protect their goods from execution.

Much as I am in favour of seeing the poor man's home protected to a larger degree than it is at present I do not care to see it achieved at the expense of the character of the occupants. Any law that is a constant temptation to dishonesty is an evil, and there is no doubt that when the day comes for legal reform on a large scale, the various questions relating to the position of the married woman in the eye of the law will have to be considered. In many cases, of course, the reforms will be towards the enlargement of women's liberty, but in the matter of holding property it is clear that where a wife or a husband is tacitly allowing credit to be obtained on his or her appearance of property that property should be available to discharge the debt notwithstanding that it is claimed as the special property of one or the other.

Menander, the Greek poet, in one of his comedies makes someone say, " To marry a wife, if we regard the truth, is an evil, but it is a necessary evil." If this was true in 300 B.C. it became more convincingly the truth in 1882 A.D., when the Married Women's Property Act became law, and the " peculiar gift of heaven " was welcomed by the unscrupulous trader as a statutory stay of execution. Since that day the Micawbers of this world have put all their available assets " in the wife's name."

The legal privileges of the married woman are not sufficiently well known. Like " the infant " she is, indeed, the darling of the law. What a fine commercial spree an " infant " could have who looked older than his years and had an elementary knowledge of the law of "infants"! Luckily they do not teach anything useful at educational establishments, and the " infant " never learns about his glorious legal status until it is too late to exploit it.

But a married woman can, and does, have a real good time at the expense of her own particular tyrant, man. Recently at Quarter Sessions a man was accused of stealing the spoons, and his wife was accused of receiving the property knowing it to have been stolen. But it was pointed out that it was one of the rights of a married woman to receive whatever her husband happened to bring home, and the judge directed an acquittal.

There are several pretty little distinctions in the criminal law in favour of the married lady, but perhaps it is not seemly to advertise them overmuch. When we come to so-called civil matters, the lady who does not know and exercise her legal privileges is indeed a *rara avis*. How many of the debt-collecting cases in the County Court are concerned with the good lady who runs into debt with the tally-man or other tradesman to the husband unknown ? True, in many of these the husband has a possible defence, but the good man is generally a sporting, careless fellow, and pays his five shillings a month in the belief that debt is a natural sequence of matrimony.

But when it comes to committing wrongs—or torts, to use the Norman slang of the law—the married woman is the only legal personality that is privileged to forget her duty to her neighbour at someone else's expense. Her unhappy husband is always liable for the damages and costs, although he may have done his best to hinder the wrong that has been done. If in his absence on the daily round the good lady slanders her neighbour's wife, or trespasses on her neighbour's garden to commit the further wrong of slapping her neighbour's infant, the husband, for the purposes of paying damages, is regarded by the law as being a joint offender. The law supposes that a wife acts under her husband's directions. When they told Mr. Bumble that, he replied in the immortal phrase, " If the law supposes that, the law is a ass—a idiot. If that's the eye of the law, the law's a bachelor ; and the worst I wish the law is, that his eye may be opened by experience—by experience."

It does seem a bit hard on the poor man certainly. If he keeps a dog the animal may have his first bite at his neighbour free of expense, and when he gets to hear about it he can send the dog away. But with a wife there is no question of *scienter*. You may not suspect that your good lady is given to slander, assault and such like indiscretions, but, if it so happens, you have to pay. Nor do I see what steps you can take to hinder the lady from trespasses which she has the mind to commit. For if you were to place her under lock and key I believe a sentimental High Court judge would grant her a *habeas corpus* that she might go out again into the wide, wide world and exercise her undoubted right of committing wrong at her husband's expense.

And I set down these disadvantages of husbandry as some sort of excuse for the meanness and dishonesty of the man who uses " his wife's name " to protect his assets and injure his creditors. I have in my mind a commercial married man auditing in his debit and credit mind the matrimonial balance sheet. " See," he says, " my liabilities under the law of husband and wife. Surely there must be some assets of the relationship in which I am entitled to participate!" Then he studies the Married Women's Property Act, and chuckles. Whether this is so or not, there is no doubt that, since the Act of 1882, " Everybody's doing it," and when the bailiffs come in the furniture and the stock-in-trade are always found to be " in the wife's name." It is a form of conspiracy, you would say, and the police should put a stop to it, but " Old Father Antic the

Law " has his answer for you there—a wife cannot be guilty of conspiracy with her husband, for husband and wife are one.

There was a story illustrating the prevalence of this custom in the precincts of Strangeways, Manchester. Mr. Isaacs, who had been absent from business for some time, returned to his workshop looking pale and white and very weak. A sympathetic neighbour put his head in at the door, and, full of pity, said :

" Dear me, dear me, you look very ill, mine friend. Vot is the matter with you ? "

" Ach," groaned Isaacs, " I have had a terrible time, a shocking bad time."

" Vot vas it all about ? "

" I vill tell you," replied Isaacs. " The veek before last two doctors came to mine house and took avay mine appendix."

" Bah ! " muttered his friend contemptuously. " I vonder at you. That vos all you own fault : you should have put it in the vife's name. Then they could not touch it."

The story might be told in a Scot's accent, or even a Welsh one for that matter, and it would represent with equal truth the prevalent outlook of mankind on the commercial advantages of matrimony. I by no means desire to suggest that " the wife's name " is made a baser use of by the eastern communities of Strangeways and Whitechapel than among the fair-haired Saxons of Surbiton and Chorlton-cum-Hardy.

There are many people who see no wrong in

doing what is within the law, and there has always been a human tendency to score off one's brother man by a smart trick since the days of Jacob and Esau. The fool will always be outwitted by the discreet ones of the world, who justify their ways by reminding us that we are only bound to obey the letter of the law, and that there is no duty cast upon us to interpret and respect its spirit.

And simple charitable folk will say that after all things may really be quite honest and straightforward, and it is only the stingy creditor who sees fraud and the ungenerous judicial mind that finds in the constant repetitions of a series of happenings an intention in the parties to whom the events occur to wrong their neighbours.

For why should not John Smith put over the door of his shop " J. Smith," and how can the pleasant, careless fellow pay his debts in these bad times, and why do those wholesale curmudgeons press for their money and weary of John's winning smile and dangling tales of future payment ? If creditors won't wait it is really very foolish in these days to sue for the money and put the bailiffs in. For friend John is away at the races and when they come and seize the stock and effects of " J. Smith " there is Mrs. Smith, dear, good lady, to whom of course everyone knows, or ought to know, the business belongs.

Is not she a married woman ? Cannot she trade in her own name ? Is not her name over the door— well, not her name exactly, but her initial—her full name is Jane Smith—and as for her husband, he has never been anything but a servant of hers, and now she is going to run the business herself!

In due course of evolution, no doubt, we shall breed this dishonesty out of the race, or else the kind of poor, simple tradesman who gives credit without inquiry will become extinct.

At present there are quite a number of people who regard laws not so much as guides to good conduct, but as difficulties to be overcome in the obstacle race of life. A learned king's counsel, a well-known expert in bankruptcy and bills of sale, told me of an interview he had with a secretary of a social society who came to ask him to deliver a lecture. The secretary explained that their members were mostly cabinet makers and small furniture dealers, and they had a meeting and a discussion every month. The king's counsel agreed to come, and asked what sort of subject they would like him to speak about.

"Well," said the secretary, "our president, Mr. X——, you may know him——"

The king's counsel shook his head.

"Well, he has been bankrupt twice—I thought you might have met him. He proposed a very good subject, and the committee were quite pleased with it."

"And what did he suggest?"

"Well, seeing we are nearly all interested in the furniture trade, he thought there would be a good turn up if you would come and lecture on the Bills of Sale Acts and how to avoid them."

And I suppose a brainy man, with a good wife,

and, what is almost as rare nowadays, a good bill of sale, can live on nothing for about as long as it can be done.

That candid poet, Arthur Hugh Clough, pointed out many years ago that the ancient decalogue did not cover all our sinful modern ways, and amended the eighth to run thus :

> Thou shalt not steal ; an empty feat
> When it's so lucrative to cheat.

And surely we may ask, Why should this miserable cheat flourish among decent citizens of to-day? Should not a man or woman be made to trade in his or her own name? In a business community it is almost impossible to make adequate inquiries before you start trading, and why, if you come to think of it, should an individual desire to trade in any but his own name ? The frauds that are committed may not be very serious, but all forms of cheating and sharp dealing are detrimental to trade, and trade, after all, is the basis of our national pre-eminence. It seems particularly undesirable in a nation that prides itself on its domestic purity that " the wife's name " should be a symbol of dishonesty. If we cannot attain to a decent code of commercial morality without it we shall have to ask our four-hundred-pound legislators for yet another statute. " One man, one name, and make him trade in it," would be well received by all the honest, rich and poor, throughout the country.

I have dealt at some length with this question of putting goods in the wife's name because I doubt if folk whose business does not take them into the

County Court have any idea how prevalent it is
and what a very present help it is to the man who
is living upon his neighbours by some semi-fraudulent
business. Every now and then the setter of flat-
traps catches a victim too strong and lusty to
remain in the trap. The shoddy gold watch is
returned, the bogus business is thrown back on
the exploiter's hands, the company promoter who
has annexed the savings of the victim by false
promises is sued for damages for deceit. In some
of these cases by pertinacity and the spending of
more money a triumphant judgment will be obtained
by the fly against the spider. But there it ends.
When the high bailiff visits the web he is politely
informed that it is part of the wife's separate estate,
every thread in the web is covered by a bill of sale,
and if you try to imprison the old spider for debt
you would find the greatest difficulty in proving
his means to the satisfaction of the Court. Bankruptcy has no terrors for the old fellow. You will
probably find that he has been there before and
rather likes its old-world dusty crannies and the
peaceable formulæ of its schedules and accounts.

No doubt it is very difficult to draft laws that the
wicked cannot wrest from their righteous purpose
and use for iniquity. But the law plays into the
hands of the knave by its verbosity and diffuseness
and the great mass and complexity of it, which the
knave studies with as great care and astuteness as
the lawyers and judges whose duty it is, within the
four corners of the law, to prevent his wrongdoing.
When it is enacted " Thou shalt not steal," the

Court knows where it stands, but that is a far more easy statute to construe than anything the parliamentary draftsman turns out to-day. If we could get a short statute of one clause, " Thou shalt not cheat," with an appropriate schedule containing a tariff of fines and imprisonment, I think magistrates could do a good deal to cleanse the cities of a great many low ruffians who make their living by swindling the poor and make the law as it stands their attorney to collect the spoils.

CHAPTER IX

POVERTY AND PROCEDURE

Therefore I counsel you, ye rich,   have pity on the poor.
Though ye be mighty at the law   be ye meek in your deeds.
The same measure ye mete   wrong or right
Ye shall be weighed therewith   when ye go home.

.   .   .   .   .

To the poor the Courts are a maze   if he plead there all his life,
Law is so lordly   and loth to end his case ;
Without money paid in presents   Law listeneth to few.

                                 PIERS PLOWMAN.

WE have moved along a little since the days of Edward III., and if Piers Plowman were with us to-day he would see no visions of " money paid in presents " to State servants, at all events not to the judiciary. Bacon was the last Lord Chancellor who indulged this evil habit, and if, as his admirers tell us, he was at the time producing his own plays on sharing terms with impecunious actors, one can understand the necessity of it whilst condemning the practice. Although we have made justice pure enough in this country and not directly purchasable, yet the rest of Piers Plowman's indictment is true enough of the present time, and law is still a maze wherein the rich are guided by the clever ones who

know the way and the poor too often get lost for
want of an honest guide.

There are many signs that the public conscience
is being slowly awakened to the iniquity of one side
in a law suit having all the legal aid that money can
buy and the other side nothing. In criminal cases
something is already done and a beginning is being
made on the civil side in the High Court to give the
poor legal aid. These reforms do not amount to
very much as yet, but they are the first steps towards
remedying Piers Plowman's grievances and, considering that it is less than six hundred years since
that excellent visionary made his moan over the law
and the poor, and the drawback poverty has in the
procedure of the Courts, there seems to have been
no very unusual delay in Government taking the
matter up. We may at least congratulate ourselves
that we have got a scheme of some sort which can be
amended and put into a business shape instead of
the Select Commission which reformers are generally
offered to keep them quiet. Old Piers would be
awfully happy—" bucked," I think, is the modern
word—if he could know that after five hundred and
fifty years we were tackling the problems of life that
worried him so greatly. In another six hundred
years or so a lot of the little matters referred to in
this book will get smoothed out. If you can get into
the habit of thinking of the world's progress in
centuries instead of months you will find it very
comforting.

Until more is known of these new schemes and
their workings we must write of the present system

as we know it, for any change in it will certainly be slow enough and it is something to understand the circumstances of the present in order to see what changes are really required.

You may remember that George Eliot in " The Mill on the Floss " describes Mr. Tulliver as saying, " that in law the ends of justice could only be achieved by employing a stronger knave to frustrate a weaker. Law was a sort of cock-fight in which it was the business of injured honesty to get a game bird with the best pluck and the strongest spurs."

I do not say for a moment that Mr. Tulliver was right, but I think George Eliot shrewdly described in his words the attitude of mind of the man in the street towards the High Court of Justice. Cock-fighting was always a popular, cruel, and exciting sport, and now that it is done away with the next best thing is to squeeze into the Divorce Court and witness a real set-to between Chanticleer, K.C., and young Cockerel, who, they say, will be taking silk himself very soon and will knock the older bird out of the ring.

Certain it is that the poor have a notion, in which there is doubtless some truth, that the fact that the other side had a better and more expensive counsellor gave them a greater chance in the legal lottery. The side that can put Carson on to bowl at one end and F. E. Smith at the other must start at a better price than the side which has to rely on an unknown amateur in the back row. Of course, A. N. Other may take some wickets, but the public have a very business-like belief that money talks, and that the verdict of the jury, like most of the verdicts in life, will turn out to be on the side which can put in the field the most expensive team.

Certainly I can say without hesitation that working men would never have got their due from the Workmen's Compensation Acts if each particular poor workman had had to fight for his rights at his own expense. It is to the trade unions and their co-operative litigation that the thanks of the workmen are due for preserving their rights under the Act.

Mr. Lysons was a Pendleton collier, and had only worked for a few days when he received an injury. This happened in 1901, and at that time the old Act said that no compensation could be recovered until a man had been off work for two weeks. It was argued before me that this being so, unless a man was employed for more than fourteen days he could not come within the Act at all. The argument did not appeal to me, but it did to the Court of Appeal, and later on again it did not to the House of Lords. So the man got his money.

But the point of the case is that had not the union come forward to take his case to the House of Lords, Lysons would have lost his compensation, and the Act of Parliament would have been construed to limit the rights of the poor for all time.

This particular case cost the union six hundred pounds to fight, and the point in dispute was whether the injured man was, or was not, to receive six shillings a week for five weeks. Several cases have run the same course. The Act is obscurely drafted and capable of many interpretations. Some of these that still stand on the books remain precedents only because the workman has not money enough to carry the case higher and has no union behind him.

And, though in the first instance a workman might often make shift to state his case in the County Court himself and rely on his own advocacy as to the facts and the judge's knowledge of the law, it is absurd to suppose he could argue a legal point in the Court of Appeal or House of Lords without assistance. Unless a trade union is ready to take up the case, the only hope of a man getting his rights is through the aid of a speculative solicitor.

Such a system has its drawbacks to the litigant and the profession, and leads to unpleasant and undesirable incidents, but it is no use shutting one's eyes to what is going on every day in every Court. Dodson and Fogg have always been looked down upon ever since Sam Weller gave them away by blurting out in Court that it was " a wery gen'rous thing of them to have taken up the case on spec. and to charge nothing at all for costs unless they got them out of Mr. Pickwick."

No doubt it is very unprofessional to make such an agreement, but with the law as it is, and the poor with rights under the law, how on earth are they to get their rights unless there is a speculative solicitor ready to risk a certain amount of out-of-pockets in the hope of getting them back with advantages from Mr. Pickwick? Unless a speculative solicitor is ready to back the poor man's case with gratuitous services and money enough for counsel's honorarium, surveyor's plans, doctor's and Treasury fees, how can the case be launched at all ?

Indeed, could one be certain that such a solicitor never undertook any case unless he was satisfied that his client had right on his side, should we not have to admit that the speculative solicitor was a ministering angel engaged in a practice of delivering the poor that cried, and the fatherless, and him that had none to help him ?

And as day by day the poor have more laws made to guide them into the way of righteousness, and more statutes are passed with the intention of making the life of the poor healthier, brighter, and better, and as, moreover, in this imperfect world the servants of the Evil One are always prowling round to cheat the poor of their rights, it would seem to follow that if Law Courts and litigation are to be the order of the day we must each of us have a panel lawyer to whom we can go when we want an injunction and our *habeas corpus* is not up to the mark.

For years and years there have been speculative doctors. No one thought any the worse of doctors because they founded hospitals and gave their services free of charge and entered a *caveat* against disease and death without first getting something on account of costs. And why should not we have legal hospitals and out-patient departments attached to the County Court where the house physician is the young man who has taken the best degrees in law and the visiting surgeon is the great leader of the legal profession ?

The idea is no more ludicrous in one profession than it is in another. Medicine has its noble traditions of charity. Why should not lawyers set an example of self-sacrifice and unselfishness ? Or is there some subtle essence in the law that of necessity destroys the favourable microbes that promote peace and goodwill among men ?

We of the long robe of the Inns of Court have always held in theory that we were there to take on the protection of any and every suitor. Please do not think when your attorney asks you for counsel's fees that you are hiring him by that golden nexus of guineas. By no means. No barrister can stoop to take wages or salary. What you are giving him is a mere gratuity, "which a barrister cannot demand without doing wrong to his reputation." And, that being so, one might expect some of the wealthier Templars to take the ideal of their profession at its face value and set up to advise and plead for the poor not only without wronging their reputation by demanding a gratuity, but by refusing to accept one.

In a recent case much was said of the noble attitude of Barrister A., who, being a political opponent of Barrister B., appeared for him when he had got into trouble—I use the phrase in no technical sense. Correspondence ensued, and some enthusiasts for the honour of the profession said that every barrister was bound to take up a case if it was offered him. I wonder what would happen if Lazarus went knocking at the doors of Crown Office Row and Pump Court with a claim against

Dives, but without a gratuity in his hand ? Would
he get anyone to advise him on evidence or
settle the indorsement on his writ ? One never
knows.

The atmosphere of our Courts is not all that it
should be. I do not refer to the physical fog which
pervades them, the smells of which the electric
fans blow about the building in the sacred name of
ventilation, but the moral atmosphere of our Courts
always seems to me to suggest that the law is an
appanage of the rich. By all means let us have
dignity, decorum, and distinctive dress, but if you
go into the High Court, although you may hear the
affairs of the poor dealt with sympathetically and
in a just spirit, the atmosphere of the Court is
well-to-do and prosperous. Everyone connected
with the duties seems to belong to the upper middle
class. There is no place at all for the working man
to play his part except on occasion in the jury
box.

And then, if the claim is the claim of a poor man
against a rich man, a special jury is empanelled and
you get at a greater cost a tribunal of the defendant's own class to hold the scales of justice. And
though I firmly believe that all do their best, and
that speaking generally justice is well administered,
yet I can quite understand the feeling of a poor man
entering a Court of Justice and finding that the
judge who lays down the law, the jury who decide
the facts, the advocates who argue the case, and the
solicitors who instruct the advocates are all drawn
from a class of the community which the working

man rightly or wrongly believes to be hostile to his outlook on life.

If I have not made myself clear, imagine yourself bringing an action against a trade union, and finding when you came into court that a well-known ex-Labour M.P. was on the bench, that the jury were chosen entirely from the working classes, and that you were only allowed to be represented by a next friend chosen from the ranks of a particular trade union.

Would you, under circumstances of this kind, even if you were convinced of the honesty and sincerity of every portion of the tribunal, feel that sense of security in its right decision which is so essential in a community where law should be respected ?

And that this is a real trouble and that the Courts are aware of its existence was shown in a recent judgment of Lord Sumner in the Court of Appeal. A learned judge in the Court below in correctly directing the jury as to the effect of the Trades Disputes Act had " added some remarks pointedly expressed which were indirectly a criticism of the Act and substantially a statement to the jury that a person who availed himself of the defence afforded by the Act was setting up a dishonest defence." These remarks Lord Sumner described as " inopportune, detrimental to the defendant's case and, perhaps worst of all, irrelevant." He concluded with quaint sarcasm : " A judge in charging a jury could never safely indulge in irrelevant observations because he could not be sure that the jury would be sufficiently logical to take no notice of them." I intend asking the Office of Works to have that painted up on the walls of my Court. It is worthy of letters of gold. Irrelevancy is certainly the worst of sins and it is a natural vice in most of us only to be kept down by prayer and fasting from the practice of it. We all dislike some Act of Parliament; the Insurance Act, the Ground Game Act, the Finance Act—none is so perfect that it has not some judicial enemies. And it is certainly very tempting when you meet the fellow in Court to give him a bit of your mind. But it must not be. The Legislature is our schoolmaster. Outside in the playground and on vacation we can express our opinions about him freely, but in school—No !

Lord Sumner is perfectly right and when he next speaks on this subject I wish he would point out with authority that this human habit of irrelevancy is the constitutional reason for maintaining the grand jury. For centuries the King's Bench judges have worked off their natural irrelevancy in charging the grand juries at assize towns to the great benefit of themselves and the local papers. This national safeguard, this barrier between judicial irrelevancy and the public at large, should not be removed in a careless spirit. Our forefathers knew a thing or two. The grand jury is really a sound instrument of constitutional mechanics. It is the safety valve for the blowing off of judicial steam.

Lawyers and judges are certainly held in higher esteem to-day than they were in the past. Gulliver describing the contemporary lawyers to his friend and master, the Houyhnhnm says: "there was a society of men among us, bred up from their youth in the act of proving, by words multiplied for the purpose, that white is black, and black is white, according as they are paid. To this society all the rest of the people are slaves. For example, if my neighbour has a mind to my cow, he has a lawyer to prove that he ought to have my cow from me. I must then hire another to defend my right, it being against all rules of law that any man should be allowed to speak for himself." In another passage he inveighs against judges in a strain of even coarser invective. "Now your honour is to know," he says, "that these judges are persons appointed to decide all controversies of property, as well as for the trials of criminals, and picked out from the most dexterous lawyers, who have grown old or lazy; and having been biassed all their lives against truth and equity, lie under such a fatal necessity of favouring fraud, perjury, and oppression, that I have known some of them refuse a large bribe from the side where justice lay, rather than injure the faculty, by doing anything unbecoming their nature or their office."

Even in 1727 the extravagance and exaggerations of these passages must have diminished the force of the satire, but one must remember that under the old forms of procedure and law of evidence all sorts and conditions of chicanery were possible, and the search after truth was clogged and hampered by technicalities that made for injustice.

Crabbe, in " The Borough," draws a picture of Swallow, the lawyer, " a hard, bad man who preyed upon the weak," but he had sufficient insight into the reality of things to see that :

> Law was design'd to keep a state of peace ;
> To punish robbery, that wrong might cease ;
> To be impregnable ; a constant fort,
> To which the weak and injured might resort.

And the main reason that the law in old days failed in a great measure to carry out its mission to protect the poor was the extraordinary mystery and obscurity of it. Where law is a jargon of technicalities foreign to the business ideas of the people an immoral man who is a lawyer has an easy task before him to defraud the weak. In our own time the worst frauds committed by lawyers have been mortgage frauds where the deeds were deposited with solicitors who converted them to their own use. Our land transfer system is a relic of the past ; it is a mystery that no plain citizen can comprehend. It is necessary for him to employ a lawyer to carry out the smallest transfer of land and it is necessary for him to rely on the statement that the land has been conveyed to him and that the title deeds are in order. The technical obscurity of the transaction opens the door to frauds that would be impossible with a modern, businesslike, public land transfer department.

And as technicalities in law and procedure were gradually abolished so we find the pictures of lawyers in contemporary fiction becoming less ignoble, though there will always be more romance in the story of a fraudulent lawyer leading a double life than in the career of a blameless practitioner who serves his clients honourably during office hours and returns punctually to his accustomed suburb at the appointed dinner hour.

Though we have done away with much legal fiction and cumbrous technicality we cannot greatly boast of the simplicity of our legal procedure. Take the County Court Practice for instance. Here is a Court primarily designed to adjudicate on the simple disputes of poor people. There are two practice books. They cost over a guinea apiece, they consist of hundreds of pages and are absolutley incomprehensible except to the trained lawyer. This being so it is clear that the lawyer is as necessary to the poor man as he is to the rich. It is a sign of grace in the matter of procedure that whilst this chapter is in the writing we have some new rules issued about giving poor people assistance in High Court actions. Up to now the procedure *in forma pauperis* has not been of practical benefit to the poor except in enabling an occasional important appeal to reach the House of Lords. It is too soon to say whether these new rules will meet their object. Shortly, the scheme is that a poor person—meaning one who can satisfy the judge that he is not worth fifty pounds—will have counsel and solicitor assigned to him from a rota. After that his case will be conducted free of costs or fees. If he succeeds the solicitor—but in no case the counsel—will get costs.

Much depends of course on the spirit in which this is worked, but it only refers to the High Court— which is not, speaking generally, the poor man's Court—and it seems unlikely on the face of it that a scheme of this kind, with no one in particular to look after it and advertise its existence, will do away with the undesirable activity of the speculative solicitor. One wishes it well, but except perhaps in relation to divorce cases it does not appear on paper to be of great practical use.

The fact is that it is not a very hopeful thing to go to lawyers and committees of lawyers for reforms unless you have the driving power of the business man behind them. Nothing was to be more disastrous according to legal prophecy than the institution of the Public Trustee. No reform has done more to mitigate domestic worries and anxiety than this beneficent institution. Lawyers and laymen nowadays concur in casting their troubles upon him and sheltering themselves and their clients beneath his protecting wing. If we are ever to have a proper system of legal advice for the poor it will, I think, have to be made an official department with a business head of affairs and attached lawyers. It might perhaps be added to the duties of Labour Exchanges, but in any case it should be a department of the Board of Trade, and it should have branches throughout the country and power to help the poor in all the Courts of the country. A device for suing *in forma pauperis* working only in London, such as is set up by the new rules, cannot be of much avail in tackling the problem of placing legal advice and assistance at the call of the poor.

I wish some experiments of a voluntary nature could be made of a more extended character than the poor man's lawyer societies that are attached to University settlements, and do good work in advising the poor. It is really in Court that a poor man wants assistance. I often think that a poor man or woman coming into a Court for the first time is like the average middle-class Englishman when he finds himself on Calais Pier without a word of French speech at his command and entire ignorance of the ways of the *douane*. How he clings to a friendly interpreter with a gold band round his hat. How extravagantly he rewards him when he and all his luggage are at length safely in the train.

And why should not we encourage an amateur legal interpreter in our County Courts just as we welcome missionaries in our police Courts. I should like to see practising in each Court an official friend of the poor, ready to state the case of a poor man or woman who sought his assistance. There is an existing section of the County Courts Act allowing a friend to appear for anyone by leave of the judge if he does not do it for fee or reward, and on that foundation something might be built.

I remember a clergyman, Father Gething, appearing for an old army pensioner against an insurance society with complicated rules, and asking to be allowed to address me, and conduct the old man's case. Sir William Cobbett, not having in his mind for the moment the section I refer to, objected. I asked Father Gething whether he was going to recover any " fee or reward " for acting in the case.

" Certainly not," replied the reverend gentleman.

" But perhaps," I continued—somewhat mischievously—" Sir William is going to contend that the word 'reward' in the statute means not only reward in this world, but the next."

Sir William smiled and shook his head at me in dignified reproof. He was not going to argue this, and with his very good will and assistance the clergyman conducted the case, and in the end secured a victory.

In the Army Courts-Martial a prisoner is always allowed a friend to advise him and to take a limited part in the proceedings, and I cannot help thinking that long before the poor man has his panel lawyer voluntary charity will be allowed to supply him with a " friend," who shall be trained in the law, but ready to give his services to the poor without fee or reward.

Many will think that the suggestions that I have sketched out of assistance to poor people are chimerical and that in any case they are likely to be costly and that the grievance, such as it is, is not worth the money to be spent on the remedy. At one time I seem to be calling out for no lawyers and here I am demanding more lawyers. The inconsistency is only apparent. In all legal reforms I place in the forefront conciliation. I want to see the French " preliminary of conciliation " applied without delay to all small cases and I want the judge of the County Court to be clothed with the duty of the French *juge de paix*, whose business it is, in the first instance, to bring the parties together and get them to shake hands. Only when that fails, or in those cases where litigation is essential and necessary to the proper determination of a real dispute, should I ask the State to assign counsel

and solicitor to the poor. If a poor man has an
honest suit with a rich man it should be a point of
honour with the Courts to see that he is not at a
disadvantage in their procedure.

But merely providing a poor man with lawyers
will not alone work the miracle. Money must be
found to pay his witnesses and prepare his case,
and this is even more necessary in civil cases than
in the defence of prisoners where, as we shall see
when we come to consider criminal matters, the
State, whilst providing legal aid, has stopped short
of providing what may be still more necessary,
financial assistance for necessary evidence, some of
which may be of an expert and expensive character
wholly out of reach of a poor man.

Piers Plowman naturally threw the whole blame
on the lawyers who went about, as he said :

> Pleading the Law,   for pennies and for pounds,
> Unlocking their lips never   for love of our Lord.

But I cannot for myself see why a lawyer or a doctor
should work for nothing any more than a business
man or an author, and, if we knew the truth, I
expect we should find that old Piers himself invented
his vision as much in the blessed hope of royalties
as " for the love of our Lord."

I do not want charity for the poor in our legal
procedure, nor do I wish to see litigation multiplied
by cheap remedies. On the contrary, I want every
effort made to cut down litigation to a minimum,
but when a lawsuit takes place I want it to be a
fair fight and no favour, with each side equally
well equipped for the fray.

CHAPTER X

CRIME AND PUNISHMENT

The penal laws of the British Empire are, by foreign writers, charged with being too sanguinary in the cases of lesser offences. They hold that the punishment of death ought to be inflicted only for crimes of the highest magnitude; and philanthropists of our own nation have accorded with their opinion. Such persons as have had no opportunity of inquiring into the subject will hardly credit the assertion that there are above one hundred and sixty offences punished by death, or, as it is denominated, without benefit of clergy.

ANTHONY KNAPP and WILLIAM BALDWIN:
Preface to " The Newgate Calendar," 1824.

THE progress we have made in the reform of criminal law in the last hundred years is really remarkable. In very recent days we have at last allowed the prisoner to give his evidence of the matter he is charged with if he desires to do so. We have, under certain restricted conditions, supplied him with legal assistance, and, best of all, there is at length a Court of Criminal Appeal.

It is interesting and encouraging when your mind has a bent towards legal reform to see how past reforms have come about. As recently as 1826 prisoners accused of felony were not allowed counsel, and the Rev. Sydney Smith, who had a winning way of stating the case of the Law and the Poor in his own day, was pleading in the *Edinburgh Review* for a reform of this matter. One would have thought then, as one often thinks now, that a mere statement of the issue would have been sufficient. This is a picture of things as they were. " There are seventy or eighty prisoners to be tried for various offences at the Assizes who have lain in prison for some months ; and fifty of whom, perhaps, are of the lowest order of the people, without friends in any better condition than themselves, and without one single penny to employ in their defence. How are they to obtain witnesses ? No attorney can be employed—no subpœna can be taken out ; the witnesses are fifty miles off perhaps—totally uninstructed—living from hand to mouth—utterly unable to give up their daily occupation to pay for their journey, or for their support when arrived at the town of trial—and if they could get there, not knowing where to go or what to do. It is impossible but that a human being in such a helpless situation must be found guilty ; for as he cannot give evidence for himself, and has not a penny to fetch those who can give it for him, any story told against him must be taken for true (however false) since it is impossible for the poor wretch to contradict it."

And yet, absurd as it seems to us to-day, the prisoner's right to counsel was not obtained without a severe struggle. At the back of the mind of those who opposed the reform was the idea that as prisoners were accused by the Crown it was an act of disloyalty to defend them. Ridiculous as that idea is it still exists in a form that is interesting only as showing that the tradition was once a reality.

CRIME AND PUNISHMENT

A King's counsel has to obtain leave from the authorities, and pay a small tribute therefore, before he can appear for a prisoner and against the Crown. Leave is never refused, but the existence of such a curious custom is only comprehensible by studying the folklore of the subject.

A hundred years ago this folly sanctioned by antiquity was a reality. The defenders of the position said it was really all done in the interests of the prisoner. His witnesses were not put on oath, and this allowed them to tell any falsehood they wished ; he was saved the expense of his counsel— as though he preferred economy to hanging—and the judge, he was told, was his counsel—an arrangement that the prisoner cannot have been very grateful for when he heard his counsel on the bench summing up to the jury for a conviction. The nonsense that was talked and written on this subject is encouraging to those who want things done to-day. Against all reforms, arguments of this kind have to be listened to and laughed out of Court, but to-day we are in a better position than Sydney Smith was, for we often find in the official world a human being ready to help on a reform when the time is ripe for it. In his day common-sense and common humanity had not permeated into Government offices, " the Attorney-General and the Solicitor-General for the time being always protesting against each alteration and regularly and officially prophesying the utter destruction of the whole jurisprudence of Great Britain." It was not until ten years after the *Edinburgh Review* article was written that

THE LAW AND THE POOR

Parliament in August, 1836, passed an Act to permit prisoners charged with felony the right to be defended by counsel. And yet there are many people who think we move too fast in necessary reforms.

Sydney Smith mentions as one of the injustices to the prisoner his inability to give evidence. This remained a disability until our own time and was only removed with great difficulty and against the advice of many learned lawyers. The folklore of the subject is quite entertaining. Our ancestors considered, from introspective knowledge of themselves and their neighbours, that no one with any interest in a dispute was likely to speak the truth about it, they therefore did not allow the parties to a suit to give any evidence at all. This was the old law in both civil and criminal cases. Thus you may remember that in the great case of *Bardell* v. *Pickwick* neither plaintiff nor defendant gives evidence, because in law at that date they were not competent witnesses. The inconveniences of this in civil matters was patent to everyone but the lawyers. Writing on the incompetency of witnesses to give evidence, Bentham said with some humour, " in the bosom of his family the lawyer by the force of good sense returns to the simple method from which he is led astray at the bar by the folly of his learning. No one is so deeply tainted with his judicial practice as to apply its rules to his domestic affairs. If you would represent madness—but a madness where all is melancholy and unintelligible—you have only to imagine an English barrister carrying into ordinary life the fictions, the rules, and the logic of the bar."

CRIME AND PUNISHMENT

Certainly we cannot believe that when Sergeant Snubbin returned to his house and found a dispute raging between his cook and his butler that he tried to find out the truth about it without hearing what either of them had to say.

In 1846 when County Courts were established, the parties and their wives were allowed to give evidence, and so obvious were the advantages of this that in 1851 Lord Brougham passed the Evidence Amendment Act extending the system to other Courts. The only thing that surprises us to-day is that there could ever have been any question about the necessity of allowing parties to give evidence if it was really desired that they should have justice.

But we still clung to the right of the prisoner to keep his mouth shut, and in our insular way boasted of his privilege. Thackeray is horrified by the examination of the prisoner in the ordinary French way. " In England, thank heaven, the law is more wise and merciful !" He sees in the French Government advocate an official seeking in every way to draw confessions from the prisoner to perplex and confound him and to do away with any effect that his testimony might have on the jury, and he thanks heaven openly that we should " never have acted as these Frenchmen have done." What really troubled Thackeray's patriotic mind was the indecency of asking the prisoner any question at all. Victorian Englishmen of all grades were peculiarly proud of our criminal administration of justice and considered the privilege of the prisoner to keep his mouth shut was the keystone of the edifice.

THE LAW AND THE POOR

Dickens approached the matter more hesitatingly : " I wonder," he writes, " why I feel a glow of complacency in a court of justice, when I hear the learned judges taking uncommon pains to prevent the prisoner from letting out the truth. If the object of the trial be to discover the truth, perhaps it might be as edifying to hear it even from the prisoner, as to hear what is unquestionably not the truth from the prisoner's advocate. I wonder why I say, in a flushed and rapturous manner, that it would be ' un-English ' to examine the prisoner. I suppose that with common fairness it would be next to impossible to confuse him unless he lied ; and if he did lie I suppose he could hardly be brought to confusion too soon."

This being the Victorian attitude in the matter it was hardly to be wondered at that the reform was delayed until our own day. Yet I doubt if anyone conversant with the criminal Courts would doubt that although there are cases where it has been to the disadvantage of the guilty to go into the witness box, it has been of enormous value to the innocent that he can give his own account of things to the jury.

There are three recent Acts of criminal law reform which have done much to safeguard the interests of innocent men, especially if they are poor. These are the Criminal Evidence Act, 1898, the Poor Prisoners Defence Act, 1903, and the Court of Criminal Appeal Act, 1907. If we could have such an outburst of legal reform every ten years in other subjects we should be doing well. But it must not

194

be thought that these reforms were obtained without trouble. Each was strenuously fought, year by year, for many many years before the energy and patience of the reformers were crowned with success.

One would have thought that the claim of a citizen, charged with a criminal offence, to give his account of the affair to the jury, if he wished to do so, was one of those matters of elementary justice that could hardly be contended against at the end of the nineteenth century, but the fight against this privilege was really a very strenuous one. Twenty years before the reform actually came the Bill had been read a second time in the House of Commons by a majority of 109, showing, at all events, that the lay mind of the country had no doubt about what should be done. In each succeeding year, when any new offence was created by Act of Parliament, there was a special clause put in to enable a prisoner to give evidence, so that at length there were some thirty or more Acts giving a prisoner the right to give evidence. This made the state of the law, as Lord Herschell said, " utterly indefensible and ridiculous." We were living under two competing systems, whose constant absurdities were made manifest in the Courts ; thus, if a man was charged with forging a trade mark he was a competent witness, if he was charged with any other forgery his mouth was closed.

Curiously enough, owing to the irony of our party system, it was the Conservatives who brought in this reform and the Radicals who opposed it. It was left for Sir Richard Webster to point to the progress of all the States of America, and the experience of our Colonies, and to ask that we should not lag behind in the good work of reform. That sturdy radical, Mr. Pickersgill, was shocked, and elaborated the quaint argument that an innocent man should be debarred this privilege lest he might be an ignorant person who would tell lies, and get confused and muddled, thereby prejudicing his chance of acquittal.

A large body of influential legal opinion was adverse to the Bill, and in the division lists voting against the reform you find the names of Sam Evans, John Morley, W. S. Robson, Lawson Walton, and other well-known Liberals. It is one of the crosses that a legal reformer has to bear that only through the services of one or other of the great parties in the State can he hope to see his pet dream materialise and there seems a certainty that, if one party is converted to a proposal, the other party makes a point of being diverted by it. Over and above that unhappy difficulty to progress there is the certainty that the lawyers, as a profession, will always offer a strong opposition to any proposition of legal reform, and, when this is defeated, will fight strenuous little rearguard actions to cripple and delay it.

The Poor Prisoners Defence Act met with less opposition. It was a comparatively small affair, and there were a few fees in it. Mr. Justice Grantham—whose merits as a friend of the prisoner and a humane judge are often lost sight of in remembering his daring dives from the bench into the sea of politics—this good judge was a keen supporter of the movement for the better defence of poor prisoners. He thought the magistrates ought to ask the prisoner what his defence was, and tell him that, if he would state it, they would do all they could to assist him in proving it, and that, if he wanted evidence, they would adjourn the case and get evidence. His ideal was that the magistrate and the police should assist a man to prove his innocence, and that any sort of reasonable defence should be followed up at the public expense.

The letter of the Act, however, only gives the poor prisoner a solicitor and counsel and a copy of the depositions. No doubt the best is done for him that can be under these conditions, but it is not the same quality of legal defence that a rich prisoner can obtain for money. Naturally, counsel who take these cases are not men of the greatest experience, and the defending of prisoners is a difficult branch of the act of advocacy. A story is told of a Scotch prisoner, who had economically pretended he was without means in order to save counsel's fees, calling out in agony as he heard his defender addressing the jury in a very unconvincing manner : " Young mun, if yo'll sit doon at once I'll give ye a feeve poun' note." Although the Act is not everything it might be, yet, undoubtedly, it is a move in the right direction and capable, under sympathetic administration, of doing much good.

The Criminal Appeal Act of 1907 has proved itself of such value already that it becomes the more amazing to read of the difficulty experienced in getting it on the Statute Book. All manner of

legal interests were banded together against it. One
of the two learned king's counsel who moved its
rejection in the House of Commons solemnly declared
that the cost of taking shorthand notes and the
expense of bringing a prisoner to London from the
north of England appalled him and, in his view,
" the machinery of the Bill must inevitably break
down . . . it was absolutely unworkable." The
second uttered mournful prophecies of ruin : " to
substitute," he said, " this most costly machinery
for the present system would deprive our criminal
Courts of their principal glory in the deep sense of
care, caution, and responsibility which was per-
vading the atmosphere of every criminal Court in
the country at the present time."

Many people seemed to think that juries knowing
there was an appeal would take less pains and care
in their duties. But a jury in a criminal case is a
body of citizens called together on a special and
solemn occasion to do a serious duty and the fact
of appeal or no appeal would have little effect on
their conduct. It was the slackness of some of
the judges rather than the possible carelessness
of juries that wanted looking to, especially in
Courts of country Quarter Sessions where the
shorthand writer and the Court of Criminal Appeal
were bound to exercise a good influence. Nothing
tends to good judicial work more certainly than
publicity, a shorthand note, and a strong Court of
Appeal easily available.

Although the criminal law has in the main been
fairly administered and equally enforced against rich

and poor there are certain classes of laws which have often, no doubt from worthy motives, been used as engines of oppression against the poor. Of these the Blasphemy Laws are a standing example. Dr. Johnson tells us that : " Laws are formed by the manners and exigencies of particular times and it is but accidental that they last longer than their causes." This is not altogether true. The fact is we have no summary machinery for removing decayed and obsolete laws from the Statute book. We want a legal lethal chamber for these old die-hards, these laws against Sabbath Breaking and Blasphemy and other old world wickednesses. A rich man may break as many Sabbaths and blaspheme at his will but he is never prosecuted for it. In the days of that great and good reformer, Charles Bradlaugh, the Blasphemy Laws were made use of to stifle the poor in the expression of their opinions in a very shameless way. Only last year a man was imprisoned under them in circumstances which gave rise to a good deal of uneasiness. He was no doubt an ill-mannered and unpleasant person, but ill manners and unpleasantness are not crimes, and to make use of these old Blasphemy Laws, to lock up the poor blasphemer only, is one of those things that does extensive harm by giving the blasphemer new fuel for his blasphemy, not only against the sacred things he does not appreciate, but also against the law which he finds ready to do injustice for the protection of these holy mysteries.

This again, like many of the things which we may

reasonably complain about in what is, as the world goes, a humane criminal law, is one of the matters handed down by our forefathers which we have not had time to set right. In the old days Unitarians and others were burned alive. Fuller in his Church History says: it was found that " such burning of heretics much startled common people, pitying all in pain and prone to asperse justice itself with cruelty because of the novelty and hideousness of this punishment. . . . Wherefore King James politickly preferred that heretics hereafter, though condemned, should silently and privately waste themselves in prison." And that is what all heretics ought to do to-day if the law were equally administered, but as a matter of fact these laws are only put in force against poor, noisy people who preach their doctrines in the market place, and are a dead letter against those who preach the same doctrines on hand-made paper bound in morocco. I can quite believe that a bye-law to hinder one man saying coarse and ill-mannered things about another man's religion in open spaces might be a reasonable police proposition ; but there must be free trade in these things and the Established Church must not have a preference. Moreover, such a law must not be extended to pulpits or printing presses or much interesting theological polemics would be lost to us. For the Blasphemy Laws in the twentieth century, protecting only one form of religion and set in motion only against the poor, nothing can be said. Foul language and obscenity can and are punishable in other ways, and the cause of religion is poorly served by being protected by laws which are only set in motion when the well-to-do are annoyed by the vulgarity and ill-manners of the poor.

There is no gainsaying that once in the dock all men are equal or very nearly so, but one may harbour a suspicion whether all men have equal opportunities of getting there. Theoretically, the dock, like the Bench and the Cabinet and all other British institutions, is approached by an ever open door ; but in practice more goats wander through the opening than sheep. Yet your sheep is a born trespasser. There are some who believe that his immunity from punishment is due to the wool on his back.

I doubt if this is altogether true. Crimes of violence and brutality are naturally the crimes of the less fortunate of mankind, and your sheep is more peaceably disposed than your goat. But when we come to the more modern crime of swindling we find that the criminal law is not very successful in punishing the fraudulent well-to-do. Fraud is a more complicated offence than larceny, and defrauders sometimes get the better of the law. Cheating is not always a crime, and successful cheating is a question of better education. That is why the rich so often keep out of the dock. The law is somewhat old and decrepit, and the modern well-to-do swindler is very much up to date. Therefore I fear it is as true to-day as it was in the days of Lord Chief Justice Coke, to say that the law " maketh a net to catch little birds and letteth the great ones go."

THE LAW AND THE POOR

If you cast your eye down the police news you will many times come upon the case of a low-down man or woman who goes round collecting for a mission that does not exist, thereby cheating the well-disposed of a few pounds or shillings. It is quite right they should be run in and sent to prison. They are pests stealing money that would otherwise relieve real distress.

But if they had had a little more money, and hired a house in some remote place, and kept half-a-dozen real orphans there, and called it The St. Anonymous Orphanage, they might have collected as many thousands a year as they liked for their excellent charity, and no one would have worried them by asking how the orphans were looked after, nor would anyone have wanted to know how much was spent on the orphanage and how much on the founder and his family, and their houses and carriages and furniture and upkeep. The poor orphan has many uses in the world. One of them is to enable the swindler to found orphanages and make his living thereby.

At first blush the crime seems the same as that of the house-to-house cadger who gets six months, but note that the uneducated man has told a lie and made a false pretence of an existing fact. The good Founder of St. Anonymous's never did that. He had an orphanage with real orphans in it. True, there were not very many of them, and the orphanage was rather a stuffy, insanitary sort of place, though photographed on end it looks imposing enough. And that is the *mot juste*, as the

French have it ; that is what the orphanage was, and what the good founder was—imposing.

If you tell no actual fibs the law does not mind you imposing as much as you like. You may transfer the savings of the working class into your pockets by promises of the wildest character and schemes of the silliest and most romantic sort, and if you do it successfully enough the nearest you will ever get to the dock will be a seat on the borough bench, from which altitude you may sentence the poor, mean criminal who never had any capital, and had no one to advise him as to the law of false pretences. This is not a fancy picture. There was at least one such a magistrate on the bench once, and for aught I know there may be some J.P.'s to-day whose wealth has been made by stealing the savings of the working classes within the law.

Certainly in this country we have been free from the subordination of the Criminal Courts to the power of gold that is said to exist in other civilised places. Any preferential treatment that exists is of a class character—snobbish if you will, but not corrupt. As an Irish barrister said to me at Liverpool—he was a great Home Ruler with a grand hatred of England and a real affection for many Englishmen : " My dear Parry, you'll never convince me that the Government ever meant to hang Mrs. Maybrick. They're a cowardly lot of snobs, and anyhow they couldn't hang a woman they might have to meet out at dinner afterwards."

And there is undoubtedly running through all our English institutions, even the administration of the criminal law, a certain amount of class snobbery which it would be better should be eliminated. Judges and magistrates are, of course, only human. The wrong doing of a man or woman of our own class naturally appeals to our bump of forgiveness more readily than that of a slum dweller whose temptations and environment we know nothing about.

Thus we can remember cases where lady shop-lifters were discovered by eminent physicians to be suffering from some extraordinary form of neuras-thenia—not insanity, of course—but one of those nervous breakdowns that made an acquittal and a rest cure in a nursing home the only appropriate course. Magistrates seem to grasp the medical facts about these well-to-do unfortunates almost too readily; but had it been a drunken woman snatching a pair of boots from a shop-nail in the street no eminent physician would have diagnosed her peculiar form of neurosis. Even if her husband had tendered evidence that of late the poor lady had been strange in her manner, he would scarcely have been listened to with much sorrowful attention. The good magistrate would have felt bound in the interests of the poor tradesman to make an example of this criminal. Such cases are not cases for acquittal, and the rest cure is generally three months hard.

There are certainly too many cases where the wealth and position of a prisoner leads to favoured treatment in the Criminal Courts. I am glad to note that these are always pilloried in the Press and publicity is given to them, and in a way nothing could be better because it is the open door that has done so much to keep our courts free from the taint of any suspicion of real corruption. I firmly believe that when these cases do occur they are generally the outcome of a spirit of humanity on the part of the presiding judge coupled to a certain extent by a class feeling of tenderness on account of the terrible downfall of a man or woman in his own social position. Such cases, too, are rare. No special note is taken of any case where the law takes its ordinary course and the rich criminal is treated in the same way as his poorer brother. These are, of course, the great majority, and there are also many cases I am glad to know where leniency and mercy is extended to the poor criminal and he is helped by societies and personal aid to regain his position among honest men.

But with all this the poor man can point to too many instances where rich hooligans running amok with a motor car in Regent Street or assaulting the police on a racecourse are let off with a fine. Here is a curious case from the London Sessions that is bound to cause a lot of talk in the mean streets. A fashionably dressed young man was indicted in an admittedly false name, and was allowed to use it for the purpose of the proceedings, and pleaded guilty. He had obtained a sable stole, value £40, from a costumier in Shaftesbury Avenue by false pretences. He had opened an account at Oxford. He received a cheque book and then withdrew his money and closed the account. He used to obtain goods which he paid for with cheques on the Oxford Bank, and cheques to the amount of £5,241 6s. 3d. had been returned marked "no account." A detective said he was a young man leading a fast life. The city police had a warrant for him for obtaining a ring value £145 and a gold watch £15. These articles it is true were returned. The Oxford police had a warrant out for him and when arrested he was attempting to obtain a valuable fur article in Dover Street. His counsel urged that his parents were people of respectability and integrity who had suffered losses, and the young gentleman was trying to keep things going in the same style he had been accustomed to, and had come under bad influences. That is the whole story, and the report ends, " the defendant was bound over, the magistrate remarking that there was no need to cause his relatives to suffer by mentioning his name."

How many poor men and women whose children have been taken away from them for long terms of years to a reformatory or sent to gaol for months with hard labour, to the knowledge of all their neighbours, will read that report, and what will they think and say of the justice of our criminal law? One pities the parents and relatives of this particular young criminal waster as one pities the parents of all children and the children of all parents when one or the other bring disgrace or ignominy on the home —but why is this one particularly undesirable swindler to be allowed the privilege of an alias in an indictment, and why is his name alone among all the prisoners arraigned at the Sessions to be kept from the world? And how hard it will be on some youngster of like criminal tendencies when he comes before a court where harsher methods prevail, and he finds that not only is his name brutally noised abroad, but offences of this character are deemed worthy of imprisonment.

One would not wish to say a word against leniency to the young however much it may savour of class-tenderness, but the concealment of a criminal's name on his trial because his parents are well-to-do and respectable, is just one of those things that the poor people treasure up and quote as an instance of the law's unfairness. At a time when every effort should be made to impress on the poor the impartiality of the law little cases of this kind, arising no doubt from motives of kindness and humanity, are exaggerated and quoted as typical of our criminal administration—which assuredly they are not.

In cases where the whole of the resources of the State are against the prisoner fair play demands that everything that can be done for him without detriment to the demands of justice should be done. In a case of murder which created a great sensation this year, the whole evidence turned on identity. Several witnesses came to the police and said they had seen the victim, a child, in company of the prisoner. Other witnesses had stated to the police that they had seen the victim in company with a woman. During the examination of the police inspector in charge of the case he was asked by the defence for these statements, the magistrate expressed his opinion that they should be shown to the solicitor for the defence, but the counsel for the Crown, a gentleman of very wide experience, " suggested that the proper thing for the solicitor for the defence to do would be to go and see the people."

I do not for a moment say that the learned counsel was inaccurate in his statement of a legal proposition. It may be that such is the law ; but if it is what does it mean ? The police have honest statements of citizens in their hands suggesting that a man has committed murder, they have equally honest statements from other witnesses that the murder has been committed by a woman. However mistaken they may believe the latter statements to be, surely fair play demands that the prisoner should have access to these statements for what they are worth. After all he is at present to be deemed an innocent man, he is not even committed for trial, and he is a citizen with as much right to the protection of the police as any other. If they have statements going to prove his innocence he ought to have access to them and be told who has made them so that he and his solicitor can see how far they help to prove his case. But no, that is not the official view. Counsel for the Crown no doubt states it correctly. The proper thing is for the solicitor for the defence to go about at the expense of the poor man he is defending and find these people out and take statements afresh. It is a denial of justice, the man has not the money to do it, his solicitor is not a charitable institution, and even if he were he probably has not money and staff for such work. In this particular case the whole of the police had scoured London for evidence to clear up the mystery. Surely when a citizen was charged with the offence public interest demands that the matter that has been discovered that goes to prove innocence should be as readily available as matter that goes to prove guilt. The present practice is to my mind a tradition, handed down from the bad old days, that needs to be swept away. We ought to free our criminal law from any shred of suggestion that the State is out to obtain a conviction rather than an acquittal. The State is only interested in the truth and justice of the verdict, and a true verdict obtained by methods of injustice is a crime against the community.

Much might be said on the inequality of punishments. The question of the advisability of corporal punishment is one upon which people hold strong and conflicting opinions. I am not a sentimentalist on this subject. I am told by some quite sane and scientific thinkers that for men, women and children of the hooligan class who have a mania for violence and destruction it is probably the most appropriate form of punishment. Its good qualities are that it is cheap; it is soon over, but irksome whilst it lasts ; and it is said to appeal to the homeopathic instincts of the hooligan class who recognise the justice of meeting violence by violence.

Against these positive merits it is very unequal in its incidence ; one victim will suffer more than others over the same punishment ; and it is brutalising, in some measure, to the flogger and floggee. Too much may be made of this last argument, for nothing can be more brutalising and deadening to all hopeful and better instincts than long terms of imprisonment.

On the whole, my instinct is against flogging, because I am an optimist and believe that though it has had its uses in the past as an educative influence we have come to a state of civilisation when we should abolish if possible all violent or cruel punishments. There was a lot perhaps to be said for thumbscrews in their day, but that day is admittedly over. My grumble about the cat-of-nine-tails and the birch is not so much that the law should put them in the cupboard once and for ever, but that if they are to be used at all, their lashes should, like God's good rain, descend on rich and poor alike.

Take the crimes for which flogging is permissible punishment to-day. For adults there is garrotting, offences under the Criminal Law Amendment Act, procuring, etc., and being an incorrigible rogue. For lads under sixteen, stealing and malicious damage.

Now the first objection to these punishments is that whether flogging is or is not to be administered depends altogether on the taste and fancy of the presiding Judge. Some think it is an advisable form of punishment; others view it with disfavour. This element of human lottery in the administration of the law should surely be kept under as far as possible. Out of a hundred and forty-five criminals convicted of robbery only three were flogged. An intending robber therefore who studies judicial "form" in the statistics will see that it is about

fifty to one against the cat, and if he is the one unfortunate surely he has a distinct grievance against
the forty-nine lucky blackguards who escape.

When only three criminals receive this punishment
in one year it is worth while considering whether
it should be continued, or, if it is to be continued,
whether it should not be extended to crimes against
women and children and other nameless horrors.
Highway robbers to-day are all of the lowest and
the poorest, but in the other category of crime there
are sometimes men of means who find their way into
the dock.

If it ever comes to be recognised, as Butler in his
beautifully prophetic account of the land of Erewhon
would have us believe, that crime is a disease and
should be treated by a family Straightener, as we
now call in the doctor, then all doubts as to corporal
punishment will disappear. The Erewhonians when
they had lapsed from the path of honesty took, under
their doctor's advice, a flogging once a week and a
diet of bread and water for three months on end
with the same heroism and resignation with which
we undergo a cure at Harrogate after a London
season. Once recognise that the birch rod is a cure
for dishonesty, violence, and malicious injury to
property, then all sensible men and women afflicted
with these tendencies would welcome the cure and
visit their Straightener as they now visit their
dentist.

But at present we are far from the realisation of
these sane, clear-sighted dreams. Flogging, as the
law uses it as a punishment to-day, is not used, I fear,

merely as a remedy or even a deterrent but rather by way of revenge. It is almost wholly used against the very poor and degraded. Even under the White Slave Act, I cannot remember any case in which it has been used against a well-to-do man. In any case it is only available against the actual procurer and not against the landlords, ground landlords, restaurant proprietors, and dressmakers, who knowingly share in the woman's earnings and live on them.

Flogging may, or may not, be an advisable form of punishment, but if it is to be used, let it be administered automatically and without fear or favour to all beasts and blackmailers and hooligans, be they rich or poor. At present the chances of a rich man being flogged for his wickedness on earth are about the same as those of the camel with an ambition to loop the needle.

CHAPTER XI

THE POLICE COURT

Squeezum. The laws are turnpikes, only made to stop people who walk on foot and not to interrupt those who drive through them in their coaches.

FIELDING : " The Coffee-house Politician."
Act II., Scene II.

WHEN Fielding was made a magistrate for the county of Middlesex in 1748 the popular notion of the office was expressed in the nickname, " The trading justice." He was paid by fees and had a direct interest in the prosperity of crime. The fees, moreover, were very small, and it was a recognised thing that he should make his office a lucrative one by methods exemplified by Mr. Justice Squeezum in Fielding's farce. Although the great writer fulfilled the duties of his office with honour, fidelity, and zeal, he has left us in no doubt about the immorality and ignorance of many of his fellow justices. It is a relief to turn from the justice room in Bow Street in the eighteenth century with its rogues and vagabonds on their way to the whipping posts of the Bridewell, and its highwaymen and thieves starting for Tyburn by way of Newgate, and to look on the comparatively civilised picture of a metropolitan police court of to-day.

THE LAW AND THE POOR

A century and a half has worked wonderful reforms for us in the world of police and police courts, but one cannot honestly say that nothing remains to be done. Direct bribery is no doubt abolished, justice is fearlessly administered, but there are still traditional methods of imposing fines and imprisonment which cause the poor to think that carriage folk go more easily along the turnpikes of the law than those humble ones who travel perforce on foot.

I am not writing of the police court as the ante-chamber of the Old Bailey. In relation to the grave crimes against society we may fairly boast that rich and poor are treated much alike. But the police court in matters within its own jurisdiction is a machine for teaching better manners to the poor. It is a somewhat harsh machine, perhaps, but in the main just and necessary at the present state of our evolution.

When folk are naughty and violent and ill-mannered and ultra-selfish, and become a nuisance to their neighbours, the police, if they are poor, take them in hand, but if they are rich they are dealt with differently. Unless they are so extravagantly and absurdly naughty as to become a public as opposed to a private nuisance, there is no necessity for the police to tackle the rich. When two " lydies " go for each other in the gutters of Whitechapel the police step in, but when the same thing happens in Mayfair, society—with a big S—maintains its own discipline.

The reason why rich folk are not so outwardly

naughty as poor folk is very much a matter of education and environment. As Lord Haldane in his valuable speech in America explained to us, there is a " system of habitual or customary conduct, ethical rather than legal, which embraces all those obligations of the citizen which it is ' bad form ' or ' not the thing ' to disregard."

Thus in the days of Sir Anthony Absolute it was " bad form " not to get drunk after dinner, and it was " not the thing " to refuse to fight a duel. These laws of conduct were not enforceable before magistrates, but they were laws all the same, and rich people dared not disobey them for fear of being " cut " by society.

And as the years roll on better education, better housing, better wages, and less of that repressive Sabbatarianism that drives the poorer youngsters into natural mischief will make the police court less and less necessary as a school of manners. The conscience and good manners of all classes attain a higher ideal every day, and the only reason the rich arrive at a better standard of outward manners than the generality of the poor is that they have been caught young and made to practise at it for genera-tions. It is not a matter entitling them to praise, but we are out to set down and discuss facts, and undoubtedly it is so.

For instance, you would expect an Eton boy to play better cricket than a St. Andrews caddie, but the caddie would probably beat the other's head off at golf. It is environment that does it, and the lesson to be learned is to improve in every way the material surroundings of the poor to the utmost of our ability. Meanwhile the police court seems to me as necessary a part of our equipment as a sewage works or an ashpit.

Crime is not only a matter of heredity and education, it is also a question of geography. This geographical distribution of crime is an intensely interesting subject. You will find that Cardigan, for instance, is the whitest county in England and Wales for crimes of all kind, whether against property, morals, or of a violent character. Glamorgan, on the other hand, is only beaten by Monmouth in records of crimes against property ; in crimes of violence Glamorgan is easily first ; in crimes against morality Glamorgan again is only beaten by Dorset, Berks, Lincoln and Huntingdon, the latter taking the 1905-09 record very comfortably. Monmouth, happily, in this latter class of crime is in a far better case than her neighbour.

If you can trace the history and causes of different crimes in different districts I believe you may hope to sterilise a county of certain crimes by moral sanitation and stamp them out just as we have rid counties of typhus and the plague. In dealing with uncivilised crimes of mischief and destruction we should always bear in mind that the poor who do these acts are very often only human beings who have not been cultivated up to modern standards. Some crimes are traditional in certain districts, and the imitative faculty being strong in criminals, heredity and mimicry work together to cause a certain historicity in crime.

THE POLICE COURT

Magistrates and others do not sufficiently study this. Patriotic county officials loudly deny what everyone who reads the Judicial Statistics knows to be true. In discussing the Edalji case I pointed out that to anyone who studied the history of crime it was far more likely that such crime would be committed by a native of the county than by a gentleman of Parsee descent. This seemed to annoy some ardent Staffordshire folk, but there is no reason why it should. Killing and maiming the cattle of others is a very ancient pursuit and has only recently been regarded as criminal. The wicked man in the Bible was often threatened with the destruction of his cattle. No doubt the righteous man was encouraged thereby to take upon himself the duty of avenging his wrongs by destroying his wicked neighbour's cattle, and the wicked neighbour, believing himself to be the righteous one, retaliated in kind. Certain it is that in border countries we always read of cattle raiding and killing and maiming, and perhaps one reason why Staffordshire is old fashioned in the cattle-maiming business is that it was a border country, and in the good old days the lords and squires raided cattle and destroyed their neighbour's farms and boundaries, and these antiquated habits remain with some as natural instincts of revenge.

In early days such acts were not considered criminal. The only malicious injury to property known to the English common law as a crime was arson. It was not until the time of Henry VIII. (37 Hen. VIII., c. 6) that it was discovered that

there were " divers sundry malicious and curious
persons, being men of evil and perverse disposition
and seduced by the instigation of the devil, who, to
damnify the king's true subjects went about burning
frames of timber ready to be set up and edified for
houses," and broke down dams and moats or cut
away lead pipes, or barked apple trees, or cut out
beasts' tongues, which seems a very ancient and
horrible form of maiming cattle. The penalty for
these latter offences was the inadequate fine of
ten pounds.

In 1722 came the Black Act which made it felony
without benefit of clergy to " unlawfully or mali-
ciously kill, maim, or wound any cattle." In 1861
a Malicious Damage Act (24 & 25 Vict. c. 97) was
passed, codifying all the law relating to such
offences, and that is the Act under which Mr.
Edalji was indicted.

I have worked out the geographical statistics of
cattle maiming in England for forty years, from
1861 to 1900, and they are extremely interesting.
In the first place it is well to know that the total
number of such crimes is rapidly decreasing. In
five years, from 1865 there were over a hundred
cases ; in five years prior to 1900 there were
less than fifty. The counties, which total more
than twenty cases each, are York, Sussex,
Middlesex, Lincoln, Lancashire and Staffordshire.
Somerset and Gloucester have nineteen cases, but
Gloucester has only one case since 1882 and Somerset
only six cases since 1870. Surrey has only eleven
cases, and only five occur since 1870. Anglesey

and Westmoreland have only one such charge each during the whole forty years. In the case of Staffordshire, in the twenty-two cases taking place from 1861 to 1900 fifteen cases had taken place since 1877, and there is never a clear five years in the period without a case.

In 1903, when the Wyrley outrages took place, it seems to me that a county with this history would have been sensible to look at home for the criminal. In counties such as Somerset and Surrey, where the offence seemed then to be dying out, the same considerations would not apply. Whereas in Westmoreland or Anglesey the expectation would be that the crime was committed by a stranger. I do not think it would be wise to press these speculations too far, but at the same time I think magistrates and police might make greater use of the wonderful statistics that are collected and published by the State at such great expense and learn useful lessons from them in their daily business.

Whilst we condemn the horrible savagery of such crimes it is only fair to remember that the law does not punish them for their cruelty, but only for their injury to property. Prevention of cruelty to animals is a far more modern branch of law, the beginning of which dates from 1822. When Lord Erskine moved his Bill against Cruelty to Animals in 1811, so absurdly sentimental did it seem to the assembled peers that they drowned his speech in a chorus of cat-calls and cock-crowing. It is well to remember when measuring punishment in the police courts that there are individuals and classes existing to-day that are scarcely more civilised than the lords and barons of a hundred years ago.

The feudal lords and their henchmen did many things in the good old days in their quarrels with their neighbours which to-day would bring them before the justices. They wounded with intent, they did grievous bodily harm to anyone who annoyed them, and they did as much malicious damage to property as seemed in their own eyes a fair set off for insults had and received. Among a certain small degraded class in our own country these traditional pleasantries of the country-side are not fully recognised to be crimes. There are a set of men among whom it is not " bad form " to commit these acts. This form of atavism requires not only pity but further and better repression at the hands of capable police.

As long, therefore, as we have these hereditary tendencies to crimes of violence and selfishness, the police court seems to me to meet a felt want. I can imagine a better world without any police court, just as I can imagine this world with a better police court.

But I should like to see imprisonment kept entirely for evil-doers, and that side of the police court work which consists in rate collecting and semi-civil proceedings transferred elsewhere. At present many are sent to gaol in the police court for the crime of poverty. In the cases of non-payment of rates or of orders on parents to pay subscriptions to industrial homes it seems a very bad policy to send a poor man to prison. It takes a man from work, it does not produce money, and it throws a family into the workhouse.

In these cases there is no pretence of proving a man's means and sending him to gaol because he can pay and won't. No such evidence is necessary. The man goes to prison because he is poor and has not the money to pay. If the State thinks fit to put a man's child in a reformatory, one would think it might stand the expense of it, without ruining the home by imprisoning the father because he cannot subscribe towards his keep.

With regard to orders for maintaining a separated wife, or affiliation orders, everyone would have less sympathy with the man who is sent to prison for not paying these. But if a man has not the money he does not make any in prison, and what these poor women want is regular weekly money.

These are special cases in which I think power to attach a man's wages up to a certain percentage would be a just and reasonable proposition. Such a law might be unpopular with mankind, but it seems fair to the women. Whether it would tend to increase or decrease maintenance and bastardy orders I have not the least idea.

" Five shillings and costs or seven days." This familiar phrase, as Count Smorltork says, " surprises by himself " the whole philosophy of police courts. Nothing is more marked in the treatment of rich and poor in the police court than the unfair incidence of fines. Take, for instance, the common case of a motor-car driver being fined forty shillings and costs for exceeding the speed limit and driving to the

THE LAW AND THE POOR

danger of mankind. If his master is a Cabinet
Minister, say, he writes a civil letter to the clerk
to the magistrates expressing his regret and enclos-
ing the needful, which is just two five-thousandths
of his official income.

But supposing he is a taxi-cab driver who owns
his cab, or is buying it on the hire system, as many
do. He, too, is fined forty shillings and costs, and
as he earns, let us say, forty shillings a week, he has
to pay one fifty-second of his income.

If he cannot raise the money his home is distrained
on, or there is the option of imprisonment. That
kind of option never worries the Cabinet Minister
or the chauffeur thereof. In the old tithe days the
parson took his tenth from rich and poor alike,
and was no respecter of persons ; all he wanted
was one-tenth of your income in cash. As between
Cabinet Minister and cabman the relation of fine
should be as two pounds to ninepence—that is to
say, if the law in the police courts desires to treat
rich and poor alike.

There is no difficulty about doing this. All that
is wanted is to enact in your statute that the fine
should " not exceed one-fiftieth or one one-thou-
sandth of a man's income." Then all would be
fined off the same mark. At present the poor man
is the scratch man, and the greater the wealth the
longer the handicap.

As to costs, they should be wholly abolished.
They are not only an odious tax on the poor, but
they give the officials of the court an unholy incentive to make the court a paying concern, and, what

THE POLICE COURT

is worse, give every clerk and officer in the police court a direct pecuniary interest in convictions. As things stand to-day a council of city men are not likely to advance salaries where their police court is losing money. A godly and righteous police court should glory in losing money year by year.

And whilst I recognise that at the head of each police court there should be a stipendiary to deal with the more important cases, and always to be within call when there are cases to try in which the local magistrates have a class interest, yet I have no desire to abolish Dogberry, nor do I take any pleasure in reading that he has written himself down an ass. In our chief cities there are now excellent stipendiaries and magistrates of all classes, including representatives of working men, and all can testify how—taking the police court system as it stands—it is worked fairly and carefully and to the advantage of all.

But these places are far ahead of the county towns and districts where the squire and parson reign supreme, and the clerk to the justices is their own faithful attorney. I believe thoroughly that these men do their best, but it is quite impossible that they can take a normal view of such horrible crimes as the rape of a pheasant's egg or the snaring of a hare. It is from the beautiful little corners of the lovely English country that the bitter cry of injustice in the police courts makes itself heard from time to time in the public Press. Why should not every hamlet have its Village Plowden to brighten life on the country side ?

THE LAW AND THE POOR

There we see, let us hope, the last of a decaying and rotten system—justice administered by a class unlearned in law, and unlearned in a far more important branch of their business—the knowledge of the works and days and temptations of the fellow sinners whose judges they have elected themselves to be. In the remote country places more than anywhere is the stipendiary a necessity. Meanwhile, why should not direct representatives of the agricultural labourer be placed upon the bench if we are not to abolish Dogberry altogether ?

While these words are being written, an effort is being made with a Criminal Administration Bill to do away with some of the abuses of the police court. The imprisonment of people for non-payment of fines is really imprisonment for poverty, and the scandal of it is at last officially recognised and the necessity of reform admitted. That, at all events, is to the good, though it is to be hoped that if the Bill at present put forward is to pass it will be widely extended and simplified.

It is quite a good thing to enact that it shall be obligatory upon magistrates to grant time for the payment of fines, but seeing that the magistrates have always had this power and never used it to any useful extent it would be well that there should be less discretion about the matter. Law for lay magistrates should be automatic and fool-proof. When you enact that a magistrate is obliged to allow time for payment of fines, " unless the Court for any other special reason expressly directs that no time shall be allowed," you are surely inviting the average justice to supply himself with special reasons why he should not carry out a law which you know by his past history he dislikes. It must not be forgotten that in Manchester, although the fees legally allowed for a summons are twelve shillings, the practice has been for fees not to exceed the fine. Imprisonment for less than five days—which in the future is not to be permitted—has for a long time not been allowed by the practice of the Manchester justices. Where justices desire to be lenient and enforce the law temperately they can do so to-day, and therefore it is clearly no use in a new statute to leave a discretion to those who will certainly abide by old and evil customs unless they are forced to do otherwise.

The statistics of the police courts show that in one year 92,000 citizens were imprisoned in default of the payment of a fine and 80,000 imprisoned without the option. The number of persons sentenced to pay fines is no less than 460,000. Every year new statutes are passed making new offences which can be committed with practical impunity by those whose purses are long enough. Under the heading Betting and Gaming, 3,346 persons were fined and only 738 went to prison. Under the heading Motor Cars, 10,631 were fined and only 36 went to prison in default; under the heading Sunday Trading, 6,654 were fined and only 12 went to prison by default. These offences are generally committed by persons with some money; but where the parties are poor what a terrible difference in their punishment. The mere giving of time to pay fines will not abolish this injustice unless the fines are made, as has been suggested, in some ratio proportionate to a man's income. If it were enacted that a fine should not exceed a day's wage earned by the prisoner, that would be a method of doing away with the burden of useless imprisonment that has to be borne by the poor. It is no use enacting that the Court in fining an offender shall take into consideration the means of the offender. I make no doubt that this is done already to a large extent by stipendiaries and the more enlightened magistrates. What is wanted is an actual printed tariff of fines fairly proportioned to the means of the offender, beyond which the magistrates may not go. Measures that depend on the sympathetic working by the members of the bench will be in many districts a dead letter, and inasmuch as the folk who go to prison in these cases are always poor people, very little will be known of their trouble except by those few persons who study blue books and statistics.

This habit of the magistracy to ignore the good intentions of Parliament and the Home Office is in nothing more marked than in the refusal of many country benches to give bail to poor people charged with offences that have to be tried at Sessions or Assizes. Many judges have called the Grand Juries' attention to the large number of prisoners who are left in prison awaiting trial, some of whom are ultimately acquitted. But this is one of the matters where magistrates must of necessity have discretion, and although they receive Home Office circulars calling attention to their duties in the matter of bail they prefer to go their own wrong-headed way and unnecessarily keep a large number of poor persons in prison who might quite safely be allowed to remain out on bail.

It is curious how history repeats itself and how a lay magistracy, as a type, always tends to act without sympathy or consideration for the poor. A hundred years ago the Yorkshire magistrates came to the conclusion that it was a most improper thing that poor people committed for trial to the House of Correction should be allowed to idle their time away at the expense of the county, so they actually required them to work for their living, and as the treadmill was the only apparatus of a commercial character in the gaol the poor untried prisoner was put to walking round a wheel in company of his convicted brother. The way in which the matter was put by Mr. John Headlam, M.A., Chairman of the Quarter Sessions for the North Riding of the County of York, is a perfect specimen of the true Dogberry temperament : " With respect to those sentenced to labour as a punishment, I apprehend, there is no difference of opinion. All are agreed that it is a great defect in any prison where such convicts are unemployed. But as to all other prisoners, whether debtors, persons committed for trial, or convicts not sentenced to hard labour, if they have no means of subsisting themselves, and must, if discharged, either labour for their livelihood or apply for parochial relief ; it seems unfair to society at large, and especially to those who maintain

THE LAW AND THE POOR

themselves by honest industry, that those who, by
offending the laws, have subjected themselves to
imprisonment, should be lodged and clothed and fed,
without being called upon for the same exertions
which others have to use to obtain such advantages."

Of course the whole question is begged when an
untried prisoner is called an offender against the
laws. The Headlam view of him always has been,
and is to-day, that the mere fact that a policeman
has arrested him is proof that he is an offender ;
this for all time has been justices' law, but it is
doubtful whether the old doctrine that a man is to
be deemed innocent until found guilty by a jury of
his peers is not still sound law and ought not to be
more fully recognised by the lay magistrates.

Of course the particular wrong that Mr. Headlam
was contending for has long been abolished, not
indeed without much argument and trouble, but we
still punish an untried man by imprisoning him
before trial, and in very many cases this is wholly
unnecessary. The idea of keeping a man in prison
is that he should be forthcoming on the day of trial.
In some serious cases it is obviously necessary to
keep a man in custody, but in many small cases if a
cheap bail was fixed there would be no difficulty in
finding the sureties and the prisoner could be outside arranging for his defence and earning money
for the support of his family until the day of the
trial.

Of 598 people acquitted at Assize Courts only
294 were allowed bail, so that there is a clear ad-

mission in the official figures of three hundred innocent persons—or persons not provably guilty— remaining in prison because the justices will not carry out the Home Office suggestions as to bail. Remember too that in some remote places there are very few assizes and eighteen of these unhappy persons remained over three months in prison awaiting trial. At Quarter Sessions the figures are even more remarkable. Of 1,586 prisoners acquitted only 688 had been granted bail. Here you have a large number of innocent men and women kept in gaol charged with offences that are not of the most serious character, and this is done not because in this peculiar instance the law itself is harsh—because the law permits bail and the government office calls on the magistrates to make use of the law—but because the law is administered by well-meaning but incompetent men who have a fixed delusion, handed down to them from their forbears of hundreds of years ago, that a man arrested for a crime by the police and awaiting trial is, to use Mr. Headlam's phrase, " an offender against the laws." Where there are no stipendiary magistrates it would not be a bad plan to give any prisoner a right to appeal on refusal of bail to a judge of the County Court who lives within the district and is of necessity a magistrate though he seldom has much time to sit at petty sessions.

Before we leave the Police Court I should like to draw attention to a well-founded complaint against police methods that the Home Office might certainly take into their consideration when they are reforming the administration of the criminal law. I refer to the practice of identification which has come so prominently before public notice in recent criminal trials. I never met a prisoner who felt that it was fairly done. For myself, I have the firmest belief that the police endeavour as a rule to do what is right and straight, but after all we must not lose sight of the fact that the police are there to clear up the crime and to run in somebody—the real criminal of course for choice—and it seems hardly right to put them at this very critical moment into the position of a judicial authority deciding the most important point for or against the man they have arrested and believe to be guilty.

I have always wondered what legal right a policeman has to put you in a row with a lot of other men and bring people to look at you. Suppose a prisoner refused to undergo the ordeal and the policeman used force to compel him, could the prisoner recover damages for assault. These are recondite, and in a sense absurd points ; but they do, I think, help one to see how wrong the present system is. At the ceremony of identification it is obviously necessary that there should be a presiding magistrate to see fair play and to take a record of what happened. It is really a part of the trial and a most important part of the trial. That a witness should identify a prisoner in a police yard in the absence of a judicial authority is clearly an unjust thing. Once he—or more especially she—has done so, the further swearing to the prisoner when he is in the dock is nothing. What the magistrate ought to see is the demeanour of the identifier when he first recognises the prisoner and especially ought a justice to be present to see that there is no suspicion of unfairness in the methods employed by the police.

We have had so many tragedies brought about by so-called identification, that it is more than time that the business of it was taken out of the hands of the police and made an integral part of the trial before the magistrate to which it in truth belongs. These reforms will not, I think, come about until we have stipendiary magistrates on the county benches, but though I wish to see this I do not want the old office of Justice of the Peace to be abolished. There is, and rightly ought to be, a keen desire among laymen to attain to this position, and it is an office of much dignity and respect and one in which a good man under sound legal advice can do worthy public service. I have been a local justice of the peace for many years and can testify to the number of occasions upon which a magistrate residing in his district is called upon for small services that would cost the applicant time and money if there was no available magistrate.

A great many lay benches with a clerk of sound learning and legal education administer excellent justice throughout the country. But there are classes of cases connected with property that would be better tried by a stipendiary unconnected with county society. I have a passion for old-world things, and grieve over the disappearance of the parish constables, the head boroughs, the tithing-men, the aletasters, the beadles, and the reeves. I do not wish to abolish the Justice of the Peace. I only wish to put him in his proper place. Of course, if he cannot be happy there, then I am afraid he will have to go.

CHAPTER XII

LANDLORD AND TENANT

At number seven there's nob'dy lives, they left it yesterday ;
Th' bum-baylis coom an' marked their things, an' took 'em a'
    away.
They hardly filled a donkey cart—aw know nowt wheer they
    went—
But they say th' chap spent his brass o' drink instead o' payin'
    th' rent.

SAMUEL LAYCOCK : " Bowton's Yard."

IN this branch of the law it cannot honestly be
said that the legal position of the poor is very
different from the legal position of the rich. Given
private ownership of land and the right of a landlord
to distrain for rent in arrear, and seize and sell his
tenant's goods to pay himself, it does not seem that
the law or the way in which it is administered is
better or worse for rich or poor. The law of distress
is, as its name implies, a harsh and cruel remedy and
the shadow of it hangs nearer and darker over the
cottage porch than over the doors of the eligible
mansion, but it is there in both places. To a weekly
wage owner paying an exhausting rent out of a
pitiful wage, the ever present right of his landlord
to distrain, whilst it nerves him to make every effort
to keep a clean rent book, must be one of the sad
and depressing elements of daily life that the middle

classes do not experience so directly. It is pleasant to record—what is in fact my experience—that whatever may have been true of the cruelty of landlords in other times and places the landlords of to-day owning cottage property are not a harsh race. They themselves, especially the poorer ones, have their own troubles. The rates have to be paid, the by-laws to be observed, the notices of the sanitary inspector to be obeyed, and perhaps the fact that they themselves have to ask for time to pay and to sue for leniency from corporations and other officials leads them to be tender with their own underlings. Certain it is that in the putting in force of the right to evict a tenant the landlord is very long-suffering. This last step is not usually taken until the rent is many weeks, or often months, in arrear. Even when an eviction order is granted, I have known many cases where a landlord renews the tenancy and collects the arrears at small instalments.

Eviction orders are very often asked for not in the landlord's own interest but in the community's. The necessity to do the sanitary requirements of public bodies is a constant source of eviction. The tenant having no neighbouring house to go to clings to the undesirable shelter he has got until the forces of the law turn him out in the interests of hygiene. Another curious cause of eviction is a woman's tongue. A lady with what is technically known as " a tongue " will set all her neighbours by the ears ; houses on each side of her domicile rapidly empty, and at length the whole street comes to the landlord demanding that she shall go or threatening to depart themselves.

The lady with " the tongue " of our day was, and as far as I know still may be, known to the law as a common scold, and according to Chief Justice Holt was punishable by ducking. Mrs. Foxby, of Maidstone, was, if I remember, the last lady who was indicted at common law for this offence and sentenced to be ducked. She moved, in Trinity Term, 1703, in arrest of judgment because they had called her in the indictment " *calumniatrix* " and not " *rixatrix* " and insisted on her motion, although Chief Justice Holt in kindly warning reminded her that ducking in Trinity Term was pleasanter than ducking in Michaelmas. As the Court pointed out, mere scolding was not the offence, it was the constant repetition that was the nuisance. In the result, after a year's litigation the flaw in the indictment saved the Maidstone lady a ducking in the Medway.

But though the common scold and the ducking stool no longer figure in the quarter sessions calendar —though it would rest with the Court of Criminal Appeal to decide if they are yet entirely obsolete— the woman with a tongue, the " *rixatrix*," or lady brawler is undoubtedly still existent and has to be dealt with by the landlord of small property by County Court eviction.

What is called a possession summons is taken out, and in the hearing of it the lady always appears and protests vigorously against the treatment meted out to her, arguing that the street is in a conspiracy against her, and that she is the one quiet peaceful woman in the neighbourhood. Any doubt as to the correctness of the judicial decision in making an eviction order is solved as soon as the order is made, when, self-restraint being no longer necessary, the full force of " the tongue " is turned upon the landlord, the judge who is in league with him, and the two stalwart members of the force who with some difficulty show the lady the door. Next to dry rot and vermin, a tenant with " a tongue " is the greatest enemy of the landlord of mean streets.

But what has long been recognised about the status of landlord and tenant, is that under present economic circumstances it is impossible for a wage-earner to obtain at the expenditure of a reasonable proportion of his income proper housing for himself and his wife and children. The duty of the State to the poor in this matter is gradually dawning on people's minds, they are waking up to the fact that it cannot be done solely by individual effort, and on this subject the law, I am glad to report, is beginning to make serious efforts to set its houses in order.

At present legislation has taken upon itself three objects : (1) The clearing of slum areas and rebuilding new dwellings, with powers of compulsory purchase granted to local bodies. (2) The granting to corporations and councils power to close insanitary houses, and to make their owners repair them. (3) The permission to local authorities to build houses for the working classes where there is an insufficiency.

We are a slow moving race. We generally do our legislative reforms by a succession of statutes vigorously fought over and hacked about by gay

party spirits whose nearest idea of patriotism is to
queer the other fellow's pitch and spoil his budding
statute by crimping amendments that he knows
will make it unworkable. We have only gone a
little way with the Housing business as yet, and if
the next statute on the matter could be put in the
hands of a small committee of both parties to draft
and bring before the House, perhaps we should get
somewhat nearer finality.

It is rather melancholy reading to pick up the
latest pamphlet of the bookstall on the Housing
Question and find much of the writer's ingenuity
wasted in trying to prove that his party, and his
only, has in the past made any effort to better the
housing of the people, and that in the future there
is only one honest capable scheme which is worthy
of consideration. There is not much real help in these
essays. Their burden is always the same. Recollect
at the Election time—" Short's very well as far as
he goes, but the real friend is Codlin—not Short."

The truth is that neither party has done very
much. The history of the matter is much as
follows. Writers of all parties and creeds in the
Early Victorian days wrote eloquently of the slum
dwellings of our great cities. Some of deeper
insight than the rest saw that all was not well,
even with the rose-covered cottage of the country-
side. It is only within our own lifetime that we
have begun to learn that it is morally and economically wicked for a nation to own slums. This
truth has not been taught us by the priests and
politicians of our time, but by our men of letters.

THE LAW AND THE POOR

Dickens knew all about it and prophesied in despair that we should have to wait for five hundred years for reform. You remember Tom-all-Alone's where Jo lives : " It is a black, dilapidated street, avoided by all decent people ; where the crazy houses were seized upon, when their decay was far advanced, by some bold vagrants who, after establishing their own possessions took to letting them out in lodgings. Now these tumbling tenements contain by night a swarm of misery. As, on the ruined human wretch, vermin parasites appear, so, these ruined shelters have bred a crowd of foul existence that crawls in and out of gaps in walls and boards ; and coils itself to sleep, in maggot numbers, where the rain drips in ; and comes and goes, fetching and carrying fever, and sowing more evil in its every footprint than Lord Coodle, and Sir Thomas Doodle, and the Duke of Foodle, and all the fine gentlemen in office, down to Zoodle, shall set right in five hundred years—though born expressly to do it."

Maybe you could not find to-day an exact replica of Tom-all-Alone's ; certainly we have swept away acres of them, but it is still worth while to read and remember such descriptions, if only to remind ourselves what the poor have to suffer if the law remains powerless and inert in the compulsory provision of decent housing. People grumble at State interference, but they forget what made it necessary. Rampant individualism led to housing workmen in the tailor's shop, described by Alton Locke " a low lean-to room, stifling me with the

combined odours of human breath and perspira-
tions, stale beer, the sweet sickly smell of gin,
and the sour and hardly less disgusting one of new
cloth. On the floor, thick with dust and dirt,
scraps of stuff and ends of threads, sat some dozen
haggard, untidy, shoeless men, with a mingled
look of care and recklessness that made me shudder.
The windows were tight closed to keep out the cold
winter air ; and the condensed breath ran in streams
down the panes, chequering the dreary outlook of
chimney-tops and smoke."

When we are wondering how far it is our right and
duty to interfere between a man and his house
property or whether it is incumbent upon the nation
to take upon itself the burden of housing its people,
it is useful to look on these pictures of England in
the glorious days of Queen Victoria and Albert the
Great and Good. The problems were there then,
but it was not the statesmen who saw them and
urged their solution.

Nor was it only sentimental Radicals who painted
in lurid colours the horrible houses of the people.
D'Israeli, in " Sybil," drew an eloquent picture of the
narrow lanes of the rural town of Marney, which
might be any country town of the South of England
—the rubble cottages with gaping chinks admitting
every blast, with rotten timbers, yawning thatch
letting in the wind and wet, and open drains full of
decomposing animal and vegetable refuse, spread-
ing out here and there with stagnant pools—these
things were common-places in the homes of rural
England in 1845.

THE LAW AND THE POOR

" These wretched tenements," writes D'Israeli,
" seldom consisted of more than two rooms, in one
of which the whole family, however numerous,
were obliged to sleep, without distinction of age or
sex or suffering. With the water streaming down
the walls, the light distinguished through the roof,
with no hearth even in winter, the virtuous mother
in the sacred pangs of child-birth gives forth another
victim to our thoughtless civilisation, surrounded
by three generations, whose inevitable presence is
more painful than her sufferings in that hour of
travail ; while the father of her coming child, in
another corner of the sordid chamber, lies stricken
by that typhus which his contaminating dwelling
has breathed into his veins, and for whose next prey
is perhaps destined his new-born child. These
swarming walls had neither windows nor doors
sufficient to keep out the weather or admit the sun
or supply the means of ventilation, the humid or
putrid roof of thatch exhaling malaria like all
other decaying vegetable matter. The dwelling
rooms were neither boarded nor paved ; and whether
it were that some were situate in low and damp
places, occasionally flooded by the river and usually
much below the level of the road, or that the springs,
as was often the case, would burst through the mud
floor, the ground was at no time better than so
much clay, while sometimes you might see little
channels cut from the centre under the doorways to
carry off the water, and the door itself removed from
its hinges, a resting place for infancy in its deluged
home. These hovels were, in many instances, not

provided with the commonest conveniences of the rudest police ; contiguous to every door might be observed the dung heap on which every kind of filth was accumulated for the purpose of being disposed of for manure, so that when the poor man opened his narrow habitation in the hope of refreshing it with the breeze of summer, he was met with a mixture of gases from reeking dung-hills."

Science, medicine, philanthropy, sanitary engineering and enlightened local government have done something to remove many of the horrible things D'Israeli describes, but one cannot say that the law has co-operated with much vigour in this beneficent crusade. Without law and compulsion the work will never be done as thoroughly as is necessary throughout the length and breadth of the land.

The eloquent outcry, from writers of all creeds and parties, demanding better houses for the people at length made itself heard within the walls of Westminster. But it was not until 1868 that the Torrens Act was passed, the first attempt of the Legislature to deal with slum property. This was followed by the Artisans Dwelling Act of 1875, which enabled local authorities to compulsorily purchase slum areas and re-build sanitary dwellings. In Birmingham, where Mr. Joseph Chamberlain was mayor, magnificent use was made of these powers to the great present benefit of the city. In Liverpool, Manchester, and other towns something was done, but as the business depended in the main on local initiative, and the spending of money, much more remained undone.

THE LAW AND THE POOR

A few small measures were passed, but they did not lead to any great practical work being put in hand, and again it was the man of letters who wakened the national conscience. I remember well in the eighties the appearance of " How the Poor Live " by George R. Sims and the interest and sympathy it aroused. There is no exaggeration in the book, but merely a graphic record of fact, and it proves with melancholy certainty the small progress that had been made since the days of Dickens, Kingsley and D'Israeli.

It was with a great chorus of self congratulation and the loud braying of journalistic trumpets that on March 4th, 1884, a Royal Commission was announced to inquire into the Housing of the Working Classes. It is almost forgotten to-day, but in its time it aroused great hopes in the breast of social reformers. Sir Charles Dilke was Chairman, the Prince of Wales himself was a working member of the commission, Cardinal Manning, Lord Salisbury, Samuel Morley, Jesse Collings, Henry Broadhurst and other great public men of the day were his colleagues.

The overcrowding, the immorality and disease and waste caused by bad housing, the terrible tax of rent on the incomes of the poor were all rehearsed in painful detail before these great ones of the earth. But when one comes to remedies and recommendations, there is nothing except the most trivial and inadequate propositions that the eminent ones can agree upon.

Their first suggestion is that vestries and district

boards should put in force existing by-laws, though who was to make them do it is not mentioned. Then they think it would be an added decency to the lives of the poor if there were more mortuaries near their homes to take the dead bodies from the already overcrowded rooms—as though the problem they were there to consider was not the housing of the quick, but the housing of the dead.

Building by-laws, sanitary inspection, and work-men's trains are a few of the Mother Partington Mop remedies that this great Commission had to offer to keep back the sea of troubles that overwhelmed the poor of our great cities in their struggle for decent existence.

One cannot blame the members of the Commission that so little was suggested. It was inevitable when one remembers that nothing at all is possible in the right direction without a great upheaval which is bound to re-act injuriously on some of the greatest vested interests in the country. A meeting of the great ones in whom the interests vest is not likely to bring about immediate reforms.

But at all events here in the pages of the printed evidence are the facts. The horrors painted by D'Israeli, Kingsley, Dickens and George R. Sims are at least patiently collated and indexed for us, and now after thirty years we should do better not to expatiate on the little we have done for betterment, but to acknowledge how much we have left undone, and show our repentance in energetic deeds. No one can recognise more clearly than I do the value of such authoritative evidence of facts and details

as are collected in the report, but the reading of
them only makes one the more impatient at the
method of government which can tolerate the
continuance of such abuses.

In 1900, little or nothing having been done, it
occurred to Lord Salisbury that it was time to have
another Commission. But it was not until 1902
that a Select Committee of both Houses was appointed to consider, in Lord Salisbury's own words,
how to get rid of " what is really a scandal to our
civilisation—I mean the sufferings which many of
the working classes have to undergo in order to
obtain even the most moderate, I may say the most
pitiable accommodation."

The problem could not be better stated. The
scandal was with us in 1885, it was with us in 1900,
and it is with us to-day. At least if we are un-
willing or incompetent to solve it let us have done
with the constant consideration and further consideration of Royal and Select Commissions which
only make the hearts of the poor sick with promises
and hopes that can never be fulfilled in our own
generation.

One cannot here set out in detail the various
Housing Acts that have been passed; there was one
in 1900, which apparently led to more insanitary
houses being closed than new cottages built. There
was another in 1903, with further new provisions and
modifications of former schemes, and lastly comes
the Housing and Town Planning Act, which deals
rigorously with owners of insanitary property. This
Act industriously made use of may help to realise

our hopes of the possibility of hygienic pleasances for the poor of future generations.

Here we have a short record of some fifty years of legislative effort—more or less honest—in which each party has sought to promote measures to help the poor who are oppressed, as Lord Salisbury said, by this " scandal to our civilisation," the want of decent housing. And yet how little has been achieved, how small the results, how disappointing to find the great men who talked in Parliament and sat on Commissions and discussed these matters with so much learning and ability passing away and leaving this problem for us to tackle, and we on our part looking idly on and still wondering what can be done. If our schoolmasters had taught us how to make bricks and build with them instead of how to read books and write more of them, better results perhaps had been already achieved.

There are many acres of houses in England built prior to 1870 that exhibit all the slum traits that have been so eloquently described in literature, and many millions of our fellow citizens live in houses which fall below the minimum standard of sanitation where the decent separation of the sexes is impossible and the general conditions of life are sunless and miserable. The amount of over-crowding in England and Wales is shown graphically enough in the census returns for 1911. Over-crowding from a census point of view means that more than two persons live in a room, counting the kitchen as a room, but not the scullery. " Thus," as the Editor of the Land Inquiry Report tells us,

" if a tenement or cottage consists of two bedrooms and a kitchen, the Census Authorities would only describe it as overcrowded if there were more than six persons living in it, no matter how small the rooms.   The Census test of overcrowding is, in fact, quite inadequate to measure the full extent of the evil, and there is great need for the adoption of a more accurate one.   Even adopting this standard, however, the Census Authorities find that one-tenth of the total urban population of England and Wales are overcrowded.   This means that nearly 3,000,000 persons are overcrowded."

No one who is constantly meeting the victims of this state of affairs, and discussing with them, as a County Court Judge has to do, their domestic affairs, can fail to be struck with the large amount of infantile mortality and disease, and the prevalence of tuberculosis and the general physical and moral weariness and debility, which may in a great measure be traced to the bad conditions in which the working classes must perforce live because there is nothing better obtainable.

The price paid for such accommodation as there is, is a cruel tax on the working man.   For the meanest shelter he has to pay anything up to twenty per cent. of his weekly income.   Imagine a man with a thousand a year spending two hundred a year in rent alone.   How eloquent would the Official Receiver be did bankruptcy supervene, as it probably would, and what homilies he would preach on the rash and extravagant folly of the bankrupt in spending so large a proportion of his income on a house.   And yet this extravagance is compulsory to a working man, who has to pay out of his wages for a mere roof over his head money that is badly needed for the food and clothing of himself and his family.

I have dwelt on this subject at some length because in most of the chapters of this book my complaint has been that the laws are insufficient to help the poor, because they have in past days been enacted by the rich, and are still being administered by the rich, without knowledge of, and sympathy for, the best interests of the poor. Here the problem is entirely different. Everyone must admit the energy and good faith of all classes and parties and officials, within the rules of the party game, in their endeavour to cope with a condition of things which is an admitted national disgrace, and a scandal to civilisation. The melancholy conclusion, however, stares one in the face. The result of interminable inquiries and committee meetings and palaver is plain unmistakable failure. The fringe of the subject has scarcely been reached, and the state of affairs which the man of letters portrayed to the shame of our grandfathers is likely enough, it would seem, to be "copy" for our grandchildren and their grandchildren to journalise with world without end Amen !

And although it would be impertinent in me to pretend to have a remedy for these evils where all the great ones have failed to bring about reform, yet I cannot help thinking that the reason of the failure is the reason of much of our legislative failure—the dread of vested interests and the permissive character of the statutes passed. What is the good of asking a town council of builders and landowners and estate agents to put in force laws that will, or at least are expected to, have the effect of diminishing their incomes? Should I, or would you, enforce an Act of Parliament with any joyful energy when we knew that the more thoroughly we did it the more we should be out of pocket? It is asking too much of human nature.

There has been a clear failure in the smaller local governing bodies in putting in force even such legislation as exists for the betterment of the district. The Rivers Pollution Acts are a standing instance of the neglect of duty by local councils. For years nothing was done to put the Acts in force, because the smaller polluters were the mill owners, who were members of the local council, and the biggest polluter of all was the council itself pouring crude sewage into the river to relieve the rates. Paliament lacked a sense of humour when it expected mill owners and sewage boards to prosecute themselves for river pollution.

Good work in housing will never, I think, be really effectively done until it is left to the initiative of a medical officer of health or a sanitary engineer, with judicial power to order things to be done and force behind him to have them done. The idea that a medical officer of health should be a servant of the casual butchers and bakers of the Town Council is, on the face of it, an absurd one. He should be as permanent and independent as are the stipendiary, the judge, or the coroner, for he requires even more than common fearlessness to deal roundly with the jerry builders and slum owners who are his aldermen and councillors, and who at present sit on a committee of appeal from his decisions.

As long as these matters are left solely to local bodies the real burden of financial consideration, the lack of personal knowledge of hygiene and sanitation among the members themselves, and the shrinking from enforcing legal hardships on the poor owners of bad property, will alone prevent effective reform. To these natural and honest forces must also be added the weight of vested interests, which deliberately obtain power on local bodies for the purpose of preventing housing reform being put into thorough operation.

Never was there a greater and louder demand by the people for a fair share of the land they live in. The countryman wants his plot and his cottage, and the town dweller a decent house at a reasonable rent. This is the " condition of England question " to-day as it was eighty years ago. Never were there more earnest and sincere people discussing what is to be done and how it is possible to transform slums into decent dwellings by Act of Parliament. We have a willing legislature, a desire to make laws for the benefit of the poor, and after many efforts the result has to be written down as failure and stagnation. It would almost seem as though voluntary effort in this affair had pronounced itself impossible, and it remains undealt with until those who are the real sufferers by the system feel strong enough to put it right.

THE LAW AND THE POOR

Carlyle in an eloquent passage cries out in his passionate way : " Might and Right do differ frightfully from hour to hour ; but give them centuries to try it in, they are found to be identical. Whose land *was* this of Britain ? God's who made it, His and no other's it was and is. Who of God's creatures had a right to live in it ? The wolves and bisons ? Yes, they ; till one with a better right showed himself. The Celt, ' aboriginal savage of Europe,' as a snarling antiquary names him arrived, pretending to have a better right, and did accordingly, not without pain to the bisons, make good the same. He had a better right to that piece of God's land ; namely, a better might to turn it to use—a might to settle himself there and try what use he could turn it to. The bisons disappeared ; the Celts took possession and tilled."

Interpreting this passage as one written in the true frenzy of prophecy, two things seem to me to take clear shape in the future outlook of the housing question. In the first place, it would seem that it will have to be settled by a Celt, and in the second place it will not be achieved " without pain to the bisons."

One would have thought that a better plan would be a small business parliamentary committee of all interests with power to enforce their decrees against owners and corporate bodies. Something permanent is necessary, akin to the Imperial Defence Committee, which knows no party politics. Are we not here in the face of a real danger to the nation ? Already endeavours have been made to take this matter out of the common rut of party politics, but these efforts have not been altogether successful, and if the matter is not settled soon there would seem nothing for it but a forcible solution and a merry set-to between the Celt and the bison, in which we may expect the Celt will get the better of the bison but we cannot be sure that the poor will get all they need even from the Celt.

CHAPTER XIII

THE TWO PUBLIC HOUSES

1. THE ALEHOUSE.

> Judged by no o'er-zealous rigour
>   Much this mystic throng expresses ;
> Bacchus was the type of vigour
>   And Silenus of excesses.
> > LONGFELLOW : " Drinking Song."

WHATEVER you may think about it you cannot travel from Charing Cross to Dijon through the hop-fields of Kent to the vineyards of the Côte-d'Or without admitting that whether the vine be a gift of good or evil it has come to stay. Bacchus is still full of vigour and has as many followers as ever. But the law has nothing to say to Bacchus. The law is after old Silenus. It lures him into a den and makes him drunk and then locks him up, and the holy Willies wag their heads at his shame and collect money for his reformation.

There are two public houses open to the poorer citizens—the Alehouse and the Workhouse. The rich man frequents neither, yet as magistrate or guardian he takes upon himself to lay down the rules by which they shall be run. These fussy, amiable, amateur bosses have conspicuously failed at their job. It is not to be wondered at. As an able Manchester business man once said to me of his partner : " He loves sitting on the licensing bench, and thank heaven he does ; it keeps him out of the office." But even if the bosses were capable and intelligent they could not hope to succeed in their work. Public institutions should be governed by the men who make use of them. The rich man's public-house is so regulated—and what is the result ? One may not approve of every detail of cookery or decoration at hotels like the Ritz in London, or the Adelphi and Midland in Liverpool and Manchester, but the average middle-class man will find in them such reasonable standard of comfort as he desires. There is, at all events, space and light and air, cleanliness, and some luxury. On proper occasions and in fit places there is music, dancing, and billiards, and you may play a game of bridge with your friends when you wish, even for threepence a hundred, in a private room. Moreover, there is always food of good quality obtainable at varied prices, and you need not take your drink standing at a counter, though you can if you wish to when there is an American bar.

Why may not the working man have similar entertainment at the Pig and Whistle ? A complete answer to that question would necessitate a study of the position of artificers and labourers in the middle ages and a short history of the ideals of the well-to-do puritans.

The rich have had two objects in view in their legislation about the working-man's public house.

THE LAW AND THE POOR

A certain section of the rich—the brewers—have aimed at a monopoly of the right to sell him ale, and nothing else, at the biggest possible profit to themselves. A second section opposing the first—the teetotal magistracy—have sought to make the public house as dreary and miserable a place as possible in order to punish the wicked man who wants to drink ale. Between the brewer and the puritan the respectable working man with a normal thirst has been jockeyed out of his freedom. Swilling and tippling in alehouses and private clubs has been encouraged; the reasonable use of ale—which Mr. Belloc rightly asserts to be the finest beverage in the world—has been crabbed and discouraged. Except an opium den—of which I have only hearsay knowledge—there is probably nothing more comfortless and degrading than the lower-class alehouse of our towns and cities.

Even in the remote days of Plato it was recognised—at all events by philosophers—that there was such a thing as thirst. "No one desires *drink* simply, but good drink, nor food simply, but good food; because, since all desire good things, if thirst is a desire, it must be a desire of something good." Further on in the discussion, Socrates addresses Ademantus thus: "Then for any particular kind of drink there is a particular kind of thirst; but thirst in the abstract is neither for much drink, nor for little, neither for good drink nor for bad, nor, in one word for any kind of drink, but simply and absolutely thirst for drink is it not?"

"Most decidedly so," replies Ademantus—who

never on any occasion stood up to Socrates and
contradicted him. " Most decidedly so."

" Then the soul of a thirsty man," continues
Socrates, " in so far as he is thirsty has no other
wish than to drink ; but this it desires and towards
this it is impelled."

" Clearly so."

If the licensing bench, and especially the teetotal
portion of it, could once arrive as far in their studies
of the subject as Socrates had done, and could
comprehend the zoological fact that man was a
mammal with a thirst, they would be on the road to
enlightenment, temperance, and reform.

Of course Socrates knew all that the puritans know
and a lot more about the rational satisfaction of love
and hunger and thirst and the irrational and con-
cupiscent desires that are attached to all natural
appetites, but in dealing with the law of licensing
in reference to the poor these considerations are
not really important. What is wanted is equality.
Grant to the poor the same reasonable facilities of
enjoyment that you grant to the rich, and leave it
to public opinion to see that they are not abused.

It is a grave disaster that the granting and regulation of licenses should have fallen into the hands it
has. Mr. Balfour's observation " that among all
the social evils which meet us in every walk of life,
every sphere of activity, the greatest of all evils is
the evil of intemperance " is useful as a peroration
to any platform speech on the subject, but only
makes the judicious grieve that with the opportunity
to do exactly as he liked and the ability to draft

255

useful legislation, Mr. Balfour did nothing whatever
to improve matters and diminish the evil of which
he was so sensible.

Section 4 of his Act does indeed enable the
magistrates to grant new licenses and to make their
own conditions as to the payments to be made by the
licensee, the tenure of the license, and any other
matters " as they think proper in the interests of the
public." Under this section if there were a licensing
bench containing a working majority of friends of
the people, men who had no social or political interest
whatever either in breweries or teetotallers, it would
seem that almost any experiment in model public
houses could be made under any regulations that
the bench chose to impose on the licensee. Mr.
Balfour was perfectly right in telling us that " love
of temperance is the polite name for hatred of the
publican "; but what is the right name for love of
the brewer ? The fact is that with these two
warring political factions in the field the ideal public
house is not for this generation. No use will ever
be made of Section 4 under present conditions,
because whoever applied for a license, and however
noble and beautiful the licensed premises were to
be, however ideal the provision of food, entertainment and drink, and whatever the guarantees of
good management, the combined opposition of the
puritans and the brewers would always strive to
defeat or destroy any effort to give the poorer classes
pure beer in pure surroundings.

The first step you have to take is to convince the
unenlightened puritan that the Alehouse is, or ought

to be, as worthy a public house as the church or the school. This might be done by means of thoughtfully prepared text books of English literature. There is no great English book from the Bible downwards that has not incidental good and holy things to tell you of " The Inn." What an appetising volume could be written of the inns and innkeepers of Charles Dickens. How he revelled in their outward appearance and the inward soul of welcome which he found there. How he rejoiced in his sane English way over " The Maypole," " with its overhanging stories, drowsy little panes of glass and front bulging out and projecting over the pathway," and honest John Willet, the burly, large-headed man with a fat face, intended by providence and nature for licensed victualling. Could we have met Mrs. Lupin anywhere else than beneath the sign of that " certain Dragon who swung and creaked complainingly before the village alehouse door " ? Could Mark Tapley have acquired his saintly outlook on life anywhere but at " The Blue Dragon," and are we not full of joy to find him returning there to live happily ever afterwards under the " wery new, conwivial, and expressive " sign of " The Jolly Tapley " ? How pleasant it is to assist Crummles and Nicholas over their bowl of punch and the beefsteak-pudding in the inn on the Portsmouth Road. Pickwick is a cyclopædia of inns, each with its own human character, good, bad and indifferent. Who has not stayed at a " Peacock " with a " mantelshelf ornamented with a wooden inkstand, containing one stump of a pen and half a wafer : a road book and directory : a county history minus the cover and the mortal remains of a trout in a glass coffin "?

One could run on in pleasant remembrances of these beautiful and delightful places by the hour, but one imagines that even the most hardened political teetotaller must really know all about them, and perhaps in his dreams strolls into " The Marquis of Granby " and sips his glass of reeking hot pine-apple rum and water with a slice of lemon in it, and awakens to the horrible imagination that his astral body has wandered instinctively into a manifestation of his master and leader, the incomparable Stiggins.

One very noticeable matter about any old-world book in which inns are faithfully pictured is that in former days there was a real race of English innkeepers, independent licensed victuallers, not mere brewers' managers. There are still a few remaining with us who keep up the old traditions, but the political forces of brewers and teetotallers have squeezed this excellent race of public servants almost wholly out of existence. You remember the Six-Jolly-Fellowship-Porters whose bar was " a bar to soften the human breast " with its " corpulent little casks and cordial bottles radiant with fictitious grapes in bunches and lemons in nets and biscuits in baskets, and polite beer-pulls that made low bows when customers were served with beer." How could there have been such an ideal haven for the weary porters but for the sole proprietor and manager, Miss Abbey Potterson, whose dignity and firmness were a tradition of the riverside?

And then the dressing down she gave Rogue Riderhood.

" But you know, Miss Potterson," this was suggested very meekly though, " if I behave myself you can't help serving me, miss."

" *Can't I !* " said Abbey with infinite expression.

" No, Miss Potterson ; because you see the law——"

" I am the law here, my man," returned Miss Abbey, " and I'll soon convince you of that if you doubt it at all."

" I never said I did doubt it at all, Miss Abbey."

" So much the better for you."

And how much better not only for Rogue Riderhood, but for all of us, if we could once again make licensed victualling a great and respectable trade, and once again have a race of people managing businesses that they could really take a pride in.

The death of the old Boniface who owned his house and bought his beer in the open market was brought about by the amalgamation of the smaller breweries in the country, and the purchase of the bulk of the licensed houses by the big breweries. The teetotallers assisted this natural evolution by harassing individual owners with trumpery prosecutions, opposing alterations and transfers at licensing sessions, and surrounding the commercial life of an individual licensee with persecution and annoyance and continued threats of impending ruin.   One man could not fight the great moneyed forces of the puritans, and the licensed holder was glad to get out of an impossible trade by selling his interest to the brewers. Most of the licensed houses in the country now belong in everything but name to the big brewery companies. Their political friends have given them a vested interest in their licenses, and the teetotallers having spent large sums of money and wasted much energy in manœuvring their opponents into this excellent position, now sit sulkily at the gates of it, and as they cannot do any effective good themselves, take earnest pleasure in preventing any enlightened brewer from making the conditions under which he sells his drink better and healthier for the community.

The result is that the poor man suffers. In the whole of this long unworthy struggle between the political teetotaller and the brewer, the higher interests of the poor and the real desires of the working classes are scarcely ever mentioned—still less considered. When he is in sufficient numbers, and is well enough off to do so, the poor man starts a club like his betters, and no doubt these are valuable institutions, but the club at the best does little for the wives and children, and is apt, unless the public opinion of it is sound, to lead a man astray owing to its very privacy. The puritan ideal is to drive the drinker into dark secret places, and as far as possible make his surroundings uncomfortable and degrading. The policy of the future is going to be to encourage the authorities—and, if necessary, get new and more up-to-date authorities—to replace the old dark, dirty puritan pub with a bright and enchanting reformed inn, fit for all classes of folk, with music, entertainment, and all manner of reasonable refreshment. Nothing can be done until we recognise frankly that for years we have been moving along a false track towards a mirage castle in the air, and that if anything useful is to be achieved by administration or legislation we must turn our backs on the past and start along a new road.

Some few facts seem beyond dispute. The mere cutting down of licenses has in itself no demonstrable effect on the evil of the drink habit. The manners and habits of all classes of people are tending to temperance and sobriety, but the consumption of exciseable articles is increasing—last year there was an increase of £5,128,000 over the figures of 1912.

What, then, is to be done? I think if we really want to do good in the matter and can approach it without a desire to make dividends out of brewery shares, or make alliances with teetotallers for political ends, we shall have to look to some extent to foreign examples for guidance in our difficulties.

All of us who have had leisure and money to see something of foreign countries know that the squalid ideal of the brewer and the puritan is not the only possible solution of such social difficulty as there is in providing reasonable alehouses. The British public-house is a national disgrace thrust by the rich on the poor by means of law. The working man has no chance of amending things, as he has no say in electing the bosses. Labour leaders short-sightedly favour the puritans' views. Certainly, our public-houses being what they are, it is a choice of evils to keep out of them.

THE LAW AND THE POOR

But why should public-houses be what they are ? I well remember at Mayence entering a beautiful public hall—it was a rainy night, or the entertainment would have been out of doors—where there was a fine string band playing excellent music. Men, women, and children sat at tables and had ham and bread and cake and beer and coffee, and those who wished to do so smoked. There was no swilling at counters, there was no forced teetotalism, there was no drunkenness ; merely domestic liberty for rational enjoyment.

Why cannot there be sufficient free trade in the beer business of this country to allow an individual or, if you prefer it, an enlightened municipality— where such exists—to copy the sane entertainments of our German neighbours ? A working man and his wife and children spend their evening listening to the band in a German beer-garden with as little sense of impropriety as Lord and Lady De Vere and the Hon. Gladys De Vere take their lunch at the Ritz, or Alderman and Mrs. Snooks lunch in the French restaurant at the Midland.

But in England these domestic felicities are for the rich alone. The brewers and puritans have given the poor man a mean tippling-house to booze in, and deny him anything better. His wife is looked upon as degraded if she joins him at the only place where he can spend his leisure, and the rich law-givers put the true stamp on their own invention by enacting that it is an unfit place for little children to enter.

The fact is that the public house should be built

in the interests of the public. There seems no great decrease in the desire to drink good ale. It is a national taste, and, if the ale be good, it is probably at least as healthy, or healthier, than drinking tea as tea is brewed in cottage homes. But in the name of liberty and equality, surely if a man wants to drink ale in moderation he should be encouraged to do so in bright, pleasant surroundings, where he can spend his evenings at a moderate cost with his wife and children and meet his friends. He should be allowed to open such a place himself if the municipality will not do it for him, and the more civilised brewers should be assisted and encouraged by the licensing authorities to build big, spacious public houses, where the poor man could obtain similar entertainment to that provided for his wealthier brother.

There is something almost shameless in the way in which the law of licensing is stretched to the uttermost for the rich and drawn to the narrow-most for the poor. One picks up a paper with an account of the latest midnight ball—the gayest event of the season—all in the interests of charity, of course. What has become of that closing time which, if overstepped by the poor, means police court for the criminals and loss of license to the inn-keeper? It has been extended, no doubt, by a complacent magistrate, and you can sit down to supper at midnight, and all night long you can refresh yourself at American bars presided over by beautiful ladies of the chorus. One gathers there will be no closing time at all, as breakfasts will be served from three o'clock. In the intervals of the dancing there are to be famous music-hall turns. At some of these fashionable dances valuable prizes are given, at others these fall to lucky ones by some form of lot—not lottery, of course, for that would be against the law, and these entertainments are arranged by eminent leaders of society who are always within the law—well within it.

It would be ill mannered to endeavour to stop so much innocent enjoyment of a class that has so little real pleasure by enforcing the licensing and other laws to interfere with their amusements. On the contrary, we should seek to use their example and better our own licensing circumstances by an appeal to their precedent. If it is good for leaders of society to sing and dance and sup after hours in their public houses, why should not the rest of society be allowed to follow their example and have their own beanfeasts in ample public houses undisturbed by the law? Of course there must be a charity! Give me an extension of license in the Old Kent Road and I will provide plenty of charities and plenty of lads and lasses ready to sing Mr. Adrian Ross's refrain :

> Care has gone to sleep till morning,
> Night's the noon of joy

For the young people of the poor are just as fond of a spree as those of the rich, and quite as ready to be charitable to the extent of their means after the same fashion.

There is an excellent letter of Charles Kingsley's written to the " Christian Socialist " some sixty years ago that might well be circulated among licensing benches by the Home Office—though I believe it is considered officially to be bad economy to address printed common sense to the unpaid magistracy. Naturally, autocrats resent or scoff at advice that has no sanction behind it. The teetotal attitude of mind and the quarrels it aroused very properly disgusted Kingsley. He took no pleasure in hearing the water drinkers calling the beer drinkers " flabby, pot-bellied, muddle-headed, disgusting old brutes," and the beer drinkers retorting on the water drinkers that they were " conceited puritans and manichees and ascetics." He saw that the quarrel would not do any good to the cause of temperance, and in his honest enthusiasm blurted out the truth, the whole truth and nothing but the truth about his teetotal friends, like the good old Christian warrior that he was.

" On my honour," he writes, " unless the tee-totallers show a more humble, gentle and tolerant spirit than is common among them I shall advise beer drinkers like myself and Mr. Hughes (Tom Brown of the Schooldays) either to flee the country, or if their cloth allows them, which mine does not, prove by self-defence that a man can value his beer, and thank God for it with a good conscience, as tens of thousands do daily and yet feel as tight about the loin and as wiry in the arm as any tee-totaller in England. Honestly, I am jesting in earnest. I regard this teetotal movement with extreme dread. I deeply sympathise with the horror of our English drunkenness that produced it.

THE LAW AND THE POOR

I honour every teetotaller as I honour every man
who proves by his action that he possesses high
principle and manful self-restraint. . . . That a
man should be a teetotaller rather than a drunkard
needs no proof. Also that a man should go about
in a sack rather than be a fop and waste time and
money on dress. But I think temperance in beer,
like temperance in clothes, is at once a more rational
and a higher virtue either than sackcloth or water."

This was true doctrine then and is true doctrine
to-day, and the sad fact that it fell on deaf ears
and is still but half understood is the reason of our
backwardness in licensing reform and the presence
of the degrading public house which the law cherishes
and protects.

Only the other day in a country town, on the
application for a license, the police superintendent
objected to the house on the ground of the small bar
accommodation. His Grace the Duke, who happened
to be in the chair, wanted to know if the proprietor
of the house would prepare a plan for enlarging the
bar accommodation. What could the proprietor do?
The police wanted to herd the drinkers into a bar
so that they could pop their heads in and see them
all at once without any trouble, the bench wanted
to do what the police wanted them to do. The
interests of the poor, the cause of temperance, the
betterment of the social life of the people were
as irrelevant to the case as the flowers that bloom in
the spring.

At many a licensing session, too, you will listen to
solemn warnings by the superintendent of police

against the public being allowed to amuse themselves with penny-in-the-slot machines or gramophones or parlour quoits or the like. Amusement is regarded with a natural horror by the puritan, and the friends of the brewer see in it a dangerous alternative to the duty of the working man to drink. One police authority threatened the license holders " that if they continued to allow these machines to be used in their licensed premises they did so at the risk of prosecution for allowing gaming." The gaming laws of England with their wholesale permission of gambling in one place and their retail persecution of gambling in another place, and their incapacity to know when a place is not a place or how otherwise, are a public laughing stock, but it is a grievous thing that they should be dragged out to drive a little harmless amusement out of the dingy tavern which is the only public institution the poor man has for rest and recreation.

As a matter of fact, these machines, if they are used for gambling, are generally used to see who shall pay for drinks. In some bars in foreign countries a dice-box is always handy for this purpose. Three or four friends come in and throw, the loser pays for drinks, and all are satisfied, and having had their drink they go. I am not upholding the custom as ideal, but I see little harm in it. In England, if three or four enter a public house, the etiquette in many places is for one to stand drinks, and for the rest in turn to offer to stand another round— an offer seldom refused—and for the rounds to continue until each has stood his corner. I would not go so far as to insist on a compulsory dice-box in every bar, but I fancy on the whole that it is an agent of temperance.

Every one who has given any thought to temperance as opposed to teetotalism, is agreed that what is wanted is the gradual elimination of bars and counters and the substitution of chairs and tables and big open rooms. In these must be provided tea, coffee, and all the usual lighter refreshments that you find in the better-class restaurants and hotels. In a big West End hotel you find every afternoon that the lounge is laid out for afternoon tea. I do not see why a working man and his wife should not have their tea in a lounge in their public house. I cannot understand why, if two friends after a day in the workshop want to have a friendly chat, they cannot find an institution where one can have his cup of tea and a muffin, and the other his glass of ale and a sandwich, and both sit at one table in a spacious room with comfortable surroundings, and if they do not heartily dislike it a gramophone to play tunes to them. That is impossible of attainment as the law now stands. If a millionaire was to offer to build in Manchester a dozen working-men's cafés on the continental plan where any decent citizen could be pleased to take his wife and children, as our French and German neighbours do, the brewers, the teetotallers, the police, the licensing magistrates and the law would see that it was not permitted.

And yet we know by experiment that in proper surroundings, reasonable facilities for refreshment do not lead to drunkenness. In the Manchester Exhibition of 1887, it being a wonderfully fine summer, and licenses having been freely given for the occasion, there was an opportunity of testing whether under proper conditions opportunity led to excess. I never heard that it did. In the Franco-British Exhibition where reasonable facilities of refreshment were also given, it is said—and I have no doubt truly said—that though eight or nine million visitors passed through the turnstiles, yet there was not a single case of drunkenness.

The problem is really a simple one, if we could only get administrators and legislators, but especially the former, to look at it in the interest of the man in the street. To the big brewery company beer is an effluent, and the public house is the conduit pipe through which they pour it into the public stomach. They have obviously no interest in ideal public houses—and why should they? They are business men on business bent. The teetotallers, on the other hand, regard the drinking of beer as a sin, and any public house as the house of the Devil. Why should they help the Devil to make his house sweet and attractive, and make the path easier for the poor sinner who thirsts after beer? At present the average licensing bench consists of " half and half " —to use a trade term—of these elements. If there happen to be a few cranks on the bench who share the feather-headed notions set down in this chapter, they can always be out-voted by a combination of brewer and teetotaller. And for my part I think we shall stick to our glorious institution of the

" tied-house " just as long as the working man intends to allow us and no longer.

When reformed public houses are taken up by the men who use the public house, and when labour demands something better, the demand will be met. For the teetotaller is nothing if not political, and when he sees where the votes are, and not before, he will begin to see the error of his ways.

Meanwhile it will do him no harm to study the statistics such as they are, and discover that the number of licenses in a district has nothing to do with the amount of drunkenness therein, and to look back on the past history of the public house and recognise that he has for many years been the friend and ally of the undesirable brewer. The good citizen's policy should be the provision of pure ale in wholesome surroundings, thereby freeing the working class from the tyranny of the public house. To the teetotallers who hinder such a policy I can only repeat Charles Kingsley's message : " And I solemnly warn those who try to prevent it that they are, with whatsoever good intentions, simply doing the Devil's work."

CHAPTER XIV

THE TWO PUBLIC HOUSES

2. THE WORKHOUSE.

Pauperism is the general leakage through every joint of the ship that is rotten. Were all men doing their duty, or even seriously trying to do it, there would be no Pauper.

Pauperism is the poisonous dripping from all the sins, and putrid unveracities and God-forgetting greedinesses and devil-serving cants and jesuitisms, that exist among us. Not one idle Sham lounging about Creation upon false pretences, upon means which he has not earned, upon theories which he does not practise, but yields his share of Pauperism somewhere or other.

THOMAS CARLYLE : " Latter-day Pamphlets,"
" The New Downing Street."

THE current cant of the day is that the alehouse leads to the workhouse. From an architectural and hygienic point of view they have much in common, and perhaps when one comes to spend one's last years amid the unloveliness and official squareness and coldness of the workhouse one will be able to look back with a sense of grateful pleasure to the more natural squalor of the alehouse. It is a zoological fact that the human pauper, escaped for the day from a workhouse, makes like a homing bird for the alehouse, wherefrom we may draw the conclusion that the public for whom our two public houses are provided by an intelligent State prefer the alehouse as the lesser abomination of the two.

I often wonder if there is any nation in the world that possesses an appetite equal to that of our own people for Royal Commissions and reports. I admit that I have the craving strongly myself—not to sit upon Commissions, for I am a working man and the amusement is one for Bishops, Law Lords, philanthropists and the leisured classes—but I buy the reports when they come out and sometimes read them—or some of them—or some part of them—and marvel at the patience and energy and research that have gone to the making of them, and sigh over the pity of it and the heart-breaking inutility of the whole business.

Here is the report of the Royal Commission on the Poor Laws, 1909. The blue cover of my copy is already turning grey with old age, the pencil marks I made in the margin when I read it five years ago remind me of the splendid reforms that spread themselves out in its pages and made one feel that after all the world was a better affair than one had hitherto believed. This report is indeed literally a monument of industry. It sat from 1905 to 1909. There are over twelve hundred pages in the report itself, which you can buy for the trumpery sum of five and six. The evidence of it is contained in many volumes, and if your library is large enough and you can afford to pay the price of a large paper set, you would have reading enough for the rest of your natural life. And what has come of it all? Practically nothing. It is not to be supposed that either the report or the evidence has ever been read and studied by our ministers and rulers. A few magazine and newspaper articles have been made of it, then perhaps a book or two are written on the subject, the origin of which you can trace to the report, and after that gradually the thing sinks by its own cumbrous weight into the dead limbo of forgotten state papers. Yet if there was a problem called the reform of the Poor Law in 1905 worthy of the consideration of the good men and women who gave up a large slice of their lives to working at it surely in 1914 there is still such a problem, and some of it is at least as urgent as the questions over which our political pastors wrangle and fight with such splendid energy. To write an essay on the law and the poor in relation to the relief of distress would be to traverse the whole ground of this famous report, but for my own part I only want to call attention to an institution typical of all the faults and errors of the Poor Law— the workhouse.

For if the rich have by their laws made a mess of the alehouse, what about the other public-house— the workhouse ? When you have no money to enable you to take your ease at your inn the only other hostelry open for you and your wife and children is the Poor House.

If there is one subject that has a more confused melancholy legal history than another it is the story of the workhouse. No doubt much has been done and something is doing, but it is difficult to see the real metal of the reformer's work for the great heaps of Poor Law dirt that our forefathers have left for us to clear away. For years the great English General Mixed Workhouse has been looking for trouble. It has not a friend even in the Local Government Board Office, and it has been condemned by all right-minded men and women time out of mind as an abomination of desolation standing where it ought not. Yet there it is. A blockhouse, invented, built, and governed by blockheads, or at least beings with wooden blocks instead of human hearts. It is mournful to read the Poor Law history of the last eighty years and to learn how little we have done to dry the tears of the widows and orphans who become, through folly, misfortune, or ill-regulated industry, the wards of the State.

And to understand how such an institution came into our midst, it is necessary to look back a bit upon the natural history of our Poor Law.

Whatever our failings may be as practical states-men capable of translating philanthropic theory into practical statutory right action, no one can deny we are a great people for ideals. And the ideal of our Poor Law has from earliest days been excellent. Coke in his Institutes tells us that it was ordained by Kings before the Conquest that the poor should be sustained by parsons, rectors, and parishioners, " so that no one should die from lack of sustenance." That was, and still is, the ideal. No citizen is to die from lack of sustenance, and yet surely since the Conquest, and even recently in our own time, some perverse person has escaped the careful eyes of the parsons, rectors, and parishioners, and crept away to an obscure corner there to die of hunger against the ordinance of Kings in that case made and provided.

Coke got this phrase from Andrew Horn, the author or editor of that excellent treatise " La Somme appelle Mirroir des Justices," which he must have compiled somewhere before 1328, though it was first printed in 1624. Horn's " Mirror of Justices," is not, I believe, regarded with great reverence by the learned as a law-book, but Coke enjoyed it and quoted it with approval, and whether or not some of its phrases were ever sound law I dare not express an opinion, but I will vouch for the excellence of Andrew's sympathies.

In writing of the criminal law he tells us that " the poor man who to escape starvation takes victuals to sustain his life, or a garment to prevent death by cold, is not to be adjudged to death if he had no power to buy or to borrow, for such things are warranted by the law natural."

I suppose it is doubtful if this was ever good common law to be acted upon in all criminal courts, but one admires old Andrew for setting it down and is glad to learn that even in the beginning of the fourteenth century there were writers on law who were trying to mitigate the rigour of the law in favour of the poor. They may not have actually stated what the law exactly was, but they had shrewd ideas at the back of their minds as to what it ought to be. If they confused the two themselves at times, and this confused other learned ones in after times, maybe no one has been much the worse for it.

THE LAW AND THE POOR

And when Horn laid down in his quaint dog French that " Les povres fusent sustenuz par les persones rectours des eglises e par les paroisiens," I fear he was writing of what ought to be rather than what was the existing common law of the relief of the poor.

I am not at all sure that leaving the matter in the hands of parsons and parishioners has not been the cause of most of the failure of the Poor Law. If you have studied parsons and parishioners as a class, you do not find them peculiarly desirous of providing sustenance for others. Queen Elizabeth —a very practical lady, much thought of by parsons and parishioners—was evidently of the opinion that you were asking too much for the poor when you said that they should have sustenance for nothing. She it was who enacted that in return for the ideal Saxon sustenance, which was apparently to be freely given, the poor person was now to give his work. Churchwardens and overseers, instead of giving free relief had power to set to work children whose parents could not maintain them, and make their parents work too if necessary. This was the beginning of the system that made you chargeable on the parish, and gave the parish a right to make you work off some of your chargeability.

In the eighteenth century came the interesting and disastrous experiment of indiscriminate out-door relief. The farmer parishioner discovered he could get a cheaper labourer by making his fellow parishioners pay some of the wages in out-door relief. A pauper was a better tenant to have, since the rent was paid out of the poor rates, a bastard child was an asset in a household, and in 1821 overseers are known to have shared out the pauper labourers among themselves and their friends and paid for the labour wholly out of the poor-rate.

The scandals that had arisen led to the reform of the Poor Law in 1834, which placed the administration in the hands of Commissioners who were to see that the law was carried out, and by a natural swing of the pendulum they turned from an indiscriminate doling out of rates to favoured paupers to a system whereby the labourer was to find that the parish was his hardest taskmaster so as to induce him to keep away from the overseers and make parish relief his last and not his first resource. The ideal that the Commissioners stood out for was that no relief whatever was to be given to able-bodied persons or to their families otherwise than in well-regulated workhouses. This was the beginning of the workhouse system which really made the workhouse a kind of prison for those who could not find work outside.

A great deal has been done since then, and especially in recent years, to mitigate the lot of the poor. Old Age Pensions, Labour Exchanges, Medical Insurance, Unemployment Insurance and the enlightened administration of some of the better Boards of Guardians have made great inroads on the negative inhumanity of the workhouse system. But unless it be in some of the more vigorous northern centres Poor Law work and Poor Law elections rouse but little enthusiasm. There are no doubt many men and women who enter into the service of the Poor Law from noble motives and do useful work, but the good they can do is very limited. The Central Authority seems to have no very settled ideals, different boards run different policies, some hanker after the flesh pots of labour cheapened by indiscriminate relief, others clamour for lower rates obtained by the inhumanity of not allowing anything but indoor relief. The guardians whose voices are raised only in the interests of the poor are scarcely heard by those who are clamouring for a lowering of the rates.

One thing all reformers seem to be agreed upon, and that is that the General Mixed Workhouse with good, bad, and indifferent men, women, and children herded together within its four walls is an abomination of desolation. Maybe it did its work in the past as part of the evolution of the Poor Law, dragging it out of a slough of corrupt and unwholesome administration, but a time has surely come when we can apply more scientific remedies to prevent the recurrence of such scandals, and there is no longer a necessity to sacrifice the lives and happiness of decent men, women, and children by the continuance of our workhouse system.

For what is a General Mixed Workhouse ? It is an institution that has been officially condemned since the Commissioners of 1834 went their rounds and made their report. Crowded together in the workhouses of that day they found a number of paupers of different type and character, neglected children under the care of any sort of pauper who would

THE TWO PUBLIC HOUSES

undertake the task, bastard children, prostitutes, blind persons, one or two idiots, and an occasional neglected lunatic. There was enough humanity among the Commissioners of eighty years ago to see that what was urgently necessary was classification ; the aged and the really impotent wanted care, peace, and comfort, the children wanted nursing, supervision, and education, hard working men and women in misfortune did not want to live in close proximity to the " work shy " and the " ins and outs." " Each class," says the Report, " should receive an appropriate treatment ; the old might enjoy their indulgences without torment from the boisterous ; the children be educated and the able-bodied subjected to such courses of labour and discipline as will repel the indolent and the vicious." This was reported of the workhouse in 1834, this is again reported of the workhouse in 1909 ; there seems every reason to believe that it will be once more reported of the workhouse in 2000.

Of course, many things are better to-day than they were eighty years ago. A different standard of sanitation and hygiene has arisen throughout the county and some of it has found its way into the workhouse. We have Poor Law schools and Poor Law infirmaries that were unthought of in those days and, as a whole, our buildings are clean and healthy; there is no ill-treatment in them as there was in the days of Bumble ; food, clothing and warmth are at least sufficient ; and in communities where there is an exceptional Board and a superior master and matron much is done to hinder the obvious evils of promiscuity. Nevertheless, the evil overshadows the good, for it is the institution itself—the workhouse—that is as radically unwholesome and unfit to-day as it was in 1834.

The evils of promiscuity cannot be exaggerated. In the larger workhouses male and female inmates dine together, work together in kitchens and laundries and in the open yards and corridors, with results that are obvious. In a fortuitous assembly of such people the lowest common denominator of morality is easily adopted as the standard. What a terrible place is a General Mixed Workhouse to which to send children or young people. One cannot read some of the passages in the report for which Mrs. Sidney Webb and her colleagues were responsible without shuddering at our own guiltiness and folly as ratepayers for allowing these things to be done in our name. " No less distressing," they say, " has it been to discover a continuous intercourse which we think must be injurious between young and old, innocent and hardened. In the female dormitories and day rooms women of all ages and of the most varied characters and conditions necessarily associate together without any kind of restraint on their mutual intercourse. There are no separate bedrooms , there are not even separate cubicles. The young servant out of place, the prostitute recovering from disease, the feeble-minded woman of any age, the girl with her first baby, the unmarried mother coming in to be confined of her third or fourth bastard, the senile, the paralytic, the epileptic, the respectable deserted wife, the widow to whom out-door relief has been refused, are all herded indiscriminately together. We have found respectable old women annoyed by day and by night by the presence of noisy and dirty imbeciles ; idiots who are physically offensive or mischievous, or so noisy as to create a disturbance by day or night with their howls, are often found in Workhouses mixing with others, both in the sick wards and in the body of the house."

This picture is foul and detestable enough, but it is perhaps in the treatment of children that the workhouse system causes the greatest unintentional cruelty. There are some 15,000 children actually living in General Mixed Workhouses. A large proportion of these have no separate sick ward for children, and no quarantine wards if there should be such a thing as an outbreak of measles or whooping cough. Young children are to be found in bed, with minor ailments, next to women of bad character under treatment for contagious disease, whilst other women in the same ward are in advanced stages of cancer and senile decay. Children come in daily contact with all the inmates, even the imbeciles and fooble minded are to be found at the same dining table with them. In this huge State nursery the nurses are almost universally pauper inmates, many of them more or less mentally defective. A medical Inspector's report in 1897, stated that in no less than " sixty four Workhouses imbeciles or weak-minded women are entrusted with the care of infants." One witness states that she has " frequently seen a classed imbecile in charge of a baby." In the great

palatial workhouses of London and other large towns
the Commissioners found that " the infants in the
nursery seldom or never got into the open air."
They found the nursery frequently on the third or
fourth story of a gigantic block, often without
balconies, whence the only means of access, even to
the workhouse yard, was a lengthy flight of stone
steps down which it was impossible to wheel a baby
carriage of any kind. There was no staff of nurses
adequate to carrying fifty or sixty infants out for
airing. " In some of these workhouses," they
write, " it was frankly admitted that the babies
never left their own quarters, and the stench that
we have described, during the whole period of their
residence in the workhouse nursery."

Seventy years have passed since it was written,
and yet the " Cry of the Children " has as much
meaning for us as it had for our grandfathers.

> The young lambs are bleating in the meadows,
>   The young birds are sleeping in the nest,
> The young fawns are playing with the shadows,
>   The young flowers are blowing toward the west—
> But the young, young children, O my brothers,
>   They are weeping bitterly !
> They are weeping in the playtime of the others,
>   In the country of the free.

And I am far from suggesting that all this evil is
the result of any personal inhumanity of Boards of
Guardians, Masters or Matrons or of their Inspectors
and Governors in higher places. It is a matter in
which each individual citizen must bear his share of
blame for he knows it to exist, and he knows that
he can have it altered if he cares to put his hand deep

enough into his pocket, or if he will forgo some of the political luxuries dear to his party heart and give up the expenditure on them to the betterment of little children.

Other European countries have managed to classify their poor. In France the medical patients go to hospitals, the infirm aged poor have special " hospices," and the blind and the idiots are separated from the little children, each having their appropriate establishments. Of course we take a great and to some extent justifiable pride in our Local Government institutions, but as the world becomes more complex and difficult, it is beginning to be seen that backward and less intelligent districts do not get the full value out of legislation and rates that a progressive and vigorous district obtains. It is one thing to pass an Act of Parliament and another thing to get a local elective body to administer it intelligently. If we could level up the worst administration of Guardians to the best, a great deal would be done, but there is no manner of doubt that the State ought to impose a time limit on the General Mixed Workhouse and to enact that after such a date no Board of Guardians shall be allowed to house men, women, and children in the unclassified barracks in use to-day. If any body of Guardians do not feel capable of carrying out such a decree the State must take their job over and do it for them.

For eighty years the law makers have been told by their own experts what their workhouses were, and why they ought to be abolished and the fact that the greatest sufferers from the iniquity are poor children who cannot voice their complaints, and exist in dumb ignorance of the wrongs that are done to them, does not make our position as the wrong-doers any less deserving of damnation.

CHAPTER XV

REMEDIES OF TO-DAY

> Ring out the feud of rich and poor ;
> Ring in redress to all mankind.
>
> TENNYSON : " In Memoriam."

WHEN Absalom cried out in a loud voice, " Oh, that I were made judge in the land that every man which hath any suit or cause might come unto me, and I would do him justice ! " he was, as we should say nowadays, playing to the gallery. Yet, sincerely uttered, what a noble wish it was. Let it stand as an expression of the still unfulfilled ideal of judicial duty and public service which we owe to-day to the poor of this country. Every man has not as yet a judicial system that does justice to every man.

And I fear that Absalom's fine saying was only an election cry in his campaign against his father, recalling to the voters perhaps David's inconsistency in the theory and practice of justice in the matter of Uriah and his wife. In those days the King, the Lawgiver, and the Judge were but one person, so that to be made Judge was to be made Lawgiver and King, and you not only administered the laws but made them as you went along. Absalom was only an office seeker, but his election address contained a noble sentiment.

THE LAW AND THE POOR

Nowadays the Judges are merely servants of the law, like policemen and bailiffs and the hangman. Nor does the King make the laws, nor are there in theory any professional Lawgivers. The people—or at least so many of the people as get on the register and trouble to vote—make their own laws, or are supposed to do so. At least they have the power of choosing their representatives and servants to make what laws they want.

If, therefore, a sufficient number of men in the street greatly desired amendment of the law in this or that direction, I have no doubt it would come about. But very few of the problems that trouble me come before the eyes of the average man in the course of his daily life, and he is scarcely to be blamed for not trying to mend that which he has not observed is broken and worn out.

One man may know at first hand the story of a home ruined by reckless credit and imprisonment for debt, another may know a cruel case of lives blighted by our unequal divorce laws, a third may have seen the sad spectacle of an injured workman sinking from honest independence to neurasthenic malingering by reason of the poisonous litigious atmosphere of the Workmen's Compensation Act.

I can never understand why men and women hunger after the tedious, unreal, drab scandals portrayed in a repertory theatre when they could take a hand at unravelling the real problem plays of life in the courts and alleys of the city they live in. Real misery and wretchedness is at least as pathetic as the sham article, and if you do your theatre-going in a real police court you may learn to become a better citizen.

Not that I advise all men and women to spend their leisure in these squalid surroundings. I recognise that the man in the street cannot at first hand study all these problems, and that is why I have set down something of the disabilities of the poor under the law, in the hope that my political pastors and masters may take an interest in these domestic reforms.

There are many, I know, who think that a judge, like a good child, should in matters of this kind be seen and not heard. But for my part I am not of that opinion, for if a judicial person knows that the machine he is working is out of date and consuming unnecessary fuel, blacking out the moral ether with needless foul smoke, and if, moreover, he thinks he knows how much of this can be put right at small expense, should he not mention the matter not only to his foreman and the frock coat brigade in the office—who arc the folk who supply the bad coal—but to the owner of the machine who has to pay for it and live with it—the man in the street?

Now there is a great deal that might be done to make the law less harsh to the poor without any very elaborate legislation, and certainly without any of those absurd inquiries and commissions which are the stones the latter-day lawgivers throw at the poor when they ask for the bread of justice.

I like to read of Lord Brougham, as far back as 1830, shivering to atoms the house of fraud and iniquity known as the Court of Chancery. I like to picture him pointing his long, lean, skinny fingers at his adversaries, and to see the abuses he cursed falling dead at his feet. Could he have had his way, the very County Court system which we have to-day would have sprung into being within a few months of his taking his seat on the woolsack, and he would have instituted Courts of Conciliation for the poor, to hinder them from wasting their earnings in useless costs.

But the petty men who walked under his huge legs and peeped about were too many for Colossus. And, to be fair to the fools of his time, the great giant was not himself a persuasive and tactful personality. Sane, wise, and far-reaching as were the legal reforms he propounded, too many, alas, still remain for future generations to tackle.

Pull down your Hansard debates of to-day, read them if you can, and say honestly in how many pages you find political refreshment for the man in the street. The small reforms of existing laws that weigh hardly on the poor are worth at least as much of parliamentary time as many of the full dress debates about ministers' investments and tariff reform and the various trivial absurdities that excite the little minds of Tadpole and Taper, but have no relation whatever to the works and days of the poorer citizens of the country.

And if I were called upon to draw up a new Magna Charta for the poor—and I could draft all the reforms I want in a very small compass—I should put at the head of the parchment—" Let it be enacted that no British subject may be imprisoned

for a civil debt." I do not believe that if Members
of Parliament would vote on this subject as I know
many of them would really wish to vote that there
would be a dozen voters in the " No " lobby, and I
am firmly convinced, though here I must own my
parliamentary friends are in disagreement with me,
that they would not injure their hold on their
constituencies.

If there were any machinery in our unbusiness-
like Parliament for dealing with social subjects on
a non-party basis, imprisonment for debt would
have been abolished long ago. The proposal is,
however, a proposal to ameliorate the bottom dog,
and the human bottom dog is poorly represented in
the great inquest of the nation. The foreign bird
whose plumes adorn the matinee hats of our dearly
beloveds, the street cur who might find a sphere of
utility in the scientist's laboratory, the ancient cab-
horse who crosses the Channel to promote an
entente cordiale by nourishing the foreigners—
all these have friends, eloquent and vigorous for the
lives and liberties of their especial pets ; but the
poor man who goes to gaol because he cannot pay
the tally-man has few friends.

There is no getting away from the fact that
political influences are against the abolition of
imprisonment for debt. I remember many years
ago—more than twenty, I fear—a learned County
Court judge laughing at the eagerness with which I
threw myself into a newspaper campaign against
imprisonment for debt. " I, too," he said, " used
to think I should live to see it abolished, and you

think that merely stating unanswerable arguments
against it is likely to lead to results.   Well, I used to
think that way about it at one time, but it is not
a matter of argument at all; it is all a case of vested
interests and nervous politicians.   Some day another
Lord Brougham will come along and sweep the thing
away as he swept away the old Chancery Courts
and many another legal abuse, but I shall never see it
done, and unless you are another Methuselah you
will never see it done."   And then with a laugh of
mock despair he added :

> Logic and sermons never convince,
> The damp of the night drives deeper into my soul.

I am beginning to think that my old friend spoke
with the tongue of prophecy, and he was certainly
right about the vested interests.

The three parties in English politics have a curious
attachment to imprisonment for debt.   They do not
allude to it much on the platform or in the House,
but it is there at the back of their minds all the same.
The Conservative opposition to the proposal is the
more straightforward and natural.   Here is a
system which enables the well-to-do to collect money
from the poor, it encourages credit giving, and is
thought to promote trading, it causes no inconvenience to the wealthier classes, it exists and
always has existed, and it works well.   Why should
it be altered, especially as there is no great demand
for change, and change is in itself an evil thing ?
Let us leave well alone.   The Liberal, off the platform, is much in agreement with the proposition of
abolition, his difficulties are purely practical diffi-

culties. He finds among his best supporters, drapers, grocers, tally-men and shop-keepers, most of them Nonconformists and keen Radicals, and all of them credit givers, carrying on their businesses under the sanction, more or less direct, of imprisonment for debt. These traders are not only voters and supporters, but they are centres of political influence. I remember in the South of England, thirty years ago, being told of a grocer in a small village who was a man whose support it was necessary for the candidate to obtain. I went along to see him and he agreed to support my friend. He was worth over two hundred votes, all of them in his debt and liable to be summoned at any moment for more than they could pay.

In politics it is absurd to expect individuals to kick against the pricks, and I do not know of any politician who, deeply as he may believe in the justice and expediency of abolishing imprisonment for debt, has ever cared to take up the matter and place it prominently before his constituents in the hope of being able to convince them that it would make for the greatest happiness of the greatest number. The general belief seems to be that the influence of the shopkeeping and travelling trading classes would be used against such a Quixote, and he would receive a severe warning to stick to the ordinary hack lines of political talk and not risk his seat tilting at windmills.

The attitude of the Labour party is even more peculiar. Outwardly and individually they, of course, being more thoughtful and experienced

THE LAW AND THE POOR

about the wants of the poor, agree very heartily that imprisonment for debt is a class institution which should be abolished. But they certainly show no great enthusiasm in taking a hand at working for its abolition. This is partly due, no doubt, to the fact that they are business men and not theorists and have other and nearer work to do. They would, I make no doubt, support any measure of abolition, but it is essentially a legal reform and they would wait for some legal authority to initiate it.

There is too, undoubtedly, at the back of the Labour mind the idea that imprisonment for debt may be a very present help in time of trouble. In the Select Committee of 1893 Mr. William Johnson, a miner's agent, gave evidence in favour of imprisonment for debt; he asserted that nine-tenths of his men did not desire its abolition and were in favour of its continuance. Later on he pointed out that in case of sickness or in the case of non-employment, " and probably in the case of strikes," credit given under the sanction of imprisonment for debt would be useful. Unemployment and sickness are now largely dealt with by insurance, and from a public point of view the idea that strikes should be financed by the small tradesmen and, in case of their bankruptcy, ultimately by the wholesale trade, is not an attractive one.

The reformer must always expect to find selfish class interests up against him, but it seems to me that the desires of those who want to finance strikes on credit and the rights of those who at present are selling shoddy on credit at extravagant prices ought not to weigh against the general public welfare. If, as I venture to think, the arguments against the last step in the abolition of imprisonment for debt are as valid as they were on former occasions, and if, as must be admitted, no evils have followed on the partial abolitions of imprisonment already made in 1837 and 1869, then the mere fact that the public is apathetic on the subject and that members of Parliament are apprehensive of interested opposition is not of itself sufficient excuse for those who are in authority in legal matters refusing to complete the reform by abolishing imprisonment for debt for the poor as it has already been abolished for the rich.

Of course, the mere abolition of imprisonment for debt would not to my mind be a sufficient protection of the poor unless side by side of it were enacted a homestead law greatly enlarging the existing exemptions from execution of the tools and chattels of a working man. The idea is that the home furniture necessary to the lives of the human beings forming the home should be incapable of being seized for debt. Make the limit twenty pounds or whatever sum you please but clearly enact that sufficient chattels to furnish a reasonable house are exempt from execution. In America and Canada these homestead laws exist and work well. It occurs to our cousins across the pond that it is a better thing to keep a home together than to sell it up for an old song to pay official fees and costs and something on account to the foolish creditor. The returns from a poor auction of a workman's household furniture are miserable reading. The landlord by distress or the

tally-man by execution may get a few shillings for
himself and pay away a few more shillings to bailiffs
and others, but the cost of it to the poor is cruel.
Tables and chairs and perhaps a sideboard that
represent months of savings and long hours of
labour are in a moment of misfortune snatched
away from their proud possessor and his home is a
ruin.

The homestead laws in Canada, though not the
same in every State, go much further than any laws
we possess to prevent the breaking up of a home.
In Manitoba, for instance, executions against lands
are abolished, though land can be bound by a judgment by registering a certificate, and the household
furniture and effects, not exceeding 500 dollars in
value, and all the necessary and ordinary clothing of
the debtor and his family are exempt from execution.
The actual residence or house of a citizen to the extent
of 1,500 dollars is also exempt. Imagine what an
incentive it would be to the purchase of house
property and furniture if a man were to know that
his cottage to the value of three hundred pounds, and
its contents to the extent of one hundred pounds,
would always be protected from bailiff and sheriff.
What a check, too, such legislation would be on the
reckless way in which credit is given.

One exception to this rule seems to me very fair.
There is no exemption of anything the purchase
price of which was the subject of the judgment
proceeded upon. Thus a man cannot buy a sideboard, refuse to pay the price of it, and claim exemption of the sideboard from execution by the furniture

dealer who sold it, though he could claim exemption of the sideboard against a money lender who had obtained a judgment against him, and wanted to recover his debt by sweeping his home away. Here in England people are driven to shifts and evasions by means of bills of sale, goods put in the wife's name, and a number of other semi-dishonest devices to protect their homes. The sight of a home broken up and the furniture that has cost so many years of saving slaughtered at a third-rate auction for little more than the costs and fees of the bailiffs is no great incentive to a working man to spend his savings on good, home-made chattels. Cheap foreign shoddy on the hire system is the order of to-day, and as a mere matter of encouragement of the better class home trade in furniture, carpets, drapery and household goods generally, we might consider the advisability of taking a leaf out of the Statute book of Manitoba.

That debt should never be allowed to utterly destroy a family and a home seems to me such a clear and sane idea that it has always been a puzzle to me to try and understand the point of view of those who cannot see the matter in the same light. I know it is a degrading confession for anyone with even the pretence of a judicial mind to have to make but it is best to be honest about it. I rather gather I am a little obsessed, or abnormal, or feeble-minded, or senile perhaps nowadays about anything that touches home or home life.

The home to me is the great asset of the nation. I do not want to see the home superseded by State barracks or common hostels or district boarding schools. On the contrary, I think individual homes are good for the development of citizens. For this reason I would protect the home from ruin by an extravagant husband or an extravagant wife in the interests of the children, who are the next generation of citizens, and whose welfare is, therefore, a debenture of the State.

Nobody would think of distraining on a pheasant's nest, or breaking up the home of a couple of partridges, or imprisoning the birds at breeding time in separate coops and cutting down their food merely because one of the birds had run up a bill for too many mangel wurzels or the other had run into debt for some fine feathers beyond her means.

Pheasants and partridges are too valuable to be so treated. Their nests are protected from any distress or execution by poachers, and their bodies are protected from arrest by watchful gamekeepers under strict laws. I want to insure under my reformed laws that the human nest should be protected in the same way, and that judges should not only be allowed, but ordered, to take care that the home is not devastated by human misfortune or even by improvidence. We want Game Laws for the poor. In future our legislators must treat them as game birds—as indeed most of them are—and not as vermin to be devoured, they and their children, by the owls and kites of the underworld in which they live.

And the second clause of my Magna Charta would be of almost simpler dimensions than the first. It would run : " Let it be enacted that the

County Courts have jurisdiction in Divorce." This
would at once place rich and poor on an equality
that is not yet even aimed at. I should not com-
plicate this matter with the overdue reforms proposed by the Divorce Commission, much as I should
like to see those enacted. They are matters of
general interest that have waited for so many
years that there is not much hardship in holding
them back further, but the institution of a new
tribunal of divorce is of vital and immediate importance to the poor. The Act would be a practically
unopposed act of one clause. It would only touch
one vested interest, the London lawyers of the
Divorce Court, and it would greatly please their
brethren throughout the country.

All details of costs and machinery could be left
to rule committees, as is the common practice in
other and more important matters that have come
to the County Courts, such as Admiralty and equity
jurisdiction, and a hundred other really difficult
and complicated matters.

And then would follow a lot of simple but important reforms that really only need the stroke of the
official pen that is never made until the man in the
street rises in his wrath and knocks the official
funny-bone on the official desk and wakens him up
to the fact that it is officially time to do some
official act.

For, of course, police court fines must be cut
down and time given to pay them, and police court
costs must be paid by the community, and bankruptcies must be made available to the poor, and

the Treasury must cease to rob the poorest bankrupts of £13,000 a year, and the limit of such bankruptcies must be raised to £250, so that poor little business men and their creditors may get what there is, rather than it should all go in costs and fees and payments to lawyers and accountants, who must give up sparrow shooting and hunt for bigger game.

And, above all, we must remember to engross in big black text on our parchment what Joseph Chamberlain said about his Workmen's Compensation Act, that it is to be worked without lawyers, or at least, that it is to be made one of the judge's duties to see employer and workman first and endeavour to bring them together before he issues his fiat that the affair is " fit for litigation."

This little programme surprises me by its moderation. How any society of business men could palaver about it in any Palaverment for more than a week passes my comprehension. I commend my new Magna Charta to a party in want of a programme. If they carried it in the first week of their Ministry and then adjourned for seven years to see how the world went on without them, they would be the most sensible and popular Government since the days of Alfred the Great.

CHAPTER XVI

Happy he whose inward ear
Angel comfortings can hear,
    O'er the rabble's laughter ;
And, while Hatred's faggots burn,
Glimpses through the smoke discern
    Of the good hereafter.

Knowing this, that never yet
Share of Truth was vainly set
    In the world's wide fallow ;
After hands shall sow the seed,
After hands from hill and mead
    Reap the harvests yellow.

Thus, with somewhat of the Seer,
Must the moral pioneer
    From the Future borrow ;
Clothe the waste with dreams of grain,
And, on midnight's sky of rain,
    Paint the golden morrow !

JOHN GREENLEAF WHITTIER.
Barclay of Ury."

I REMEMBER in my youth being told in the words
of Marcus Aurelius : " Be satisfied with your business and learn to love what you were bred to."   At
the time I may have resented the advice, but I
have lived long enough to see the wisdom of it.
Personally, at that period, I should have liked
to have been an engine driver or at least a railway
guard ; later on in years I had thoughts about

299

carpentering; and in course of time water-colour painting, etching, playing the fiddle, and even golf seemed possible of attainment. But when you really learn that these higher ranks of life are closed to you by your own natural limitations and find out that your business in life is to be a drab official in an inferior court, then Marcus Aurelius is indeed grateful and comforting.

One can, after many years of it, learn to love even the County Court. You have much the same outlook and experience of life and human nature as the old bus driver. Every day brings you new passengers who accompany you for a few minutes on the journey of life, and you get to know many old ones and have a friendly crack with them over their domestic troubles. Moreover, at moments your daily job brings you in near touch with the joys and sorrows and trials and daily efforts of poor people, and once in a way perhaps you can be of use, which to a child and to a grown-up who has any of the child left in him is always a jolly thing. When you have really got quite accustomed to enjoying your work the natural garrulity which your friends lovingly attribute to senile decay stimulates you to make them partners in your joy. The narrow circle in which you spend your daily life has become your only world. You find yourself quoting with approval " with aged men is wisdom, and in length of days understanding," and you begin to believe you are the only person who really does understand. Childlike, you find dragons in your path that you want to slay, pure and beautiful souls are oppressed, and you fancy that you can release them from bondage; there are giants of injustice and persecution in the land whose castles you mean to turn into peoples' palaces. Then you sit down to write your fairy tales again—but no longer for the children nowadays, since they are all grown up. These fairy tales are for journalists, philanthropists and politicians who make fairy tales and live on fairy tales; and believe me, there are no more essential fairy tales than stories about legal reform. Only to the writer are they real, and to one or two choice child spirits who never grow old and still believe in a world where everyone is going to live happily ever afterwards. The way in which Master Ogre, the Law, swallows up the poor is quite like a real fairy tale, and it would have even a happier likeness to the fiction of the nursery if we could tell of a Jack the Giant Killer cutting off the wicked monster's head and rescuing his victims.

I am under no delusions that this little volume is going to do any particular good in any particular hurry. I know by historical study that the way of reform lies through official mazes of docket and précis and pigeon holes, that legislative decisions are hatched out in some bureaucratic incubator that the eye of common man has never seen. I reverence the mystery that surrounds these high matters. It is really good for us that we should know so little of the reason why things are no better than they are. And then how good our rulers are to us in the matter of Royal Commissions and Blue Books! At our own expense we may really have as many of these as we ask for. I wish I could get folk to understand what a lot of sterling entertainment there is in blue books. All the earnest ones, all the clever ones, all the cranky ones of this world set down their views and opinions on any subject at any distance from that subject, and wrangle and argue and cross-examine each other, and then the good Government prints it for us all verbatim and sells it to us very very cheap. Practically, I dislike the shape of a blue book, and æsthetically they do not match my library carpet when they are lying around, which is a disadvantage, but I must own that if I were banished to a desert island I would rather have my blue books than much of what is called classical literature.

The evidence is the best reading—and when one comes to the final report I generally find the minority report to be the thing one is looking for, as it is usually the minority who want to do something. But in some subjects, divorce for instance, things are moving so hurriedly during these last few hundred years that actually there is a majority in favour of legislation and reform.

Not that this makes the slightest difference as to any actual reform being done. The feeling of security that nothing is ever going to come of it makes it a safe and reasonable thing to print the most advanced views at the expense of the State. The physical weight and size of these volumes have been carefully considered and the whole format cunningly designed to repel readers. Nothing ever comes of blue books, and I do not suppose anything

ever will come of them. When I turn over their
dreary pages I find myself humming Kipling's
chorus—

> And it all goes into the laundry,
> But it never comes out in the wash,
> 'Ow we're sugared about by the old men
> ('Eavy sterned amateur old men !)
> That 'amper an' 'inder an' scold men
> For fear o' Stellenbosh.

Dickens had the same impatience of the heavy
sterned brigade and invented his immortal Circum-
locution Office, and doubtless genius is entitled to
deride these substantial State institutions. Personally, I find them very English and valuable.
The more energetic of us may take our pleasure in
giving friendly shoves to these heavy sterned
Christians, but their inert services to the community are not to be undervalued. But for this
immovable official wall who knows what reforms,
unnecessary and ill-advised, might have been
carried through. If Lord Brougham could have
had his way much that I am writing about to-day
would long ago have happened. The heavy
sterned ones sitting on the lid prevented the opening
of the Pandora box with its promises of affliction
for the human race in the shape of legal reform.
They have left these things over until to-day and
brought me amusement for idle vacation hours.
At least, let me be thankful to them and sing their
praises.

I remember when I was planning out these chapters
being the victim of a most terrible nightmare. A
newspaper with a King's speech in it was thrust

before me and every one of the reforms I had already
written about was promised to be passed within
the Session. I remember smiling in my dream,
knowing what parliamentary promises were, and
then as I was gliding down the Strand a silent
phantom newsboy handed me an evening paper.
There it was in black and white, every bill was
passed—there was nothing left to write about. I
awoke with a cry. It was a terrible shock, and it
was some moments of time before I could realise
that such a thing was absolutely impossible. And,
of course, when you think of the large number of
things that you want done and recollect that
nothing ever is done that a man really cares about
in his own lifetime it was absurd of me, even in a
dream, to believe that anything was coming
between me and my little book. Indeed, I have
hopes that for many years to come it may be
regarded as a popular primer about legal reform
for future generations who wish to while away idle
hours in the luxury of vain imagination.

I should like to interest the man in the street
about legal reform and to see him at work remedying
some of the more obvious of the existing abuses I
have referred to, but I am under no delusion that
such reforms would bring about the millennium.
It is good to do the pressing work in the vineyards
on the slopes of the mountain, but it is permissible
for poor human man to have his day off now and
then to climb on the hilltops and gaze out on the
limitless ocean of the future and indulge in wild
surmises of the after-world.

REMEDIES OF TO-MORROW

The remedies of to-day are really tiresome parochial affairs compared to the remedies of to-morrow and hardly seem worth troubling about when one considers that even if you passed them all this year in a century or two your new statutes would be out of date and only fit for the scrap heap.

Bacon tells us that Time is the greatest of all innovators, but he does not explain to us why, unlike all human innovators, Time is in no hurry about it. I have quite distinct beliefs, which to me are certainties, as to how Time will reconcile the law and the poor in the centuries to come, when our social absurdities and wrong-doing will not even be remembered to be laughed at. The law will never be a really great influence for good until it is utterly conquered, put in its proper place in the world and based on the principle of Love. In other words, when the Law of Love receives the Royal Assent no other law will be necessary.

Nineteen hundred years ago a new principle was introduced into the world. It was the principle of unselfishness, and its apostles were labour men. In relation to man's personal life it has made some progress, but in practical social politics its business value is not yet fully recognised. Still, a beginning has been made, and that old snail, Time, is doubtless satisfied with the pace of things. Let us remember hopefully that two thousand years ago unselfishness as a basic principle of life, doing to others as you would be done by, promoting peace and good will instead of strife and ill will—these ideas as business propositions were as unknown then as railways, telegraphs, motor cars, and aeroplanes. A vision of to-day would have been a wild fairy tale to Marcus Aurelius, a vision of two thousand years hence would be incomprehensible to us.

One does not mean, of course, that unselfishness had never before been preached as an ideal, but a society based on the common quality of all its members placing the interests of others above their own was a new notion, and the novelty of it has not yet worn off. Nevertheless, love and unselfishness have achieved sufficient lip-service already to make me hopeful of their future, and I foresee a time when they will be the foundation of the laws of the world, and the preamble to every statute will be " Blessed are the Peacemakers."

Some day when the Chinese send over a mission to heathen England, missionaries will go about the country destroying all the boards on which are written the wicked words " Trespassers will be Prosecuted." But I hope we may not have to wait for a foreign mission to teach us our duty.

This phrase, typical of the law of to-day and eloquent of the claims of the rich to fence the poor off the face of the earth, must utterly disappear when the new spirit of the law is made manifest. We have no sense of humour. On Sunday we intone to slow music our desire to forgive our enemy his trespasses ; on Monday we go down to our solicitor to issue a writ against him for the trespass we have failed to forgive. The old notice threatening prosecution is really already out of date. It ought, of course, to read, " Trespassers will be

Forgiven." For my part if I met with such a notice,
I should hesitate before I walked across the owner's
land ; whereas to-day, when I am threatened with
prosecution, my bristles go up, I scent a right of way,
and as like as not proceed in my trespassing out of
pure cussedness. There are a lot of other folk besides
myself who are built that way. I know a little girl
of five whose chief glory in life is to walk " on the
private," as she calls it, when the park-keeper is not
looking. It is that constant " Don't ! " and " You
mustn't " that rouses the rebel in us. The less for-
bidding there is, the easier the path of obedience.

I hold no brief for trespassers. I know it is
naughty to trespass. But in the present state of
my evolution there is so much of the original monkey
in me that when that " monkey is up," to use a
phrase dear to Cardinal Newman, I go astray. So
do many of my best friends.

I have the same belief in the evolution of the
moral world and its onward movement that I have
in the revolution of the physical world and its
rotary movement. For this reason I expect my
great-grandchildren of two thousand years hence
to be much better behaved than I am. You can see
it coming along in your own grandchildren unless your
sight is getting dim. And I am quite clear that my
own manners are an improvement on my great
grandfathers, who lived in caves, and, when they had
disputes, made it clubs, and battered each other
strenuously until it was proved which had the
thickest skull, when he of the toughest cranium was
adjudged to be in the right.

THE LAW AND THE POOR

The vigorous legal procedure of the cave men sounds laughable enough to us nowadays, but does anyone think that two thousand years hence superior unborn persons will not be smiling superciliously over the history books that record the doings of our judges, our hired counsellors, our sheriffs, our gaolers, and our hangman?

It was only in the recent reign of good Queen Bess that the ordeal of battle was given up. The abolition of that old-world lawsuit must have been painful to the conservative mind. And there was a lot to say for it. From a sporting point of view, what could be better than to go down to Tothill Fields in Westminster, as you might have done in 1571, to see A. B. battering C. D. to the intent that whichever knocked the stuffing out of the other gained the verdict?

If you look at it from a healthy, open-air point of view, maybe it was better for everybody than sitting in a stuffy court and listening to two bigwigs splitting hairs to the resultant financial ruin of one of their clients. One reason, no doubt, that trials by battle were abolished was that they gave the poor at least as good a chance as the rich.

I remember a good story—it is an old one, but still quite good—of a noble lord and landowner who met a collier trespassing in the neighbourhood of Wigan.

" My good man," said my lord, " do you know you are trespassing? "

" Well, wot of it? "

" You have no right to be walking across my land."

" I'm like to be walking across somebody's land, I've noan o' me own."

" Well, you must not come across mine."

" How do I know it is yours, and who gave it you ? "

" Well, this land," replied the noble lord, " belonged to my father and grandfather and his father for many generations."

" But how did thi' first grandfeyther get it ? " persisted the collier.

" Well, as a matter of fact, it was granted by the King for services rendered. I may say," my lord added proudly, " that my ancestors fought for this land."

" Did they, now ? " said the collier, " then tak off thi' coat an' I'll feight thee for a bit."

One can see from this anecdote that it would never do to return to ordeal by battle. And though individual fighting by violence to assert rights is out of date and not permissible, yet in the affairs of the collection of human beings known as nations the horrible waste of armaments and the menace of war are living evidence of the ultimate tribunal to which we still appeal.

No one really believes that force and violence are sane remedies for the evils of the world, and the whole history of mankind shows a gradual decline in the practice and use of them. In each succeeding generation our children will be nearer the truth than we are, and further on the journey towards the end when the rule of Love and Unselfishness will be the only law of the Universe, and will enforce itself without judges, juries, or policemen.

THE LAW AND THE POOR

And lest anyone should say that all this is the mere vague raving of prophecy, let me set down a short, practical catalogue of what I expect the remedies of to-morrow to bring about in, say, two thousand years. In the first place, the disabilities of the poor that I have written about in these pages will all have been abolished and forgotten. Crime will be regarded as a disease, and it will be as inhuman to treat the criminal with harshness as it is to-day to torture lunatics after the methods of a hundred years ago.

Every citizen will have a right to sufficient food, clothing, housing, and entertainment in exchange for reasonable hours of work. The spirit of humanity will so greatly have been improved that it will be very little necessary to extort proper conditions for the lives of citizens or to protect the weak from exploitation by the strong. Litigation and war will be out of date and replaced by conciliation and arbitration. In a word, the reign of love and unselfishness will have commenced.

We may not even see my beautiful world from afar, but this need not dismay us, for we know it is there, and we know that every effort we make to serve the cause of the poor helps to clear the path through the desert along which the coming armies of victory will march in triumph. The cause of the poor has always been the greatest cause in the world, and the generation that has at length understood it, and fought for it and won it, will find itself standing at the open gates of the promised land.

INDEX

ABINGER, Lord Chief Baron, his judgment in *Priestley* v. *Fowler*, 77, 78, 95, 96

Ademantus, 254

Administration orders in bankruptcy, 119—124

Alehouse, the, 252—270

" Alton Locke," slums described in, 238

American judiciary and working classes, 93, 94, 95; and workmen's compensation, 103

Appeals, cost of, 175

Artisans Dwelling Act, 1875.. 241

Asquith, Right Hon. Herbert Henry, on workmen's compensation, 87

Attorney-General v. *The Edison Telephone Co.*, 83

BACON, Lord Chancellor, 305

Bail, unnecessary refusal of, 226; statistics of this, 228, 229

Balfour, Right Hon. Arthur James, on intemperance, 255, 256

Bankruptcy, 106—124; failures due to extravagance, 115—117; not open to the poor, 118; administration orders, 120 ; exorbitant Treasury fees, 122—124

Bell, Alexander Graham, 82

Belloc, Hilaire, 254

Bentham, Jeremy, on legal evidence, 192

Bias in judges, 96—103

Bills of Sale Acts, 168

Black Act, 1722..218

Blasphemy Laws, 199, 200

Blue Books, 301, 302

Bradlaugh, Charles, 199

Bridewell, the, 9—10, 213

Bright, John, 99

Brougham, Lord, on imprisonment for debt, 48, 49; on the Evidence Amendment Act, 193 ; on Chancery reform, 287, 288

Butler, Samuel, 211

CADAVAL, Duke de, arrested on mesne process, 46

Capias ad satisfaciendum, 37, 44

Carlyle, Thomas, on history, 21 ; on language, 108, 110 ; on fools, 153 ; on land question, 250

Cattle maiming, 216—219

Chamberlain, Right Hon. Joseph, on workmen's compensation, 87—90 ; on administration orders, 119, 120 ; his housing work in Birmingham, 241

INDEX

Chancery Court, and Lord Brougham, 287

Children, treatment of, in workhouses, 280, 282

Closing time, regulations for rich and poor, 263, 264

Clough, Arthur Hugh, 169

Cobbett, Sir William, 186

Coke, Sir Edward, Chief Justice, his description of *peine forte et dure*, 11 ; 201, on early Poor Laws, 274, 275

Collier, Sir Robert, on imprisonment for debt, 55, 56

" Compleat Constable," The, 4—7

Conciliation in trade disputes, 110

Conciliation, preliminary of, in France, 187

Corporal punishment, advisability of, discussed, 209—212

Costs in police court, abolition desirable, 222

Cottenham, Earl of, his Insolvency Bill, 1837..45—47

County Court procedure, expense of, 184

Court of Criminal Appeal Act, 1907..194, 197, 198

Crabbe, on lawyers, 183

Cranmer, Thomas, Archbishop of Canterbury, on divorce, 125, 126, 127

Crime and punishment, 189—212

Criminal Appeal, Court of, 189

Criminal Evidence Act, 1898.. 194—196

Criminal Law Amendment Act, 210

Cruelty to Animals Bill of 1811..219

Davey, Lord, on workmen's compensation, 92

Deane, Mr. Justice Bargrave, on divorce, 137

Debt, imprisonment for, Old Testament view of, 22 ; New Testament view of, 24 ; Greek law of, 27 ; Roman law of, 31 ; in Papal Rome, 34 ; in time of Henry III., 36—39 ; in eighteenth century, 41, 43 ; in " Pickwick," 45 ; mesne process, 45 ; debates on, in 1837..46 ; in 1869..50—57 ; evils of, 59—68 ; arguments against abolition, 69 —71 ; none in Germany, 71 ; nor in France, 72 ; wastefulness of system, 72 ; encourages improvidence, 157—160 ; in police courts, 220, 222 ; political views on abolition of, 288 — 293

Debtors Act, 1869..41, 49—57, 158

Debtors' prisons, 41—47

Dendy, Mr. Registrar, on divorce in County Court, 146

Denman, Lord, speech on imprisonment for debt, 46

Dickens, Charles, on imprisonment for debt, 45 ; on the living wage, 108 ; on the evidence of prisoners, 194 ; on slums, 238 ; on inns and innkeepers, 257—259

D'Israeli, Benjamin, slums described in " Sybil," 239— 242

Distress, law of, 233

INDEX

Divorce, 125—151 ; in time of Edward VI., 125—128 ; Act of 1857..131 ; hard cases of poor, 133—141 ; necessity of using County Court, 144—146, 297

Dogberry, abolition of discussed, 223, 224

Edalji, 217
Edward VI., 126
Edward VII., 126
Eliot, George, 174
Elisha, and imprisonment for debt, 22, 23
Elizabeth, Queen, her Poor Law, 276
Employers Liability Act, 1880 ..86
Erewhon, treatment of crime in, 211
Erskine, Lord, and cruelty to animals, 219
Eviction, 234
Evidence, prisoners right to give, 193 ; Criminal Evidence Act, 1898..194 ; of Crown not available to prisoner, 207—209
Exekestides, 27

False pretences, 202, 203
Fielding, as a magistrate, 213
Fieri facias, 39
Fines in police courts, unfair incidence of, 221, 222 ; time for payment of, 224 ; statistics of, 225 ; abolition of, 297
France, no imprisonment for debt, 72 ; divorce law, 143, 147 ; preliminary of con-

ciliation in, 187 ; poor law, 283
Fuller, on burning of heretics, 200

Geographical distribution of crime, 216
Germany, no imprisonment for working men debtors, 71 ; divorce in, 147
Gilbert, Lord Chief Baron, 37, 39
Goldsmith, Oliver, 13, 14
Gordon, Cosmo, Archbishop of York, on divorce, 128
Gordon, Mr. Justice, of Australian Labour Court, 110
Governor of gaol, charity to poor debtors, 65
Grand jury, 181
Grantham, Hon. Mr. Justice, 101 ; on poor prisoners defence, 196
Gray, Professor John Chipman, of Harvard, 80 ; on judge-made law, 81

Haldane, Viscount, 66, 215
Hale, Sir Matthew, Lord Chief Justice, 100
Halsbury, Earl of, on workmen's compensation, 92
Hard labour for unconvicted prisoners, 227, 228
Headlam, John, an old-fashioned Dogberry, 227, 228, 229
Herschell, Lord, on prisoners giving evidence, 195
Hogarth, 10, 15
Homestead laws of America and Canada, 293, 294, 295

INDEX

Hood, Tom, 108

Horn, Andrew, his "Mirror of Justices," 275

Housing question, 236—251 ; Royal Commission, 1884.. 242 ; Select Committee, 1902 ..244

IDENTIFICATION of prisoners, present methods criticised, 230, 231

Imprisonment for debt. *See* Debt.

Innkeeper, independence of, 258

JEREMIAH, and the living wage, 108, 113

Jessel, Sir George, on imprisonment for debt, 50

Johnson, Dr., 4 ; on the poor in England, 13, 14 ; on public executions, 15, 16 ; on imprisonment for debt, 70 ; on the formation of laws, 70

Johnson, William, miners' agent, his views on imprisonment for debt, 292

Judge-made law, 79—85

Judgment summonses, statistics of, 60, 63

Judicial irrelevancy, 180

Judson, Frederick N., author of "The Judiciary and the People," 94

Justice of peace, utility of lay justices, 231

KELVIN, Lord, 82

Kingsley, Charles, 108 ; on slums, 238 ; on teetotallers, 264—266, 270

Kipling, Rudyard, 303

LANDLORD and tenant, 233—251

Land transfer system, assists fraud, 183

Leniency to well to do in criminal courts, example of, 205, 206

Licensing, class regulation of, 253 ; section 4 of Act of 1904..256 ; effect of reducing number of licences, 261 ; extension of hours for rich, 263 ; prohibition of amusements, 267

Living wage, 108, 109, 110

Lysons v. *Andrew Knowles*, 175

McMAHON, M.P., on imprisonment for debt, 55

Malicious injury to property, 217, 218

Manitoba, homestead laws of, 294, 295

Marcus Aurelius, 299, 306

Married Women's Property Act, undesirable use of, 161 —170

Matthew, and imprisonment for debt, 24, 25

Maule, Mr. Justice, on divorce, 129

Maxwell, Rev. Dr., 13, 14

Mayence, public beer drinking at, 262

Medical officer of health, status of, 248

INDEX

Menander, on marriage, 163
Mesne process, arrest on, 45 ; abolished, 49
Mesnil, M. Henri, on divorce, 143
Moryson, Fynes, 8, 11, 34, 35

NEWMAN, Cardinal, 307

ORDEAL of battle, 308, 309
Overbury, Sir Thomas, 11
Overcrowding, 245 ; census statistics of, 246

PARRY, Serjeant, 99
Peine forte et dure, 12
Pepys, Samuel, 4
Pickersgill, M.P., on prisoner giving evidence, 196
Pickwick, and imprisonment for debt, 45, 47
Piers Plowman, on debt, 75 ; on law and poor, 172, 173 ; on lawyers, 188
Police courts, abolition of fines, 297
Poor law, 271—284 ; Royal Commission, report of, 272 ; in time of Elizabeth, 276 ; in eighteenth century, 276 ; in 1834..277 ; general mixed workhouses, 278—284
Poor man's lawyer, necessity of, 184—187
Poor Prisoners Defence Act, 194—197
Priestley v. Fowler, 76—79
Procedure and the poor, 172—188

Public houses, 252—270. And see Licensing.

RAILWAY Conciliation Boards, and their working, 111, 112
Raleigh, Sir Walter, 1, 3
Regina v. Thomas Hall, 129
Registrars of County Courts and private practice, 72, 73
" Reformatio Legum Ecclesasticarum, The," 125
Ridley, Sir Matthew White, on workmen's compensation, 87
Rivers Pollution Acts, 248
Roe, Gilbert, author of " Our Judicial Oligarchy," 86, 94
Rogues and Vagabonds, 4—7
Ruskin, John, 108

SABBATARIANISM, evils of, 215
Salford quarter sessions in 1824..17
Salisbury, Earl of, 244, 245
Schuster, Dr., on German system of debt collecting, 71
Scold, common, trial and punishment of, 205
Scots divorce, 126
Scott, Sir William, 15
Seisachtheia, The, 29
Selden, John, on marriage contract, 150
Shop lifting by ladies, 204
Sims, George R., his " How the Poor Live," 242, 243
Sittlichkeit, 66
Slums, legislation against, 236
Smith, Judge Lumley, on divorce costs, 148, 149

315

INDEX

Smith, Rev. Sidney, on prisoners' right to counsel, 190, 191 ; on prisoners' inability to give evidence, 192

Smith, Sir A. L., Master of the Rolls, on workmen's compensation, 89

Smollett, 9, 42

Snowden, Philip, M.P., and the living wage, 109 ; on strikes, 111

Socrates, on thirst, 255

Solicitors, speculative, 175

Solon, and imprisonment for debt, 27—31

Starkie, Sir Thomas, 17

Stephen, Mr. Justice, decision in telephone case, 82

Stipendiary magistrates, want of in country, 223 ; necessary in interests of justice, 231

Sumner, Lord, 180, 181

Swift, on lawyers, 181, 182

Taylor, Jeremy, his prayer for debtors, 75

Teetotallers, persecution of licence holders by, 259 ; their ideals, 260 ; Charles Kingsley's views of, 264—266, 270

Telephone, legal position of, 82, 83

Tennant, Mrs., report on divorce, 136

Thackeray, on prisoner giving evidence, 193

Torrens Act, 1868..241

Treasury fees on Administration Orders, exorbitancy of, 121—124, 298

Twelve Tables, The, 32

Tyburn, 7, 15, 16

Vinogradoff, Professor, 84

Warrington, Harry, imprisonment for debt, 45, 46

Webb, Mrs. Sidney, her report on poor law, 280

Weston, Richard, trial of, 11, 12

Whipping, punishment of, 6—9, 209—212

Witchcraft, 100

Workhouses, 271—284. *And see* Poor Law.

Workmen's compensation, 76—105 ; history of the law, of, 76—84 ; employers liability, 86 ; in Court of Appeal, 90—93 ; in America, 94, 103 ; 162, 286, and conciliation, 298

Wyrley, cattle maiming at, 219

York, Archbishop of, on divorce, 136, 137

BRADBURY, AGNEW & CO. LD., PRINTERS, LONDON AND TONBRIDGE.

The List of Titles
in the Garland Series

1. Walter Besant. **East London.** London, 1901.

2. W.H. Beveridge. **Unemployment. A Problem of Industry.** London, 1912.

3. Charles Booth. **The Aged Poor in England and Wales.** London, 1894.

4. Clementina Black, Ed. **Married Women's Work. Being the Report of an Enquiry Undertaken by the Women's Industrial Council.** London, 1915.

5. Helen Bosanquet. **The Strength of the People. A Study in Social Economics.** London, 1903 (2nd ed.).

6. A.L. Bowley and A.R. Burnett-Hurst. **Livelihood and Poverty. A Study in the Economic Conditions of Working-Class Households in Northampton, Warrington, Stanley, and Reading.** London, 1915.

7. Reginald A. Bray. **Boy Labour and Apprenticeship.** London, 1911.

8. C.V. Butler. **Domestic Service.** London, 1916.

9. Edward Cadbury, M. Cécile Matheson and George Shann. **Women's Work and Wages.** London, 1906.

10. Arnold Freeman. **Boy Life and Labour. The Manufacture of Inefficiency.** London, 1914.

11. Edward G. Howarth and Mona Wilson. **West Ham. A Study in Social and Industrial Problems.** London, 1907.

12. B.L. Hutchins. **Women in Modern Industry.** London, 1915.

13. M. Loane. **From Their Point of View.** London, 1908.

14. J. Ramsay Macdonald. **Women in the Printing Trades. A Sociological Study.** London, 1904.

15. C.F.G. Masterman. **From the Abyss. Of Its Inhabitants by One of Them.** London, 1902.

16. L.C. Chiozza Money. **Riches and Poverty.** London, 1906.

17. Richard Mudie-Smith, Ed. **Handbook of the "Daily News" Sweated Industries' Exhibition.** London, 1906.

18. Edward Abbott Parry. **The Law and the Poor.** London, 1914.

19. Alexander Paterson. **Across the Bridges. Or Life by the South London River-side.** London, 1911.

20. M.S. Pember-Reeves. **Round About a Pound a Week.** London, 1913.

21. B. Seebohm Rowntree. **Poverty. A Study of Town Life.** London, 1910 (2nd ed.).

22. B. Seebohm Rowntree and Bruno Lasker. **Unemployment. A Social Study.** London, 1911.

23. B. Seebohm Rowntree and A.C. Pigou. **Lectures on Housing.** Manchester, 1914.

24. C.E.B. Russell. **Social Problems of the North.** London and Oxford, 1913.

25. Henry Solly. **Working Men's Social Clubs and Educational Institutes.** London, 1904.

26. E.J. Urwick, Ed. **Studies of Boy Life in Our Cities.** London, 1904.

27. Alfred Williams. **Life in a Railway Factory.** London, 1915.

28. [Women's Co-operative Guild]. **Maternity. Letters from Working-Women, Collected by the Women's Co-operative Guild with a preface by the Right Hon. Herbert Samuel, M.P.** London, 1915.

29. Women's Co operative Guild. **Working Women and Divorce. An Account of Evidence Given on Behalf of the Women's Co-operative Guild before the Royal Commission on Divorce.** London, 1911.

    bound with Anna Martin. **The Married Working Woman. A Study.** London, 1911.